Won't you come along with me . . . Down the Mississippi?

HE RAMBLED!
'TIL CANCER CUT HIM DOWN

by

JAN SCOBEY

DISCLAIMER

This book is presented solely as a work of historical and cultural interest. The story has been researched thoroughly. If somehow, there should be conflicting information available, I would greatly appreciate hearing from the reader.

All photographs used have been furnished by the photographers or owners of the photographs. No premeditated usage of photographs, articles or quotations were made that did not represent the owner's or the originator's wish, intent and consent.

If any photograph or article was used without the consent of the owner or originator, this usage was unintentional and not deliberate. I would appreciate hearing from anyone who wishes to set the record straight and if any error was made, I will do my best to give proper credit in the following editions.

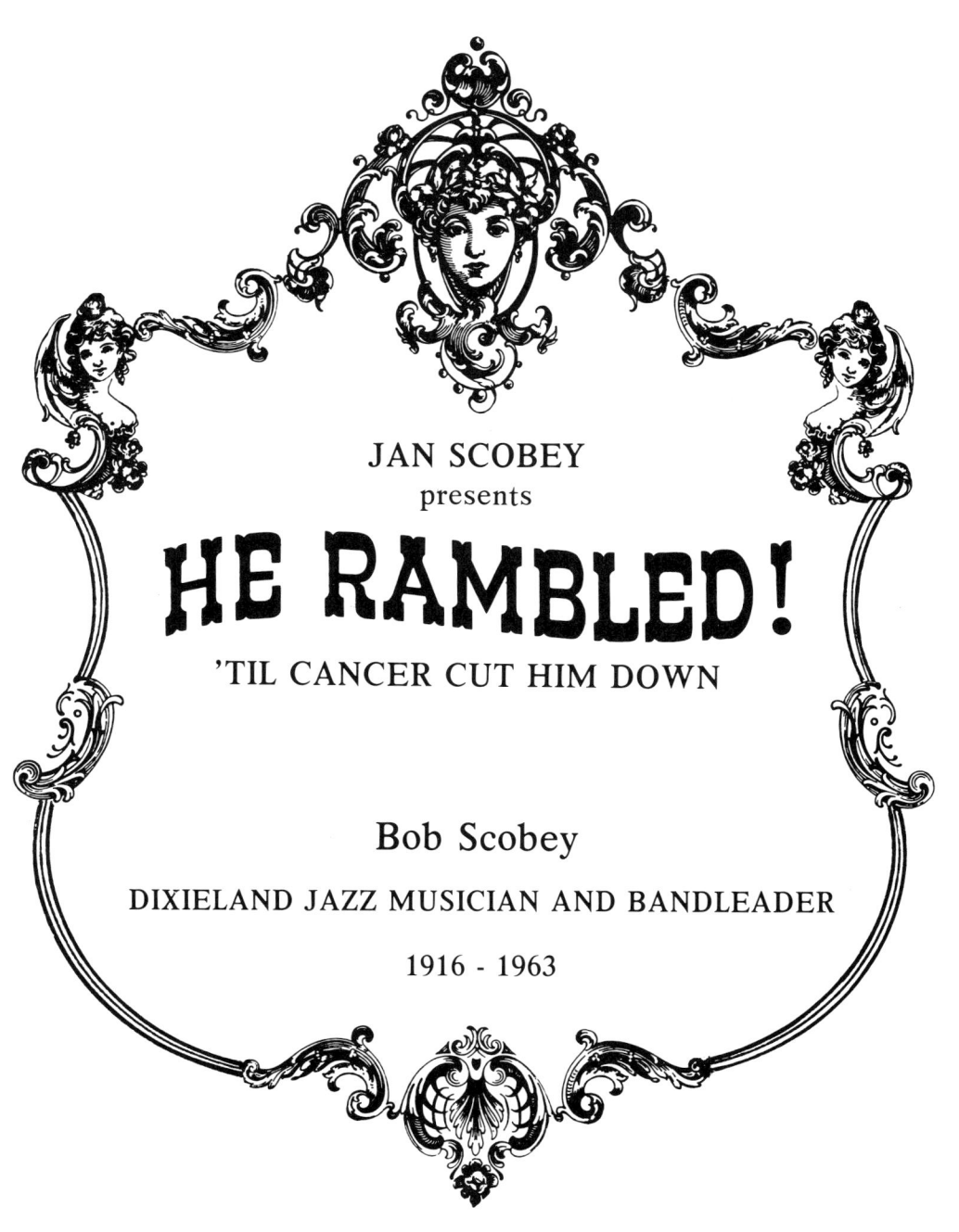

JAN SCOBEY
presents

HE RAMBLED!

'TIL CANCER CUT HIM DOWN

Bob Scobey

DIXIELAND JAZZ MUSICIAN AND BANDLEADER

1916 - 1963

THIS BOOK IS DEDICATED TO HUMANKIND

IN MEMORY OF BOB SCOBEY

First Edition—December 9th, 1976

PAL PUBLISHING
P.O. BOX 807
NORTHRIDGE, CALIFORNIA 91328

Copyright © 1976 by Jan Scobey

All rights reserved, except for review. No part of this publication may be reproduced, utilized or stored in a retrieval system or transmitted in any form or by any means, electronic, mechanical, photocopying, recording, now known, or hereafter invented or otherwise, without prior written permission of the author and publisher.

Library of Congress Catalog Card Number LC 76-544-44
ISBN 0-918104-01-7

GRAPHIC DESIGN

GENE PALENO

SPECIAL ACKNOWLEDGEMENT

TO

GENE

My husband and partner

for all his help, patience,

understanding and support.

LETTER OF ACKNOWLEDGEMENT

When I began my research material for this book, I found boxes and piles of old photos and letters. It was really so very little of all that Bob Scobey experienced. I wrote to his fans and friends for their recollections, and like a kaleidoscope of memories; the letters, phone calls and photographs came to me from all over the world.

They were bits and pieces of a man's life, recalled once more, that became complete as the months passed, filling in the forty years of Scobey's life before I met him, in a way my memory alone could never see him.

I give thanks and credit to the people whose lives have become part of this book. These were entertainers who accompanied Bob on his walk through life, and the friends and family who helped him reach his dream, to bring *'HAPPY MUSIC'* to all corners of the world.

Many people, who touched Bob Scobey in his life-time and whom he touched, contributed to this book. Because of them I gained a multi-dimensional view of Bob I never had, although I loved him, married him and embraced him until he died.

The roster of contributors is very lengthy and so I have listed each one at the end of my story. Thank you all, for this special gift to me and humankind.

Happiness always,

Jan Scobey

CONTENTS

DISCLAIMER	2
DEDICATION	4
GRAPHIC DESIGN	5
SPECIAL ACKNOWLEDGEMENT	6
LETTER OF ACKNOWLEDGEMENT	7
INTRODUCTION	10

VOLUME I

PART ONE

1.	THE HOTTEST MUSIC IN THE WORLD!	15
2.	DON'T TAKE AWAY MY HORN!	19
3.	JAZZ! JAZZ! JAZZ!	33
4.	AIN'T GONNA STUDY WAR NO MO'	53
5.	SWINGIN' DOORS	67
6.	JAZZ AND SEMANTICS	85
7.	FOR EVERY SOMETHIN' THERE'S ANOTHER SOMETHIN'	103
8.	TRAVELIN' SHOES	111

9.	I NEED A HIT RECORD!	127
10.	A GOOD MAN IS HARD TO FIND	145
11.	TROUBLE IN MIND	155

PART TWO

12.	LOVE ME OR LEAVE ME	167
13.	COME RAIN OR COME SHINE	181
14.	BLUE SKIES	191
15.	THAT'S A PLENTY	205
16.	RIVER, STAY AWAY FROM MY DOOR!	225
17.	THERE'LL BE SOME CHANGES MADE	235
18.	STORMY WEATHER	249
19.	WE CAN DREAM, CAN'T WE?	277
20.	ST. JAMES INFIRMARY	291
21.	TRIBUTES TO A TRUMPETER	295
22.	BOB SCOBEY'S DISCOGRAPHY	306
23.	A WIDOW'S EPILOGUE	318

SPECIAL ACKNOWLEDGEMENTS	336
ABOUT THE AUTHOR	339
ILLUSTRATION AND PHOTOGRAPHY CONTRIBUTORS	340
INDEX	341

INTRODUCTION

I have wanted to write this book for fourteen years. My husband, Bob Scobey left behind so many impressions and memories when he suddenly died of cancer in 1963. I determined his life and death should not go unrecognized by humanists. My experiences are narrated to you as honestly and as close to the objective truth as was humanly possible. These were times of joy and happiness that suddenly, without warning, gave way to sadness and despair, as Bob's illness progressed.

I hope this book will bring you a better appreciation of Bob Scobey's 'Happy Music', and I know you will be entertained. But my first and most compelling reason for the writing of this book is to offer you a greater understanding and some ways of coping with the human condition at a time of crisis.

If a single sentence or thought I have related, can spirit you on, or inspire and help you through your personal trials more successfully, then it was worth the time, energy and emotion it took for me to tell my story.

If you are in the midst of a personal struggle, try to remember that we are each our own star. A practical hope for success must start with and depend on OUR OWN EFFORTS. Even during troubled times, the struggle ALWAYS brings rewards and greater happiness in a future time you would otherwise never have known! Each tragedy has within it the seeds of a future VICTORY!

Bob Scobey left us a valuable musical legacy—one that deserves to be documented. He was a gifted artist and his personal warmth and character, his integrity and inspiration endeared him, very specially, to those who knew him.

Robert Alexander Scobey earned his right to be remembered because of the way he lived. Fortunately, today, we have musical recordings which preserve an artist's particular sound. Scobey's compositions are his improvizations to music already written. In his lifetime, Bob Scobey appeared on about thirty-one albums and many Ep's, long playing records, 45's and 78's, so his music really got around. During his last years, he played all over the world, recorded, and appeared on radio and television.

At the moment of his most grim defeat, with unfailing cheerfulness and courage, in the face of death, he gave us the measure of his greatness. Our situation was unique. However, we can all share in another's moving, eventful experience—perhaps to our own benefit.

Part One is devoted to the life and musical career of Bob Scobey before I met him. His personal philosophy and friendships left a warm, lasting impression with his fellow musicians, family, friends, and fans.

Part Two tells of my personal relationship with Bob, when I entered his life and during the dark days of Bob's battle with cancer. It is a graphic, frank account of death. However, it also shows the drive a man can have with a horn he just won't put down.

If somehow I missed reaching you, before this edition, for any memorabilia you may have of these times, I ask you now for your help, so I may keep future editions up to date. Any criticism and suggestions by the readers are solicited to aid in maintaining an increasingly high standard of comprehensiveness, authority and usefulness in future editions.

While I was writing this book I found myself coming to strong conclusions that will help anyone who may be told they have cancer. I found myself compelled to research all I could to help future sufferers. I have simultaneously published Volume II, 'CANCER? WHAT YOU CAN DO!' which deals with Bob Scobey's suffering, as a case history. This work has been thoroughly researched and includes the latest findings in help for the sufferer. Many periodicals and medical journals print interesting and useful hypotheses seldom viewed by the non-medical person. Volume II is a handbook for the prevention and treatment of illness, and specifically, cancer.

When the last page was written, the book closed and I had once again lived through those days of good times and bad, I realized Bob Scobey gained the final victory after all. His immortality is evident in his recordings, in the memories of all who loved him, and now through this book.

Happiness (Victory) always,

Jan Scobey

VOLUME ONE

PART ONE

1 THE HOTTEST MUSIC IN THE WORLD!

IN NEW ORLEANS, ON THE WAY TO THE cemetery, they used to play sad———but coming back—Oh, my! The music was happy! The music was gay!

If you and I could turn again to yesterday and stand in the shade of the moss covered cypress trees, on the crumbling, brick sidewalk in Storyville, and listen—very carefully—we might hear in the distance, the sound of brassy blues, coming slowly toward us, carried on the balmy Mississippi Delta air. Sad and slow, the procession drifts past Canal Street, gradually winding it's way toward St. Louis Cemetery #2 on North Claiborne Avenue. The music plays softly as the musicians walk slowly . . . just a few steps at a time———stop———a few more steps———a long pause.

The hearse, drawn by two bays, is draped in black lace, and the weeping family and friends follow. The music, a prolonged, dirgelike lament, sets the pace, as the feet-scraping, shoulder-drooping caravan trails behind.

Heads pop out of windows from upper story buildings, from stores and alleys. Men, women and children run out to join the caravan, leaving behind the jambalaya, red beans and rice, cooking on the stove: and the ironing still unfinished. Excitement grows!

"Who died?" "How many bands?" "Which way are they going?"

Trumpets are raised to pour out the melancholic sounds of 'St. James Infirmary Blues'! Everyone is stretching to see how grand the funeral, how important the deceased.

JUNE 12, 1963

I was dead tired. I had been tired for so long. For months I had nursed and cared for Bob. Now the hours and days seemed to be getting longer, with only brief moments of rest. Adrienne, his daughter, was attending Bob now, so I could at last steal a few hours of badly needed rest. I fell into a deep, weary sleep . . .

Suddenly, my mental alarms woke me to a wide-eyed alertness. I heard Bob gasping, struggling to draw breath, choking in the 3:00 a.m. darkness. As I arose in swift urgency to help him, I realized Adrienne was in my bed, sleeping.

"She should be on watch with her father," I thought in sudden panic.

"Damn it, Adrienne!" I screamed.

BOB SCOBEY at Bourbon Street on State Street in Chicago, 1961.
©Jan Scobey 1976

2 DON'T TAKE AWAY MY HORN!

ANY STORY ABOUT A GREAT MUSICIAN IS only a shadow of their substance—until you hear them play. This is especially true of Bob Scobey. Robert Alexander Scobey (1916-1963) played trumpet. A solid Dixieland Jazz Horn... 'Bourbon St. Parade', 'When The Saints Go Marching In', 'London Blues', 'Skit-Dat-De-Dat', 'Didn't He Ramble!'. You name it, Bob Scobey played them all. His sound has a crisp, happy, carefree resonance full of anticipating, syncopating rhythm.

To understand his beginnings, we must go back to 1916. America was preparing to unload hundreds of thousands of young, American soldiers on European soil to fight on the battlefields of World War I. Robert Alexander Scobey was born on December 9th, that year, in Tucumcari, New Mexico. The times were unsettled and the following year his parents moved to Stockton, California. The post war years were a frenetic rush to life and all kinds of music was popular.

There were no professional musicians in Bob's family, but his mother, a music lover who played a little 'parlor' piano wanted to develop music appreciation in her children and so she bought Bob a cornet for his ninth Christmas.

"I exhibited the usual amount of interest for a boy, taking out the horn on days when my grade school band rehearsed. Once in a while, at home, when I was lazy, my parents would threaten to sell it if I didn't use it. They knew how to reach me—then, I would practice!"

At fourteen Bob put down his cornet for a stronger love. He wanted to play trumpet because there was something magical about it to him. He heard a more penetrating, commanding, voice-like sound, and from that moment on it became his chosen instrument, almost a part of his flesh and blood.

At Berkeley, the musical director took an interest in Scobey's talents, realizing his aptitude for the horn, and urged him to study with good teachers. Bob took lessons from Joseph Weiss, the band director, and because of Bob's broad range of interest in music he sought out teachers such as Dave Rosebrook, who was featured soloist with the Goldman band. Bob kept looking for more guidance and he received advanced instruction from Ben Klatzkin, lead trumpet player with the San Francisco Symphony, which furthered his musical capabilities immensely. Bob's musical

BOB SCOBEY - 1946
Yerba Buena
Jazz Band
Courtesy of George Fletcher

education was thorough, and he acquired great technical skill at an early age.

Upon graduation in 1934, Bob had a conflict to resolve. He liked chemistry and mathematics, but, aside from being unusually talented, music was fun! The lure of night life and knowing many musicians were making more money than highly trained scientists, plus the deterrent of four more, long years of college settled the question. Bob Scobey had made his decision, the scene was set and a rip-roaring musical career began!!!

Wade Thomas was dating Bob's only sister at this time (they later married). Wade had been playing with Kay Kaiser's band and was offered a job in Hawaii. He preferred teaching on the mainland, so he turned over the job to Bob. Bob was all of nineteen, but Wade knew he was ready as a professional and as Wade said:

"Bob had it all together and was well on his way. He was always talented, and fit right in!"

These were depression years and a job of any kind was hard to find. With the music business in it's hey day, Bob was lucky, at such a tender age, to have been so well appreciated by his peers. It was a short gig but it led to other jobs.

In the late 1930's, at 22, his first serious, steady job, after joining the union, was at the State Hoffbrau Restaurant as a side man in the house band. He was making $85.00 a week working as a musician! I imagine he must have thought, *"How sweet it is!"* That was top money!

It was customary in those days to play a few nights here and there, running the gammut of musical experiences. Bob Helm, clarinetist; who played quite a lot with Bob in these early days, put it this way:

". . . . Scobey first made an impression on me by his ability to punch out a sparse, driving lead in the ensemble choruses and his solos were always interesting!

"Before the '40's jazz revival, a full time player had to take a wide range of music jobs to live. Most of the jazz players worked them all—the Chinese New Year, funerals, celebrations, birthdays, weddings, christenings and Bar mitzvahs in the Bay Area. Besides these casual jobs there were the hotel bands, night clubs, shows, dime-jigs, ballrooms, theatre pit bands, marching and concert gigs.

"The late thirties was a period of highs and lows. The lows could be attributed to the uncertainty of steady employment and the nature of it, if offered. In those poor times it didn't take much to make a high—people were easily pleased.

"All dance bands were expected to play the 'stage, screen and radio pops' of the day; however, the manner in

BOB HELM - 1946
Yerba Buena Jazz Band
Courtesy of George Fletcher

which the tunes were played, the arrangements and the leader's interpretation made the performances a high or low.

"A couple of high performance ballroom bands that Bob and I worked in, that come to mind, were Jack Trent, (Horace Perazzi) and Lu Watter's Sweet's Ballroom Band.

"The four taxi dances, called 'dime grinds' by the musicians, were Oakland's Home-Sweet-Home, for a lot of players. There were memorable nights when these small bands, sometimes composed entirely of jazz refugees; had a chance to play more than the usual two minute (or less) tunes, and at the rate of 30 to 50 an hour. This went on for five or six hours at a crack!

"Another high point would be collecting daily wages from the concession's pin ball machines at the Musician's Union while sweating out potential contractors. The Scobey-Helm System of using shoe leather to negate the 'tilt' made the use of extensive 'body english' possible . . . ."

About this time Turk Murphy, a young trombonist, also searching for his future, met Bob Scobey in Seattle.

". . . . I was with a band playing at the old Club Victor and Bob came into town from San Francisco in a pick-up band, doing one-nighters under Horace Perazzi. This was in 1936. He and I were involved with most of the records made by the Lu Watters band and Bob played on the first records made by my own group on Jazzman label. Bob and I had left the Watters band about the same time.

"Gee, Bob was a fine musician! He needed no great amount of training or work to play the way he did. I enjoyed

TURK MURPHY - 1946
Yerba Buena Jazz Band
Courtesy of George Fletcher

his company on the many things the band did as a group. Scobey was a great fan of horse racing, and I went with him to the track on several occasions. He could pick some winners! . . . .''

Bob Scobey welcomed every opportunity to play in every conceivable band.

"I was in the sweetest and in the hottest bands in San Francisco, and they were some swingin' days," he said. *"I took more to jazz than any other form of music."*

Scobey could really swing musically with scores by Scott Joplin, for instance. His 'Maple Leaf Rag' rendition of Joplin's work is one of his finest recordings on Jansco Record label. The brilliant improvizations and almost symphonic-like involvement are the highlights of Bob's style.

TRUMPET

As played by: BOB SCOBEY
JANSCO - Vol. II - 6252
©Jan Scobey 1976

MAPLE LEAF RAG

SCOTT JOPLIN

MAPLE—2

MAPLE—3

JELLY ROLL MORTON
Courtesy of the Los Angeles Public Library

    Bob had a keen appreciation of the many changes in jazz compositions. Ferdinand 'Jelly Roll' Morton was another favorite of his. RCA recorded an album featuring Scobey that devoted much of the repertoire to 'Morton' compositions. Bob shared the same awareness for 'King Oliver's'—'Snag It', 'Dippermouth Blues' and 'Dr. Jazz.'

JOHN PHILIP SOUSA
November 6, 1854 - March 6, 1932
Gale Research Company Book Tower
Courtesy of the Los Angeles Public Library

During Scobey's early days, he would fall asleep listening to records of other artists. He built his repertoire quickly and with his ear tuned to the greats.

Often he related to me the deep feeling of mutual respect musicians had for each other and the close brotherhood between them—just one big happy family! It really bugged Scobey that the musicians' unions were all segregated into black and white locals. In Los Angeles, it was local #767 for blacks and Local #47 for whites. The same thing occurred in cities all across the country. Petrillo, who was head of the National Union at the time, delayed the natural trend toward integration within the unions. He was typical of countless others before him, with the segregationalist attitude of the country.

Jamming, working with black musicians, building friendships, and discovering each other's unique musical innovations, Bob looked forward to jobs where he worked with blacks despite the ignorance of others. He idolized 'Louis Armstrong' as well as the music written by black artists such as 'Scott Joplin' and 'W.C. Handy'. These composers and musicians were the creators of the only music that is truly, naturally American. The Blues and Jazz! . . . They were firmly established in music as early as the start of the 20th century.

W.C. Handy wrote, 'St. Louis Blues', way back in 1914.

W. C. HANDY
Courtesy of the Los Angeles Public Library

BOBBY HACKETT
Courtesy of Ed Lawless

HARRY JAMES
Courtesy of Harry James

This single tune has sold more in sheet music and recordings than any song before or since. There were many others like 'Friendless Blues,' 'Careless Love,' 'Beale St. Blues,' and on. These tunes were all a part of every Dixieland Book. As it went, whites and blacks were prevented from intermingling during this era.

When at last the country's growing civil rights awareness brought some lowering of the barriers, the locals begrudgingly united. People on both sides, black and white, continued to struggle in cold war fashion to keep their own autonomy. Blacks, especially, wanted to preserve their hard-won gains. They feared, justifiably, they would be swallowed into the white union. Regardless, in 1953, Los Angeles almalgamated. In Chicago the change was delayed for ten more years. The union and city fathers were not enlightened in these matters, to say the least. Bob revealed his deepest feelings whenever he recounted the unfairness of the segregational policies in America. Bob often remarked,

"Music is our most valuable tool of communication. It is something all of us can understand and can certainly use to

reach the goal of world unity." That's how Bob felt about music and I wholeheartedly join him.

There were other horn players Scobey favored and surely the lingering sounds from these fine musicians helped him to develop his own unique style. Harry James' clear, strong tones; the melodic flow of Bobby Hackett's trumpet, and the perfect pitch of Leon 'Bix' Beiderbecke, all left their musical mark on Bob. When the guys were in town, everyone would get together, jamming into the wee hours of the morning. There was always a place to jam; always some spot to sit-in and play!

Scobey's idolized favorite, personally as well as musically, was *"Louis 'Satchmo' Armstrong"*. 'Armstrong' was the first, great jazz soloist who changed the style and sound of all the other hornplayers. Bob and Louis were friends. They probably only had a chance to get together socially a dozen times in their lives; between sets or after gigs when time would allow. Both of their careers took them to all parts of the world, and they very rarely happened to be in town together. When fate did bring a reunion, Louis and Bob exchanged 'gem stories' and limericks, as well as talk music.

On these chance meetings I would tag along, just observing their camaraderie. This happened only four or five times while I was with them, but I could see it was always a treasured occasion. They showered a deep love on each other and Bob would affectionately call Louis 'Pops'. They would sit around in the dressing rooms, just cutting up and laughing out loud. They truly enjoyed their own 'Mutual Admiration Society'. It was beautiful!

Many artists touched Bob, yet, Bob, like all creative geniuses, was always his own man, and after traveling a distance with each of them, he went on to develop and create his own, distinctively, new brand of Jazz!

LOUIS (SATCHMO) ARMSTRONG
Courtesy of Louis 'Satchmo' Armstrong

into a primitive, social music that was to be known one day as 'jazz'. From Africa, Spain, France and England they came, sometimes via the long, devious routes of the Creoles and Cajuns, and from the aboriginal Americans, the Indians.

"The irrepressible rhythmic drive, out of the Congo, distorted the soft, sensuous Creole songs, the quadrilles, polkas and marches popular in those days. The blues and spirituals—products of African chants superimposed on Anglo-Saxon hymns—worked their way in from the fields and the back-shacks. The Mississippi carried the piano rags upstream from Memphis and St. Louis; and in the heart of the old town was the formidable symbol of Old French culture—the Opera.

"New Orleans was a parading town. After the Civil War, brass bands flourished, most of them consisting of five to seven pieces or more, when the occasion warranted. They played for funerals, piled onto wagons to advertize functions or tout political candidates, and at night, they played for dancing. The original bands found it impossible to carry a piano on their wagons, but the other instruments compensated for the piano by evolving melodic-rhythmic parts for themselves.

"Bolden's band consisted of cornet, clarinet, trombone, drums, bass and guitar. In later bands, when times got bad, a piano might have been brought in to replace bass and guitar. Jazz, with the possible exception of the modern 'cool' school, has never completely forsaken the forthright, 'brassy' sound of the New Orleans brass band.

"In New Orleans, it was possible for a completely original, unorthodox style to develop because, first, most of the musicians could not read music and had only enough technical skill to get the basic characteristic effects from their instruments. Having no prescribed parts to follow, they evolved their own roles in the ensemble according to what they instinctively felt was required. As in any brass band, trumpet or cornet carried the melodic lead and concentrated its attack mainly on the strong beats. The clarinet would play a more mobile counter melody, filling in on the weak beats and phrase endings with rapid figurations

up and down the stick, trombone would accent the off beats and propel the rhythm with huffs, puffs and glissandi that, in the hands of a master, served also to fill in the harmony with the cornet.

"The New Orleans clarinet style was uniquely a Creole product. With few exceptions, the pioneer clarinet men had French blood and were the only legitimately trained musicians in the early bands. Their technique and ability to think out a fluid, somewhat operatic part for themselves determined the role of the instrument in the traditional ensemble.

BASIN STREET, STORYVILLE

"The development of the piano in jazz was hardly regarded in New Orleans; however, the men who were to transform ragtime into jazz found work in Storyville, the famed red-light sector of the town, of which the most celebrated street was Basin Street. The rags of 'Scott Joplin' and some others were popular good-time music, but the young ladies of the various establishments often preferred the blues.

"This dual repertoire situation created such influential stylists as 'Tony Jackson', 'Clarence Williams', 'Richard M. Jones' and most significant—'Jelly Roll Morton'. The latter, in particular, did a great deal to enlarge the jazz repertoire, composing dozens of great vehicles such as 'Milneberg Joys' played by the Scobey band, 'King Porter Stomp' and many others.

"Bolden's progeny, some of whom were old enough to have played with him, included the late 'Bunk Johnson' and 'Joe 'King' Oliver'—trumpets or cornets. 'Louis Armstrong', jazzdom's all-time great, undoubtedly derives from 'Bunk' and 'Oliver'.

"'Alphonse Picou' was perhaps the first important clarinetist. It was he who first played the now traditional clarinet part of 'High Society', and was skilled enough to adapt from the piccolo part of a standard march. He also composed several of the New Orleans classics.

"'Big Eye' Louis Nelson' was another of the early style-setters, and these men were followed by 'George Baquet', 'Johnny Dodds', 'Jimmy Noone', 'Sidney Bechet' and 'Albert Nicholas', and still later by 'Barney Bigard', 'Edmund Hall',

George Lewis', and 'Joe Darensbourg'.

"'Zue Robertson' is believed to have been the great original on slide trombone, although much more is known of 'Honore Dutrey', who was with 'Oliver and Armstrong', and 'Kid Ory'.

"In the early days, the emphasis was on the ensemble. Solos were rare and brief, sometimes confined to 'breaks'. Certain purists continue to hold forth that the early, archaic jazz is 'the only true jazz'! The fact is that 'New Orleans Jazz' continued to develop along lines of greater individual freedom, at first without sacrificing any of the cohesive ensemble feeling. Most of the early patterns and breaks were worked out by a certain few musicians, then memorized by others and repeated by all ad infinitum. The real creative freedom and the resultant era of the great individualists developed gradually and sometimes, admittedly, to the detriment of the stylized mellow-as-old-wine ensemble.

"It's quite possible that the ensemble grew as far as it could under the benevolent 'King Oliver', and that the solo star tradition grew along with the career of King's disciple, 'Louis Armstrong'. Louis' own original 'Hot Five', with 'Ory', 'Johnny Dodds', 'Johnny St. Cyr' on banjo and 'Lil Hardin Armstrong' on piano, might have been called an ensemble virtuosi, but as 'Louis' became more and more the symbol of jazz, the emphasis on ensemble deteriorated. By the thirties, 'Louis' had taken to fronting big bands which served merely to showcase his solo horn.

"The term 'Dixieland', for many years, was applied to white groups that played in the New Orleans manner. The word itself is said to have stood for 'New Orleans' long before it was fastened on the entire area south of the Mason-Dixon line. It derives from the word 'Dix' which had been printed in bold type on a series of $10 bills issued by a certain New Orleans bank.

"The first Dixieland music, it is said, was minted by 'Jack Laine's Ragtime Band', which was 'improvizing' in the manner of the Negro bands around the end of the 19th century. Actually, the original Laine bands had all of their numbers, mostly rags, worked out note for note. The band played for minstrel troupes as well as for the usual social, commercial and political functions. Laine himself played an alto horn, and his basic instrumentation also included a cornet, trombone, clarinet and drums. On occasions he would add guitar, string bass and possibly violin. One of the clarinet-playing Rappolos (not the famous Leon) was with him in his first band, and later bands were training ground for most of the New Orleans white pioneers, including the 'Brunies Brothers' and the members of the 'Original Dixieland Jazz Band'.

HEADING NORTH

"In 1915, the Laine 'school' graduated 'Tom Brown', who took a crew to Chicago where it was billed as 'Tom Brown's Dixieland Jass Band, Direct from New Orleans'. The overwhelming success of this outfit sent several Chicago club owners on expeditions to New Orleans searching for similar bands. Brown, who sold his music with the aid of considerable clowning, took off for New York and a string of vaudeville engagements, and returned to Chicago to find another New Orleans musician, 'Yellow' Nunez, who was riding high. Out of a series of personnel swaps emerged the 'Original Dixieland Jazz Band'.

"The 'ODJB' made the first jazz recordings in 1917, and opened in New York at Reisenweber's, a fashionable spot off Columbus Circle. Dixieland had arrived! It set the country on fire, and then the band took off for England, where the boys had an effect comparable to that of the Norman invasion.

"Another white outfit, the 'New Orleans Rhythm Kings', hit Chicago four years later than the Original Dixieland boys, and brought with it three of the most formidable instrumentalists jazz had produced. There were 'Leon Rappolo', whose legitimate background was similar to that of the French-derived Creole school, and the gutty tailgate trombonist 'George Brunies', and the Oliver-inspired trumpet lead, 'Paul Mares'. Later, the significant drummer, 'Ben Pollack', was brought in. The New Orleans Rhythm Kings were to provide much of the repertoire, and most of the inspiration for a group of Chicago high school kids, who one day were to burst out with their own brand of Dixieland. These included such future stars as "Jimmy McPartland', 'Bud Freeman', 'Dave Tough', 'Eddie Condon', 'Joe Sullivan', 'Gene Krupa', and 'Frank Teachemaker'. Into their orbit also came the late geniuses 'Bix Beiderbecke' and 'Benny Goodman'.

"In Chicago, jazz moved away from a strict diet of two-beat rhythm, and new, steady four/four time produced a new kind of drive. This Chicago version of Dixieland was hard boiled, aggressive and swaggering, like Chicago itself. It had, and still has tremendous vitality. In fact, for some years it made the jazz public forget there was an older, rich jazz heritage.

"Although New Orleans musicians continued to play New Orleans music in New Orleans, the gustier Chicago brand, and the big swing bands that grew out of the thirties, drove some of the key traditionalists right out of the music business. Then, in 1939, a most significant book appeared—'Jazzmen'—compiled by Fred Ramsey, Jr., and Charles Edward Smith. This was perhaps the first important attempt *to document jazz history, and it succeeded in awakening interest in the origins of the art in the men who created it.*

"On a tip from 'Louis Armstrong', the editors went looking for old 'Bunk Johnson' and found him working in a Louisiana rice field. Jazz collectors chipped in and outfitted Bunk with a horn and a new set of teeth, and at 64, Bunk made a spectacular comeback. He appeared in New York, San Francisco, and of course, in New Orleans, where he found a group of cohorts who were younger, but born and bred to the tradition.

"Meanwhile, the New Orleans spirit sprang up, with almost unprecedented strength, in the unlikely city of San Francisco. Not that New Orleans was entirely new to California. When the Navy Department closed down Storyville in 1917, several of the displaced jazzmen worked their way west. There was 'Dink Johnson', the drummer of the Original Creole Band, who went there to work with his own Louisiana Six. And 'Kid Ory's Brown Skinned Jazz Band', with 'Papa Mutt Carey' on trumpet. 'Jelly Roll Morton' himself was in California between 1915 and 1923, later moving to Chicago, and then back to the Coast in 1938, (finally dying there in '41). 'King Oliver' took seven pieces to San Francisco in May 1921 and worked out a six month contract there before his historic run in Chicago (with 'Louis Armstrong' on second cornet.) When Louis himself arrived on the Coast in 1930, it was to front a big band.

"'Mutt Carey' made California his home after 1919 and even Ory settled down to semi-retirement there on a chicken farm in 1933. The drummer 'Zutty Singleton', after working around New York with some of the swing stars in the '30's, settled in Los Angeles. The guitarist 'Bud Scott', who had played with 'Buddy Bolden' in 1906, went west with 'Ory's first band . . . ."

About 1940, in San Francisco, some young musicians were about to re-introduce the old New Orleans jazz to the world. Historians had written the YERBA BUENA JAZZ BAND formed in 1938 or 1939. Actually, the nucleus of the band had played together on the same gigs, in a larger band. Meanwhile, they talked about forming a new Jazz band of their own. They continued to sit-in and jam at the 'San Francisco Hot Music Society' meetings which were held at 20 Annie Street in San Francisco. The group developed such a following that the 'Dawn Club' was formed at the same address to permanently house the new venture—the 'YERBA BUENA JAZZ BAND', but it did not occur until 1940.

Kid Ory's Creole Jazz Band

Personnel:

KID ORY — Trombone and Leader

MUTT CAREY, *Trumpet*
JOE DARENSBOURG, *Clarinet*
BUSTER WILSON, *Piano*

BUD SCOTT, *Guitar*
ED GARLAND, *Bass*
MINOR HALL, *Drums*

NOW PLAYING NIGHTLY*

at the

JADE PALACE

6619-6621 Hollywood Boulevard

Courtesy of Joe Darensbourg

THE GREAT BRASS TRIAD

SCOBEY! WATTERS! MURPHY!—These three brass men, who rocked San Francisco almost as much as the 1906 Earthquake, formed a great triad. Their early interest in jazz sparkled San Francisco with a brass team that reminisced of the 'King Oliver/Armstrong' days in New Orleans. The 'Yerba Buena Jazz Band' was formed in 1940 and they were one of the first to leave the then currently popular, fourteen piece big-band-sound in favor of a smaller musical unit.

They searched out old music from books, music stores, the Library of Congress, old records or they made up their own tunes. Here were enthusiastic youngbloods trying to recapture the sounds of the twenties and the San Francisco Barbary Coast days. What a solid brass team!!! The trio was a strong section in the 'YBJB'. The driving force behind them, their dynamics and ensemble playing, were hard to contain. It kept their listeners at a high peak of happy enthusiasm. SCOBEY, WATTERS, and MURPHY, were trendsetters with their new revival team. They were applauded throughout the United States as their message made a cross country flight via recordings.

PACIFIC STREET OF 'BARBARY COAST' DURING CHAMPAGNE DAYS

Courtesy of the Los Angeles Public Library

THE GREAT BRASS TRIAD   MURPHY - WATTERS - SCOBEY   Yerba Buena Jazz Band

Courtesy of George Fletcher

Other important members of the group at that time were, 'Ellis Horne' and later 'Bob Helm', clarinetists; 'Wally Rose', piano; 'Harry Mordecai', banjo; 'Dick Lammi', bass; and 'Bill Dart', drums. The entire group gradually separated from the 'YBJB', and the members, SCOBEY and MURPHY formed their own bands. Harry Mordecai speaks:

". . . . I considered Bob to be the best man around to play in the 'Yerba Buena Jazz Band', night after night, in a band better measured dynamically in decibels rather than from 'pianissimo' to 'triple forte'. Bob's personality can be summed up as alert and quick of wit, easy to talk to and well read. I first knew Bob while a member of the 'San Francisco Hot Music Society' during the World's Fair at Treasure Island in San Francisco during the late 30's.

"I thought Bob possessed a sharpness of intellect and a real keen sense of business acumen. One case in point was his refusal to invest in the ill fated Hambone Kelly Corporation. Instead of joining the co-op he preferred to play with us as a salaried performer along with Bill Dart and Clancy

HARRY MORDECAI
Yerba Buena Jazz Band
Courtesy of George Fletcher

Hayes. Then later, his sense of fairness was shown to me when he had his lawyer seize some record masters which were held until we were paid in full before he allowed them to be issued.

"Bob didn't use much tobacco or liquor when I knew him. He really enjoyed golf and was especially interested in horse races. He approached them scientifically with books and charts on the 'nags' and track conditions.

"Though his political views were Marxist, I'm sure they weren't the violent overthrow type. Incidentally his views caused many a heated discussion as the rest of the band had little love for the red doctrines. It didn't interfere with the music, however, and left no hard feelings. Once he offered me $500 that within the next five years the capitalist in the United States would suffer the worst depression in history. I never collected, but now after 30 years his 'Marxist wet dream' may yet be coming to pass . . . ."

SCOBEY'S POLITICS

In Bob's 16th year, Black Friday on the New York Stock Exchange was already three years in the past. It was 1932, and the bleakest year of the Great Depression. Bob was sharp and mature enough to understand what was happening around him. He knew what it meant when he read that 270,000 families were being evicted from their homes.

The average wage earner (if you even had a job) was earning a little more than $16.00 a week which had to pay for food, heat, a roof over their family's head, clothing, medicines, and other necessities of life.

Young Bob's questions multiplied when he had heard of and had seen; tired, hungry men, whose only crime was to walk a picket line; being beaten by paid thugs and hoodlums. Big business all across the country, steadfastly refused to cut the prices of their products to the struggling consumer. Instead, they continued to slash wages and cut payrolls which 'snow-balled' the effects of the depression. Hundreds of strikers were clubbed, beaten, and shot at by private police forces, national guardsmen and strike-breakers hired by the big bosses. These violent criminal activities were all the while supported and condoned by those in power.

Like thousands of other young Americans growing up in the midst of this national anguish, Bob was ready to listen to any solution to the national problem. He was impressed with the promise of an equal and fair distribution of wealth as Karl Marx had taught.

In New York, 35,000 hungry citizens filled Union Square to hear communist speakers preach the new gospel of 'share the wealth'! Meanwhile, another group of 2500 starving veterans and their families, after being jailed for begging for bread on the Senate steps, left prison singing the words of the communist 'L'International' they had recently learned.

> *"Arise ye prisoners of starvation,*
> *Arise ye wretched of the Earth,*
> *For justice thunders condemnation,*
> *A better world's in birth."*

Children were singing:

> *"Mellon pulled the whistle,*
> *Hoover rang the bell*
> *Wall Street gave the signal,*
> *And the country went to hell!"*

That year, Andrew Mellon was Secretary of the Treasury and Representative Wright Patman asked the Congress to impeach Mellon for high crimes and misdemeanors.

While President Hoover was piously offering his opinion that *"a little poverty strengthened the moral character of the masses,"* old women were scrabbling for food in garbage cans!

The numbers of thoughtful, enlightened American poets, writers, musicians and artists, and other young people were legion and growing. America was on the verge of revolution in those years, and a Marxist, 'share the wealth', philosophy seemed, to youngsters like Bob, a simple answer to the problems of the countless, starving millions.

For this reason, some of Bob's closer friends, in later years, were left with the impression that he was a Marxist. He was not.

I would listen (with half an ear), to Bob discuss his deepest, social feelings with friends. He never raised his voice. Bob pursued his arguments of belief with a quiet conviction and a deep sincerity.

"Karl Marx said the numbers of the poor always grow more rapidly than the wealth of a country. The rich guys— the real rulers of America, have always decided the rules— and these rules don't ever give an edge to the poor people."

No matter who he spoke with, they would listen attentively for you could tell Bob really and truly believed it. He thought our elections didn't actually elect.

"The voters are always given a limited choice of leaders, already selected by powerful interests." he remarked one evening in the dressing room. The guys objected, hot and heavy to the idea they weren't picking their own candidate. The big election at the time was Kennedy vs. Nixon and everyone had chosen sides.

Bob mused over their comments a while, then he smiled and said, *"Well, I think a lot of those guys mean well, but when a million dollars worth of lobbiests are spreading influence and pressure to pass a certain law, the small guy doesn't have a chance.*

When Bob grew older and more prosperous and famous, he enjoyed all the blessings of Capitalism. One of his greatest joys and proudest possessions was a string of new cadillacs. He would buy a new one every few years. In later years he was striving to own a night club business. Bob was an entrepreneur, creating his own wealth within the system. However, he never forgot or abandoned his gut beliefs and convictions.

Scobey's seemingly Marxist attitude was more a desire for a fairer distribution of wealth and equal opportunity, a better circulation of money. Bob touched 'high society' as bandleader and probably realized, except for amusement, the wealthy and upper levels of society generally looked down on even the most famed of entertainers. The 'upper class' were clannish and snobbish, and maintained a very strict, social separation between themselves and the musicians. He believed those who control great wealth and power in this nation, have an obligation to make possible and encourage the poor, the uneducated, the underprivileged every opportunity to acquire a fair share of the 'good life' if they are willing to work for it. If he lived today, he would be a working champion of the civil rights movement and the underdog.

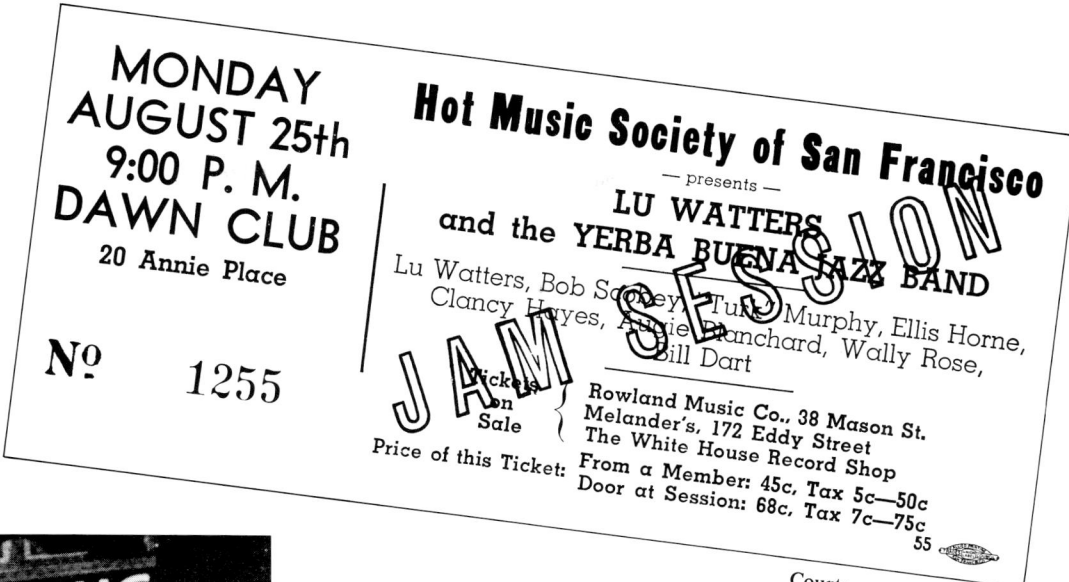

Courtesy of Pete Tamony

DAWN CLUB
Courtesy of Ed Lawless

NEW ORLEANS JAZZ REVIVAL

The 'Yerba Buena Jazz Band' appeared for the first time, as an entity, at Number 20 Annie Street, in the heart of San Francisco. The Dawn Club housed the Great Brass Triad of the Yerba Buena Jazz Band.

NESUHI ERTEGUN

Scobey and Watters alternated on lead parts, and SCOBEY, WATTERS and MURPHY were the most powerful brass team in all of Traditional Jazz History. With the live broadcasts through station KGO radio, the 'YBJB' kept gaining ground and popularity.

Pearl Harbor was still a year in the future. In San Francisco there was a sudden flare-up of interest in Jazz. Maybe it was always there, but the West Coast was isolated from live jazz except for the occasional appearances of such traveling bands as 'Louis Armstrong', 'George Lewis', 'Kid Ory' and others. When it happened, the 'YBJB', with its high degree of development in their style of jazz, was able to take full advantage and cause a revival with little or no competition.

In 1941 the first recordings of this band were mastered on Jazzman Records. The bandsmen's execution of these recordings was impeccably clean. They would carefully write out the charts, get the notes down in their heads and then throw away the charts before recording. This gave the ensemble playing a powerful, harmonic sound, but still allowed them freedom for improvization.

Nesuhi Ertegun, now director of Warner, Elektra, Atlantic records, produced these first recordings on his Jazzman label.

"... . I had recently come to the United States from Europe. I was passionately interested in New Orleans Jazz and tried to hear it wherever it was played. The impact of the 'YBJB' was unbelievable and indescribable. I had never heard anything quite like it before and in fact have heard nothing like it since. Those young musicians actually played New Orleans music, not Chicago or Dixieland. The obvious influences were 'King Oliver', 'Louis Armstrong' and 'Jelly Roll Morton'; and yet the sounds they produced were totally different from these great names of the past.

"In the first place the band was extra-ordinarily loud

LU WATTERS
Yerba Buena Jazz Band
Courtesy of George Fletcher

when it wanted to be loud. It was, undeniably, the loudest eight piece band (without use of electronic devices) in the history of music. The two trumpets, both musicians of extraordinary talent, Scobey and Watters, played together with uncanny understanding, looseness and rapport. These recordings the band made, give a very incomplete idea of their power and drive and swing.

"It was fashionable at the time, in critical circles, to expound on the stiffness and 'monotony' of the old 'YBJB' but this opinion was mostly held by people who never heard the band in person. It was strange, actually, because the rhythmic impetus of the band was established by, and came from, the horns. The two trumpets, the trombone, and the clarinet pushed forward with such controlled intensity that they forced the rhythm section to swing along with them.

"All in all, this was an unforgettable experience for me and later on I realized the important contribution to the overall sound of 'Wally Rose', of 'Dick Lammi', of 'Clancy Hayes', of 'Squire Girsback' and of 'Bill Dart'.

"I realized that the centre of the rhythm section was formed by the two trumpets, 'Scobey' and 'Watters', and that Dart made ornamental comments around the beat, apparently on strict instructions from Watters.

"I got to know all the members of the 'YBJB' and became quite friendly with most of them. When I moved to the West Coast a few years later, these friendships grew, especially with 'Turk Murphy', 'Bob Scobey', and 'Bob Helm'.

"Scobey was quite different from the other San Francisco musicians. He was less of a purist, less fanatic about old jazz, more practical, more down to earth and often more rational. The future interested him more than the past, although he never denied his roots and never ignored them.

"His ambition, as far as I could tell, was to become a

BILL DART
Yerba Buena Jazz Band
Courtesy of George Fletcher

DICK LAMMI
Yerba Buena Jazz Band
Courtesy of George Fletcher

JACK BUCK-SQUIRES GIRSBACK
FREDDIE HIGUERA-BOB SCOBEY
Jamming in Golden Gate Park
Courtesy of Bill Napier

WALLY ROSE
Yerba Buena Jazz Band
Courtesy of George Fletcher

commercial musician in the best meaning of the word. I mean by this, that he wanted to be heard by the greatest number of people possible, and he wanted to sell as many records as possible. He had much faith in the public's taste, he was convinced his music was good, pleasing and 'mainstream-contemporary', and he was absolutely certain that success would come if he could only expose his music to vast audiences.

"I never saw him really angry, although I was to spend a lot of time with him, especially during record sessions when things can get rather tense; he was always laughing and joking with the other musicians; he never lost his sense of humor and of proportion, and kept going straight ahead because he was sure success would come.

"I did quite a lot of recordings with him, first for my label, 'Jazz Man' and later for 'Good Time Jazz', where I was working for Les Koenig. I remember especially, a session in San Francisco with 'Darnell Howard' and 'Burt Bales', among others, which was a dream of a session where everything clicked, and the interplay between Bob and Darnell and Burt, who had never played together before, nor rehearsed, was absolutely tremendous. We cut four sides in two hours, and as producer, I had practically nothing to do because it was all happening by itself. I just sat back in the control room and enjoyed the music!

"That was in 1949 or 50, and because of Bob, I did the only 'vocal' I have ever attempted. There was a spirited argument between the musicians as to who should shout 'Oh Play That Thing' at the right time on 'Dippermouth', and Scobey settled the discussion by saying 'Let Nesuhi do it', and I did (This is an example of Bob's skill at human relations and solving people problems).

"I felt that in some of his later bands 'Scobey' didn't always play with musicians who were really worthy of standing beside him. He was a most underestimated musician, with a purity of tone on slow numbers, and drive and bite on fast tunes, which set him aside from most of his contemporaries. Broadly speaking, he came from the 'Louis Armstrong' tradition, but then what trumpet player, or rather what musician, didn't?

There was an incredible sense of time and space and majesty in Bob's phrases . . . ."

WORLD WAR II

Another trumpet blew for Bob and 3,000,000 other young American men on December 7, 1941. The drums and the bugles sounded the alarms of war and for the 'YBJB" their careers were interrupted.

By 1942 they had to dissolve the band to meet their

patriotic obligations. They scattered through all the military groups, into the Army, the Navy and the Air Force. America was involved and at war—World War II. Noel Drady, a jazz fan was there!

". . . . I met Bob at the World's Fair. He was in a big band and one of the members of the small jazz group that would step out front and play some great music. When the war broke out, an attempt was made to keep the band together by an officer from the Naval Station at Livermore, California. Watters and several others from the band were accepted by the Navy and were able to stay in the Bay Area. Bob, however, ended up in the Army. Bob would always sit-in when he was home on leave . . . ."

Scobey served three years, six months, and seven days in the Third ASF Band. Happily for him, classed as he was, in a civilian pre-war occupation as 'Band or Bandsman', it gave him an opportunity to keep his hand in music.

He was decorated with 'The American Theatre Service Medal', 'The Good Conduct Medal', and the 'Victory Medal' (which meant that he never went overseas, kept out of the brig, and was stuck until the war was over.) His discharge shows no wounds received in action except perhaps from a boot camp training sargeant who was impartial to all new recruits in that regard.

The war was over and Bob was ready and eager to get back with his buddies and play jazz!

4 AIN'T GONNA STUDY WAR NO MO'

SEPTEMBER OF 1945, THREE MONTHS before Bob was to be discharged, signaled the end of the war-years' prosperity. A series of strikes began at Ford and General Motors. Bob's one-time $85.00 a week, huge earnings, just before he was drafted, was a thing of the past now! Times were getting worse. By March, the workers "rebellion" had started paralyzing the lumber, oil, utility, steel and coal industries.

January 27, 1946; after several hours of rounding up his personal possessions, Bob walked out of the gates of Fort Washington, California separation center, eager to resume his civilian life.

> *I'm goin' to lay down my swo'd and' shield,*
> *Down by the riverside, Down by the riverside*
> *Down by the riverside.*
> *I'm goin' to lay down my swo'd and' shield,*
> *Down by the riverside.*
> *Ain't goin' to study war no mo'!*

He immediately looked up his old pre-war buddies; 'Turk Murphy' and 'Lu Watters', and within a few weeks of his discharge they were all back together at the Dawn Club on Annie Street in San Francisco, swinging better than ever before!

I wrote to Lu Watters, inquiring about this period, but at the time he was too ill and on medication. (Ironically Scobey, Clancy and Watters all suffered with cancer in later years). His wife, Pat recalled those days with a little warm nostalgia.

". . . . One thing that stands out were the many kindred spirits that gigged around the Bay Area. Although Bob was quite a bit younger than most members of the band, he played so well, he fit right in with the group. I was happy to be a part of those fun-times. The boys were a super hit!

"At the Grand Opening of the Dawn Club, the crowds jammed in to hear the supreme sounds of the newly re-organized 'YERBA BUENA JAZZ BAND'. (By the way, Yerba Buena is also spanish for 'good grass'!) It was good to listen to them again, after the more than three year break-up. These were good times for everyone!

"Well, for nine months, everyone had one big ball! Then in January of '47, Disaster Struck! The Dawn Club folded.

Courtesy of the Los Angeles Public Library

Too many thieves! . . . ."

Scobey was the driving force behind the 'Yerba Buena Jazz Band', yet he was never given credit for his leadership in any later chronicles. How could this happen?

Like much of history, many stories are told and evolve that color the truth. So it was with 'the Yerba Buena Jazz Band'. I had a feeling of uneasiness, perhaps intuition, there was more to the story. Something wasn't quite 'right' about the history of San Francisco Jazz.

I wrote to Lu Watters, Turk Murphy and all of the musicians of that era—each one, who I felt knew something more about the infancy period of the 'YBJB'. No one seemed to want to write about those days or change the history books.

My search continued through the year, then I wrote to Pat Watters asking, *"How in the world did the group arrive at the 'YBJB' name?"* She told me it was San Francisco's original city name and didn't add any other details at the time. I accepted what she had to say but was still left with the feeling, I did not have the whole story.

During a conversation with a friend of hers, she related my inquiry about the 'YBJB' name origin and her friend asked her if she *"told me the truth?"* That spirited her to send me a communication and luckily it reached me before I went to press . . . .

". . . . I thought of something else in connection with the name 'Yerba Buena'.

The band started as a cooperative venture.

There were to be no stars, no spotlights, no music stands, no funny hats.

That's why a name was chosen, so that the band could be booked as the 'Yerba Buena Jazz Band'—like the Casa Loma Band (before your time, but very popular in the pre-war years—not, however, a jazz band.)

A friend reminded me when he said 'Did you tell her the truth? . . . ."

Pat

So, at last, the mystery unravelled. Watters had always been given credit, erroneously, for the start of the group when in fact it was a joint venture. I can understand how it might have happened; the need by a historian to identify the group with a single, easy to remember, name. Later writers picked it up automatically.

The enthusiastic group initiated the revival and their teamwork was the cause of their sensational popularity. I could hear it in their recordings. Watters never played music after the band separated. The true driving force and the lion's share of the credit must, in fairness and in accuracy, go to the men who continued to play, Bob and Turk. Bob Scobey went on to make the largest contribution through his diversification and most often recorded personality of all the members of the 'YBJB', and Turk Murphy was a very close second.

YERBA BUENA JAZZ BAND
Courtesy of Duncan P. Scheidt

Left to right:
Harry Mordecai
Turk Murphy
Bill Dart
Lu Watters
Bob Scobey
Bob Helm
Wally Rose
Dick Lammi

This removes nothing of the credit that is due all of these young men who gave so much of themselves. It just puts into clearer focus, the revival of Jazz around San Francisco and later throughout the world by the men who struggled to keep it going.

Besides live broadcasts direct from the club, in June of 1946 and on six successive Mondays, the fellows met in the Avalon Ballroom on Post Street off Van Ness in San Francisco, and the recording sessions, under the West Coast label, resumed once again.

Two mikes were set in front of the band on the stage. The sound was carried, via leased telephone wire, to the distant recording studio several blocks away, where direct disc masters were cut. In the early days, the studios were too small and crowded with technical equipment to hold a band, so telephone transmitting was a commonly used way of

". . . . I remember now, back at the Dawn Club, there was a hot controversy among the regular fans: Who was better, Lu or Bob? Among the orthodox, purist traditionalists, Bob was considered perhaps a bit too flexible or facile, if not flashy. Bob was so much more informal in personal style that to many fans, he was suspect. They were so serious about the music and the old records, that they were convinced it should be grim. I was a victim of this attitude, for a while, but then broke away from it.

"Bill Napier (then Bill Ashbury) and I, among the young players, joined a sizable group of listeners who decided Scobey was better, that he was more flexible (and hence better, not worse) and played a more lyrical, 'Louis-like' horn.

"There was (and still is) a rigid, reactionary, orthodox prevalence among the 'YBJB'' followers. When Bob put his own band together at 'Victor & Roxie's', many of these types felt he wasn't carrying on 'the tradition' because he played in too 'swingy' a way and played 'non-classic' tunes such as 'Pretty Baby'. I liked him for doing this, but I felt slightly 'wicked' and rebellious for preferring his style since the orthodoxed, Lu Watters crowd thought it was wicked . . . ."

JIM GOGGIN

These were times when a lot of kids would hang around the clubs to listen to the music. Jim Goggin is now a Bank of America Vice President in San Leandro, but he was, and still is, one of the multitude of loyal jazz fans that carry on a love for American Jazz.

". . . . Bob is about the only person I have ever known who could knock me out by just humming. I well remember him humming a few bars to emphasize a point of music in conversations with me.

"I was extremely keen on Bob, and I followed him to the places he played like the Tin Angel, The Pioneer Inn, Victor and Roxie's, and the Hangover Club. I liked his idea of finding a new freedom in music. The warm, relaxed sound he obtained was superb. Some of my favorites are: 'All The Wrongs', I still get chills when that record is played. 'Strange Blues', I think is better than Wingy's . . . ."

Bob was not always relaxed though. Some of the things that nettled Bob were sloppiness and an unprofessional attitude.

". . . . One time, at an afternoon session, his group was doing 'Sobbin' Blues' and somehow it became 'Wang Wang Blues' before they were through. This was one of the few times I saw Bob become irritated.

"On a Good Time Jazz recording date, to get the right tempo for '1919 Rag', Scobey, Murphy, Napier, Bales, Newman, Girsback, and Ward marched around the studio so they could get the timing they wanted. It was a hilarious sight and I understand everybody in the studio was chuckling. That was the same session they forced out 'Harry James' Orchestra' who ran overtime. A number of the guys from James' band stuck around to listen to their session.

"Bob loved golf and horses but he always seemed to have more luck with golf. Stan Ward, the drummer, used to supplement his income by betting on horses and he tried to get Bob to adopt a more conservative approach. 'Bet the horse to show rather than just to win', Stan would caution Bob.

"When Lu Watters left 'Hambone Kelly's', Bob tried to provide live jazz for minors, which was a noble idea, but you just can't sell that much coke to make it feasible. But how many would have even tried? . . . ."

BILL NEWMAN
Courtesy of Ed Lawless

SQUIRES GIRSBACK
Courtesy of Ed Lawless

TURK MURPHY
Courtesy of Shortie Short

BURT BALES
Courtesy of Ed Lawless

JOE DARENSBOURG
Courtesy of Ed Lawless

Joe Darensbourg, a great jazz clarinetist, first met Bob in San Francisco while he was still with the 'YBJB' at the Dawn Club. Later on, Joe joined in at Hambone Kelly's.

"*. . . . I used to go and 'jam' with him quite often. In fact, the whole 'Kid Ory's Band' used to go. One of the highlights I can remember was when Bob played with 'Kid Ory' at the Hangover Club. He had replaced 'Mutt Carey' and I was in the band at the same time.*

"During my musical career I ran into Bob several times. As you know, I played with 'Louis Armstrong's Band' and when we were in Chicago I would always go visit and sit in with Bob at his club. One time we were in London and I ran into him. We laughed and talked about the days of San Francisco and also Seattle with 'Johnny Wittwer' at the China Pheasant.

"When I had my hit record of 'Yellow Dog Blues' Bob called me and wanted me to play with his band, but I was getting ready to join the 'Louis Armstrong All Stars' at the time and had to turn him down.

"Bob was a very fine musician, among the very best, as well as a nice fellow. I always enjoyed playing with him as you could always follow and understand what he was playing . . . ."

Larry Quilligan, a jazz devotee, lived in the Bay Area while he was assigned to Alcatraz as a correctional officer.

LARRY QUILLIGAN
Officer at Alcatraz

"*. . . . I saw Bob in 1947 during a visit to California. We got to be friends after my assignment to Alcatraz two years later and when he was playing with Watters at Hambone Kelly's.*

"Hambone's was, as you may have heard, a good place to eat. Lu himself, held forth in the kitchen as well as on the bandstand. At that time I was single, residing in BOQ (bachelor officer quarters) on Alcatraz and usually eating prison food. So you can imagine how important food was to me. Hambone's featured old-time silent movies nightly, followed by about a half hour of solo piano (with many rags) by 'Wally Rose', just before the full band came on, fortissimo, at about 9:00 p.m.!

"It is simply impossible to convey in words my memories of Hambone Kelly's, or of the band, or of Bob and his playing at that time! It was unique, it was intensely moving, to the point of being thrilling, and it was an emotional jag the like of which I never experienced before or since! For one that did not experience it, there is just no way to describe it effectively! The food, the movies, the camaraderie, the fun and especially the music had to be experienced! You either

liked the music at Hambone Kelly's or you went elsewhere. Even the juke-box, played at intermission and at other times, had only the records of 'Jelly Roll Morton', 'King Oliver', 'Louis Armstrong' and other such primitive and righteous records on it - take it or leave it! Bob had 'Louis' for a musical model and it told in his playing. Yet, in spite of that (or because of it!), his tone had its own freshly minted and definitive sound!

"The late, super clarinetist and violinist, 'Darnell Howard', played with many of the old, great bands, including 'King Oliver'. He told me many times how fond he was of Bob's playing and how much the 'YBJB' reminded him of the old days with Oliver. High praise, I'd say, coming from such a great musician as Darnell Howard!

DARNELL HOWARD
Courtesy of Ed Lawless

"I shared with Bob a love of the limerick, bawdy and blasphemous, and he would regale me at intermissions with an inexhaustible store of them which he cited from memory, ad infinitum . . . ."

I recall a few limericks too. I do remember at the time though, some of them were a little raw for me as I was a bit prudish in my younger years. Bob always had someone laughing.

Most people interested in the printed word have come across at least one limerick in their life. F.A. Wright, in a book titled Greek Social Life, suggests that the limerick goes back to Aristophanes (448?-?380 B.C.), the greatest of the Greek comic poets. And there was a fad of unlaundered limericks of which Bob had the greatest pleasure in telling:

> *There was a fat lady of Clyde*
> *Whose shoelaces once came untied*
> *She feared that to bend*
> *Would display her rear end,*
> *So she cried and she cried and she cried.*
>
> *Anonymous*

> *On a maiden a man once begat*
> *Bouncing triplets named Nat, Tat and Pat;*
> *'Twas fun in the breeding*
> *But hell in the feeding;*
> *She hadn't a spare tit for Tat.*
>
> *Anonymous*

> *An accident really uncanny*
> *Befell a respectable granny;*
> *She sat down in a chair*
> *While her false teeth were there,*
> *And bit herself right in the fanny.*
>
> *Anonymous*

It seems most limericks were written about the female by men. This gives me the golden opportunity to write several myself as a humorous tribute to Bob who really appreciated a good limerick.

> *Dear Rodney once spied a new fling,*
> *Proud beauty that made robins sing.*
> *When he took her to bed*
> *She turned on 'Carson' instead;*
> *"Next to 'Johnny' you haven't the zing!"*
>
> *Jan Scobey*

There once was a braggart named Roy,
Who thought he could bring ladies joy,
Although he could get 'em
He soon would upset 'em
Roy's joy . . . was simply a toy.

Jan Scobey

A lot of musicians jammed at the Hangover Club, including Kid Ory and his band. Often times, band members fluctuated and perhaps four or five bands intertwined using the same side men as jobs came up.

Bob enjoyed listening to fine records. He loved 'Louis Armstrong', 'J.P. Sousa' marches, and 'King Oliver'.

As I'm writing, I am listening to 'At a Georgia Camp Meeting' and Wingy Manone's 'Memphis Blues'. I can hear why Bob dug these sounds. 'Sobbin Blues' by King Oliver and his Dixie Syncopators—there it was, that strong sense of timing—one of Bob's signatures.

When he left the 'YBJB' he made a most important choice and decision which changed his professional direction profoundly and affected his musical career. He wanted to explore and develop his own unique sound of jazz.

Watters was a stickler for the 'oom-chuck' beat of traditional jazz. Bob had a new, looser style. These musical ideas needed expression. Bob enjoyed sticking to the lead of a tune and, of course, traditional jazz; although it held a good deal of ensemble playing; in the 'YBJB' the jazz choruses would go on, seemingly forever—each guy taking a solo, each tune.

Bob found this monotonous. He felt it would wear and tear an audience down and preferred an even larger library of music than the traditional 'dixieland' book. Bob believed jazz should be simple, direct and musically interesting. Nothing is more difficult, and it requires tremendous musicianship to be successful in this fashion.

Watters had quit playing, partly because he had a serious heart condition and partly because the music business demanded a certain amount of traveling.

About a year after Hambone Kelly's closed, Bob re-opened it as 'Alexander's'. Poor Bob! He tried to make it on cokes, without booze, and it just couldn't go. It takes a lot of liquor sales to support a seven piece band. Providing live jazz to minors, drinking cokes, was a lost cause for the band from the start, but then again he may have had trouble getting a liquor license after a 1940 bust:

SAN FRANCISCO CHRONICLE . . . December 25, 1940
"*. . . . ENTERTAINERS HELD ON NARCOTICS*

HANGOVER CLUB
Courtesy of Ed Lawless

CHARGE! Police arrested two night club entertainers Robert Scobey 24, 1331 McGee Avenue, Berkeley, and Charles Spencer Haerr 31, 2911 Sixteenth Street, on charges of possession of Narcotics. They said they seized $2000 worth of marijuana in Haerr's room . . . ."

**Entertainers Held
On Narcotics Charge**

Police arrested two night club entertainers, Robert Scoby, 24, 1331 McGee avenue, Berkeley, and Charles Spencer Haerr, 31, 2911 Sixteenth street, on charges of possession of narcotics. They said they seized $2000 worth of marijuana in Haerr's room.

DEC 25 1940

These years were the learning years—and in many ways! Bob found out he could not hold a liquor license with an arrest for a felony. Bob was not involved in the narcotics situation, he just happened to be visiting when the arrest occurred and a few months later, the charge was dropped, and his record cleared.

Left to right: Paul Lingle, Hotso Casey, Bob Scobey, Squires Girsback, Turk Murphy

5   SWINGIN' DOORS

> *Bring the good old Trumpet boys,*
> *We'll sing another song.*
> *Sing it with a spirit,*
> *That will start the world along.*
>   (*Marching through Georgia 1865*)

BOB SCOBEY REACHED A NEW HIGH IN HIS career, in 1949—he was to lead his own band of men who would happify the world with their rollicking music!

Scobey considered rhythm the most important of all the elements of music, and he wanted his band to play with great rhythmic looseness, still maintaining force and drive. Bob believed these two qualities, properly combined, would result in a singularly relaxed, yet powerful, new approach to music and with this purpose in mind, he opened at Victor and Roxie's in Oakland, California.

His faith was justified. The club and Bob's band were a smash hit, and you couldn't get another soul in the place! They came and they stayed, jammed in, elbow to elbow, everyone digging the sounds!

What was to have been a short engagement developed into a three year stay. Scobey was on his way to greatness as his ideas met with instant and rapidly growing, public support.

Bob was recording on his own label now, Ragtime Records, and his popularity boosted sales across the country. Larry Kostka, drummer, has these early recordings:

"*. . . . If you listen to enough of Bob's records, right at this time, you can hear he was trying to emerge and develop a more swinging style of music than what he was able to play in the old 'YBJB'. They were restricted by very tight rhythm, that really did nothing but clunk, clunk, clunk.*

"*Bob was getting away from this. You could tell by the way he was playing, by the swing in his horn. He was trying to push the band with his direction . . . .*"

Jack Buck and Bob played together on a steady basis after Bob formed his own band. They were tight friends as well as brothers in music.

"*. . . . The Old Frisco Jazz Band, that I was part of, had broken up. When Bob got the job at 'Victor and Roxie's'; 'Hotso Casey', 'Gordon Edwards', 'Burt Bales' and I were in*

CLANCY HAYES
©Jan Scobey 1976

GORDON 'GRAMPS' EDWARDS
Courtesy of Ed Lawless

**CLANCY HAYES
MINSTREL EXTRAORDINAIRE**
Courtesy of James van Thijn

JACK BUCK
Courtesy of Ed Lawless

the band. The fans dug us.

"One night, 'Clancy Hayes' strolled by and he stayed to play and sing. Victor heard him, and put him on the payroll. Now we were really cooking, rolling, and we were getting huge crowds. It turned into a roaring, three year stand. The personnel of the band changed over the years, but Bob, Clancy and I played together from then until Bob moved to Chicago . . . ."

Swingin' Doors, Swingin' Doors, he said,
"Young man, don't go through those swingin' doors.
You can wine 'em, you can dine 'em,
And they'll steal your stick and diamond,
And they'll throw you through them swingin' doors.

. . . Clancy Hayes

These fun lyrics were written by 'Clancy Hayes', artist superb, who played and was featured with 'Bob Scobey's Frisco Jazz Band' for 16 years.

They had a musical combination that grooved together and meshed winningly. Clancy Hayes was featured with Bob on 18 albums and they recorded for Good Time Jazz, Verve, R.C.A. and Jansco.

Clancy Hayes was born in Caney, Kansas, on November 14, 1908, the seventh son of a seventh son. His parents were both musical and his Dad led the local band for fourth of July parades. All of his older brothers were musicians.

"I just grew up in an orchestra," laughed Clancy.

For a while he toured with his brother's band, then in 1926, he moved to San Francisco. During the early years of his career, he worked for NBC when they opened their local studios.

The next 20 years, until his fateful meeting with 'Scobey', were a rounding out and maturing of his singing style and musical ability on the banjo and guitar.

In their early recordings, using many of the traditional charts and adding the spice of currently popular works, 'Scobey' and 'Clancy' achieved international prominence via record sales.

To me, 'Clancy Hayes' was 'Minstrel-Extraordinaire'. He was a one-man minstrel show, poet and musician. Some of his own compositions 'Travelin' Shoes', 'Huggin' and Chalkin', 'In New Orleans', 'Ten To One It's Tennessee', 'Parson's Kansas Blues', and 'Swingin' Doors', were requested as often as 'Ace In the Hole'. Just like minstrels of yesteryear, he was anxiously welcomed by his fans as he traveled across the country.

When Clancy belted out 'Silver Dollar Blues' or 'Chicago', while being accompanied by Bob's brassy, powerful trumpet; the combination was pulsating. Clancy is one of the great folk singers of all time. He vocalized all the 'Happy Sounds' of the 'Scobey Frisco Band'. He was tops! His execution of the guitar was lyrical and his banjo was pure "Mississippi - summer day - show stopper'.

It was his singing style that was really unique. Clancy had a phenomenal memory for the words and music, and was a veritable encyclopedia of jazz and American folk tunes. He knew them all! Everyone who knew anything about Clancy, thought of him as a walking library for this form of specialized music. He compiled his own music folio of many old, old songs and he knew all the verses as well—which was a rarity. He had also written several hundred of his own compositions.

The Examiner reported on one of Clancy's and Bob's steady TV appearances. They aired on the Bay Area TV Station KPIX every Tuesday at 10:30 on 'Clancy's Corner'.

SAN FRANCISCO EXAMINER

".... They sound off their explosive, rooty-too-toots with a flourish: Clancy Hayes, the big, bald banjo player and dixieland singer; and Bob Scobey and his 'don't call it' Frisco Jazz Band. This is what the networks should bring into view instead of those summer replacement shows! ...."

Through the years, the public became so accustomed to seeing and hearing Bob and Clancy together in their performances, they were often thought of as one person.

Occasionally band members would shift around. During this period 'Jack Buck' played trombone and doubled on piano. Famed 'Darnell Howard', was in the Scobey Band

GEORGE PROBERT

HANGOVER CLUB
TURK MURPHY, BOB SCOBEY,
ALBERT NICHOLAS
Courtesy of Ed Lawless

from time to time.

Darnell was a clarinetist as well as a violinist, and most of his recognition came from playing the clarinet. In his early musical career, he played with 'King Oliver' at the New Orleans Plantation Cafe and he later fluted for 'Earl Fatha Hines', in 1928, in Chicago at the Grand Terrace Ballroom. Darnell Howard also did several recordings with Bob.

Burt Bales, who was added to the band at Victor & Roxie's, when the money got better, did a lot of Scobey recording sessions at Jenny Lind Hall. The year following, When Nesuhi Ertegun supervised a recording session of 'The Scobey Story' several new faces were added to Bob's roster to assist in various musical spots. 'Albert Nicholas' recorded and played at Victor and Roxie's, and jammed at many of the jazz spots around San Francisco. His experiences were especially steeped in musical history.

'Albert Nicholas' was one of the lucky ones, as he put it, to enjoy being part of the early New Orleans Jazz Tradition. When he was a kid, he would be thrilled just to walk along and carry a jazzman's music case during a parade. Jazz touched his heart and he quickly mastered the clarinet. At a tender age he was in the full swing of music, playing with 'Manuel Perez' and 'Paul Barbarin' at Tom Anderson's Cafe in Storyville, located at Basin & Iberville Streets, just a few doors and steps from Mahogany Hall.

In 1925, 'Nicholas' played with a young reed section including 'Darnell Howard' and 'Barney Bigard' in 'King Oliver's Dixie Syncopators' ensemble at the Plantation Cafe.

With professionals like Howard, Buck, Bales and Nicholas the Scobey band got to the hearts of his followers.

How does a band come together to make the rare amalgam of meshing musicians creating great music? The leader is the prime mover, of course. He must have the ability to select talented professionals, make the administrative details, and to hustle for work. Beyond that, a good side man will often come to the leader's attention on his own, as George Probert did!

". . . . I had gone up to the Bay Area to see what was going on. I called my old friend, 'Burt Bales', and he had invited me to come and sit-in at 'Victor and Roxie's', where Bob had his group. A few sets passed and Bob enjoyed my sound. He asked me if I would like to join his group. I naturally jumped at the chance, however, I still had to wait out my union transfer. To help me live, Bob gave me all the band tips for the next three months, until I finally got my Local 6 card and officially joined the band.

"When we opened at the Greenwich Village in Palo Alto the end of 1950, that started my career. I worked for Bob and

GEORGE PROBERT

ALBERT NICHOLAS
Courtesy of Ed Lawless

was part of the band on and off until August of '53. It was Bob who gave me my first, big chance with his kind offer and help . . . .''

It was more than occasionally that the band members shifted around. 'Dick Lammi', played bass and a solid tuba, 'Freddie Higuera' and 'Gordon Edwards' alternated their rolls of drumming with Scobey's band.

Once in awhile, probably a little too often for the leader,

BOB SCOBEY
Courtesy of Marilyn Napier McGwynn

Bob's sidemen would get sick or were otherwise indisposed. The leader, in a situation like this can be in a tough spot, especially if all the other cats who play a particular instrument are booked up or just not in town. The leader has to start sweating, get on the phone, and hope someone turns up. Sometimes you are blessed with a pleasant surprise and your substitute, who happens to be in between gigs, turns out to be a star in his own right. Jim Goggin helped Bob out on one occasion.

". . . . I was active in the local jazz society and often hired Bob for afternoon sessions held at Cook's Union Hall in Oakland. One time, after such a session, we all went over to 'Victor & Roxie's' and 'Jack Buck' became ill. This meant Bob would be the only front line member as he didn't have a clarinet man either at the time. Bob asked if I could go get

ALEXANDER'S JAZZ BAND
Victor and Roxie's
Left to right: BOB SCOBEY, JACK BUCK,
CLANCY HAYES, ?, BILL NAPIER
Courtesy of Marilyn Napier McGwynn

MARILYN
NAPIER
MCGWYNN

'Albert Nicholas' who was in San Francisco, which I did, and then I sat back and heard some of the greatest music ever.

"Nick and Bob really spoke the same language. Those wonderful Ragtime label records with 'Albert Nicholas' were made with very few takes and they sound just as good today. 'Burt Bales' considers these records to be tops too.

"Sometimes the party mood would get going and once I even had occasion to join the guys with my washboard on one of the sets at the jazz society sessions. Wow!! What times we had! . . . ."

Marilyn Napier McGwynn knew Bob, worked with him as cashier, bookkeeper and was one of the 'family' for years.

". . . . I was at 'Victor & Roxie's in 1951. I had a real problem getting in the club unless I tagged along with someone who could pass for an adult. Conveniently located to the club, with connecting doors, was a coffee shop. Most of my early exposure to Bob and his band was sort of second hand, listening through the 'Swingin' Doors'. (I wonder if

Clancy wrote his tune 'Swingin' Doors' while at this club)?

"Bob and the guys would spend their intermissions with us in the coffee shop. After we became friends, he would leave the door open so we could see as well as hear them. Through this association, I did manage to get on the 'right' side of those 'swingin' doors on various occasions. Of course, I was enthralled and in a trance, with the sound of the band.

"You know 'Papa Scobey' had one generous quality. He always treated everyone as if they were really and truly important. We all loved him dearly.

"Sometimes, and it would really get to Bob if it happened in succession, personnel changes, at times were frequent. Bob didn't like the members of his band to drink to excess while playing, also there were personality conflicts that played a big part . . . ."

BOB MIELKE
Courtesy of Ed Lawless

'Papa Scobey' as he was tagged, had been instrumental in inspiring and helping many a young musician to a place of recognition and fame in their careers.

Bob Mielke reminisced of the way Scobey sparked his musical interests.

". . . . When I was only 14, I caught the group live, in 1940, I guess. My brother and sister were quite a bit older and they let me tag along with them and sneak in the club. We were attracted there by the live broadcasts. Later, I became a regular weekend attendee. They put me in a dark corner and sold me cokes.

I took up the trombone as a result of the 'YBJB' inspiration, when I was 16. I stood in awe of the musicians, and finally Bob allowed me to sit-in and even hired me to sub on a few weekends. At the time, I felt I was a neophyte and was scared, but I sure was thrilled to be able to sit-in and flattered to be asked to play on the gig at all. Bob was friendly and supportive. He was relaxed and sought to put me at my ease.

"I did appreciate that, but accepted his encouragement in a negative light. Since I saw myself as strictly a neophyte, the fact Bob let me sit-in, and even hired me, lowered my esteem for him at the time. If he couldn't figure out how limited I was, what could he know?

"I know now that was a perverse reaction———encouraging young players is only to be admired and one measure of a man's personal security and stature . . . ."

Mielke saw first hand, Bob's inaugural attempt to create a larger band to reach for the big band sound, that stayed so popular.

HEIDI SWETINA

". . . . I was involved in one recording date—April, 1952, the one at 'Jenny Lind Hall'. On that session one of my favorites we recorded was 'Peoria' among others. This was also Nesuhi Ertegun's baby. It was Scobey's first venture into a larger band—he added two trombones to create a three part section. 'Jack Buck' scored simple chord back-ups and ensemble for the three trombones. I was thrilled, flattered and nervous to be on this date.

"I worked with Bob on weekends at the 'Pioneer Village' in Lafayette for a while. I didn't get to know Bob or others of his generation at that time except superficially, because I was running scared then and couldn't feel on an equal footing. I was slow to mature, to really professionalize; and not feeling equal, was closed-off. I wished I could have known Bob later when I gained more confidence . . . ."

Bob hired female vocalists for his band. Another example of Bob's continual search for the magical formula that would give him the sudden, total success he was striving for.

Heidi Swetina, pictured here in all her regalia, was the *"Voice that wouldn't travel"*. She enjoyed the Bay Area too much. Heidi sang with Bob while he was in Frisco, but never when he left town for Vegas, Chicago or New York. Much of the memorabilia from the clubs Bob played in, during his tours, was sent on to Heidi and because of her faithful cataloging she had them available.

Heidi and her husband Sam were introduced to Bob back at the Dawn Club and they remained fans and friends ever since. They were often guests in his home and would listen and criticize various recordings, upon request, before Bob issued them.

Heidi sang with many bands in the Bay Area and was also tagged as *"the girl with the trombone voice"*. She really could belt them out.

DOUG AND BARBARA KEELING

". . . . I wished 'Bob Scobey' had stayed in Lafayette, California. The dance floor was so large, and it was jumping out there in the '50's. We tried to out dance Scobey's band but we would always tire first . . . ."

When the band played in Lafayette, Barbara Keeling worked along with Bob and Clancy, putting on 'a charleston exhibition' to songs like 'Yes, Sir That's My Baby' and 'Charleston', stirring up an interest of the Roaring 20's dance favorites.

". . . . Can't help thinking of Clancy too! He used to call me Miss Question Mark because of a funny shaped feather I wore in my hair as part of the costume. I remember, Bob wanted to hire me for an appearance at the Palmer House in

Chicago and I couldn't make it because I was newly married. Sure miss both Clancy and Bob. Those were the swinging days!...."

Female vocalists, dance acts, comedy acts; Scobey never quit looking and trying for the magical key. I think he knew he had it deep in the very core of his music, but he was impatient and couldn't run with it, fast enough.

Totaling up the receipts from the few nights at the El Rancho and extra one-nighters which were sparse, along with a few recording sessions, Bob found it necessary, at times, to take on jobs away from music . . . carpet cleaning, painting, and whatever. It was all he could do to scrape funds together between musical jobs.

Russ Bernard of Oakland caught many of Scobey's 'Opening Nights'.

BOB SCOBEY, RUSS BERNARD, EARL WATKINS
Victor and Roxie's
Courtesy of Russ Bernard

". . . . I thought it would be just another dixie band, and from right out in front of the club, I could hear this horn had a style of its own. During intermission, I asked Bob to come to my table. After talking a while, when he was ready to do another show, Bob asked me what tune I would like to hear. I requested 'Careless Love'.

"After that night, everytime I would walk into a club where he was appearing over the years, he always remembered my favorite, and would say, 'Here's Careless Love for brother Russ'. He never missed once. I would follow him around town for all of his opening nights. A couple of them, I remember well, were the El Rancho and Showboat. We talked about music all the time, and his uncanny ability. When I was in on opening nights, he would come over and ask me how the acoustics were. It made me feel important.

"I did see Bob one day, and this was the only time, quite down in the dumps and discouraged. He was selling insurance! It wasn't like him at all. He confided in me and said he was thinking of quitting the music business altogether. He couldn't get work for his band. I would like to think the encouragement I gave him that day helped. However, Bob always impressed me as being a man of ability, and his determination left me without any doubt that he would succeed.

"I remember one time at the El Rancho Grande, when we were talking, he was thinking of giving up smoking because of cancer. The next time I saw him he had quit smoking for good!

"About music, I didn't know a B-flat from a hockey puck. I think that is why so many people enjoyed Bob's music. He played to please the audience. He played for the people who came in to hear him, actually people that loved him and his music. I think this is what made him so outstanding. I feel, too many musicians today play to entertain themselves and it always turns me off. I know when Bob asked my opinion it was not based on my technical knowledge because I had none. To him, I represented the audience. Bob knew its all well and good to have some professional critic give you a good rate, but in the final analysis, the audiences are the ones you have to please . . . ."

'Ernie Lewis', currently Assistant to the President of the American Federation of Musicians in New York played for quite a while with Scobey and is on several recordings.

ERNIE LEWIS
Courtesy of Merkle Press

". . . . I met Bob through 'Earl Watkins' when they needed a piano man while playing at Peggy Toke Watkins Club, 'The Tin Angel', on Embarcadero Street.

"That summer Bob got an engagement to play the 'Blue Note' in Chicago and we broke the house record for attendance. We also appeared at the "Typhany Club' in Los Angeles at which time the band recorded at the Police Academy, every day, for a whole week—for Pacific Records.

"One of the nicest recordings I made with Bob was 'Mobile' with 'Clancy Hayes' doing the vocal on it. I also remember that 'Sweet Georgia Brown' came off well.

"Bob was one of the finest musicians I have ever played with. He knew what he was playing at all times. His band had a good feeling in it and everyone in the band gave their all when we hit the bandstand. Bob won't be forgotten because there were just too many good times! . . . ."

During the session's intermission or break, the mesmerized 'Shelly Manne' is looking on, while 'Jesse Fuller' plays his own invention, the *"Fodola"* as he called it. This picture was taken during a recording session with 'Claire Austin', 'Shelly Manne' 'Stan Wrightsman', 'Barney Kessel', and 'Morty Corb' . . . Bob Scobey's Group backed 'Claire Austin'.

'Jesse Fuller' was there to record his 'One Man Band', during their breaks. The photo captures the respect and

FODOLA
Courtesy of Shortie Short

SHELLY MANNE
and JESSE FULLER
Courtesy of Shortie Short

enthusiasm when brother meets brother. That's music for you, the only true communication between people. 'Pud Brown', at the left, is also looking on, quite engrossed. 'Jesse Fuller' has a harmonica in his mouth, a guitar in his hands and he's working the cymbals with his feet.

STAN WRIGHTSMAN and BOB SCOBEY
Recording Session - 1956
Courtesy of Shortie Short

BOB SHORT and PUD BROWN
Courtesy of Shortie Short

STAN WRIGHTSMAN
Courtesy of Shortie Short

JESS STACEY, BOB SHORT, PUD BROWN
Courtesy of Shortie Short

This Christmas Day was spent performing for the inmates at the San Quentin Prison. Often times, Bob was playing at charitable functions, gratis; many entertainers will donate their time and talents. It's one profession that gives freely in order to happify people going through tough times, be it for Easter Seals, American Cancer Society, or a place like San Quentin.

BOB SCOBEY'S BAND, CHRISTMAS DAY, 1955
San Quentin Prison
Left to right: Jesse Tiny Crump, Clancy Hayes,
Squires Girsback, Bob Scobey,
Freddie Higuera, Bill Napier,
Jack Buck

Courtesy of Heidi Swetina

Courtesy of Shortie Short

Newsmen were becoming more aware of Bob and Clancy. Ted Krec, of the Independent Press caught Bob's performance at the big Gene Norman Concert, where the stage was studded with stars . . . 'Louis Armstrong', 'Sidney Bechet', 'Joe Darensbourg' and many others.

TED KREC

". . . . My wife and I got tickets to 'Gene Norman's Jazz Concert' at the Shrine Auditorium in Los Angeles primarily because we wanted to hear 'Sidney Bechet' and his soprano sax.

"'Bob Scobey and His Frisco Band', with 'Clancy Hayes', were also on the program and got a bigger, better, louder applause than even old Sidney. They were tremendous!

"On that autumn evening, many of the nation's big names in the field of Dixieland Jazz had joined forces to present an 'Annual Jazz Concert'. 'Sidney Bechet', grand old man of the soprano saxophone, was there as were many of the top-notch New Orleans musicians.

"Truly it was a night to remember. Trumpets were screaming through intricate melodies and trombones were 'smearing' all over the stage. And the audience, packed solid from orchestra to top balcony, was having a ball.

"Then it happened. A slender, dark-haired young man with a shiny trumpet came on stage with his band. Another man, older, heavy-set, but striking in a white suit, positioned himself at a microphone. He carried a banjo and lost no time getting right to work with it. The band raced through a fast number and the audience cheered. Another number and the applause was deafening.

"The young man with the trumpet was 'Bob Scobey' and the big fellow with the banjo and the happy manner was his right hand man, 'Clancy Hayes'. That night was the beginning!

"I had set up an interview with him for our Sunday supplement, I remember very clearly that I met him for drinks in Hollywood and we talked for quite a while. My impressions of him at that inverview concerned themselves mostly with his nervous energy and drive. He had that all-powerful drive, that get-up-and-go that reflected itself in his music. I never had met anyone quite like him! . . . ."

Bob used the professional name for his band as 'Alexander's Jazz Band' at this time! A few years had gone by and no one was using the name 'Frisco Jazz Band', so Bob decided on the new name for his group. When he first advertized his band that way he received a lot of static and feedback from the people who had originally used the name, even though they were no longer working.

Bob was not above using promotional ideas and

GENE NORMAN CONCERT
BOB SCOBEY - TRUMMY YOUNG - LOUIS ARMSTRONG
Courtesy of Larry Kostka

gimmicks if it helped put his band in front of people. He was never mean and calculating, rather, he was always open-handed and spontaneously genuine, but he loved a joke. So crafty Bob, with obvious tongue-in-cheek delight, for a while ran his ads, 'Don't call it' Frisco Jazz Band!

6 JAZZ AND SEMANTICS

N THE SECOND HALF OF THE FIFTIES, BOB was spreading out to new fields and his happy music was being heard in new places. He was traveling, hitting all the whistle stops, large and small. Scobey and his band were doing it all; the big-time 'Flamingo' in 'Fun-City', Nevada; sophisticated 'Zardi's' in Hollywood; the famed 'Blue Note' and 'Preview Lounge' in Chicago; even far off 'Gotham City' at New York's hip hangouts—the 'Roundtable' and 'Basin Street East'.

Bob and Company took off on a tour of the colleges with renowned lecturer 'Dr. S.I. Hayakawa' to musically illustrate the lecture series on Semantics; 'The Meaning of Jazz'. Best of all, Bob opened 'Storyville', his own night club!

Like most bands, especially the larger ones, personnel continued to fluctuate. Side men came and went for a variety of reasons, but two men remained with Scobey for most of Bob's entire career. They were the songster, 'Clancy Hayes', and the phenomenal 'Bill Napier' on clarinet.

'Bill Napier' was the man who played most of the unique, stimulating clarinet solos on many of Bob's albums, a genuinely powerful virtuoso. Bill looked back down the dusty years to the long shadows of things that were:

EL RANCHO GRANDE,
LAFAYETTE
BILL NAPIER - BOB SCOBEY
CLANCY HAYES
Courtesy of Marilyn Napier McGwynn

". . . . One Saturday night, recently, a group of us were walking to the Sheraton Palace Hotel where I was playing in the Tudor Room. I side-tracked my wife toward a dark,

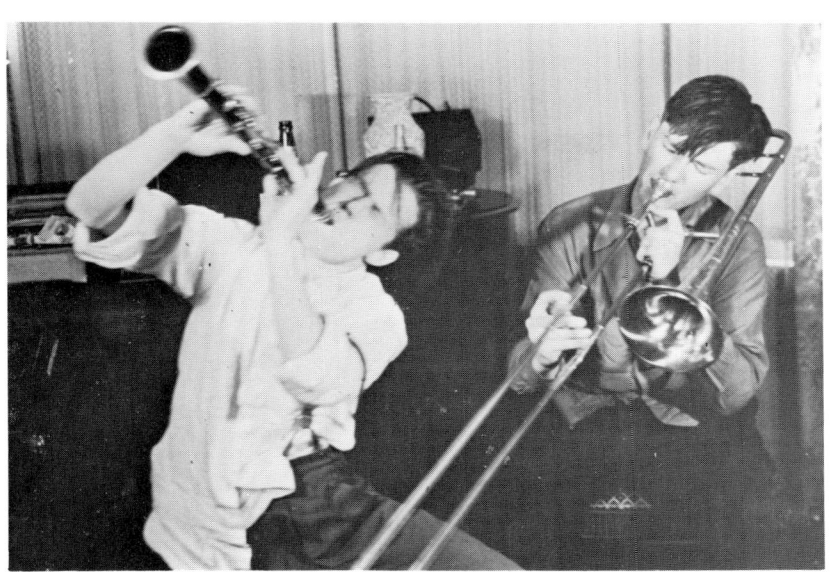

BILL NAPIER - BOB MIELKE
Courtesy of Bill Napier

BOB SCOBEY'S FRISCO BAND
EL RANCHO GRANDE - 1955
Left to right: Bill Napier, Bob Scobey,
Clancy Hayes, Jack Buck,
Dick Lammi, Bob Hotaling
Courtesy of Marilyn Napier McGwynn

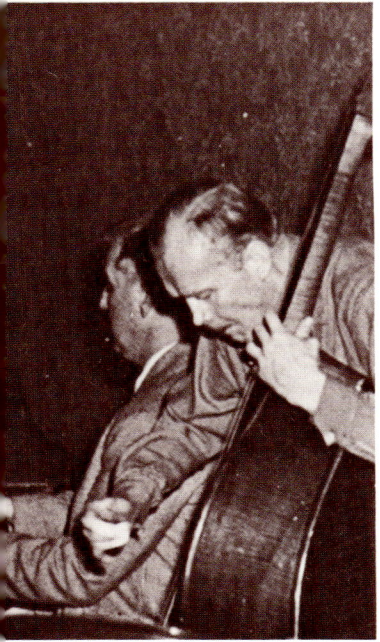

KPIX - TV
JACK BUCK, BILL NAPIER, BOB SCOBEY, CLANCY HAYES
Courtesy of Marilyn Napier McGwynn

empty room, then tried the door, and my wife said, 'Bill, what on earth are you doing, taking me down this dark, scarey alley and looking into empty buildings?

"I replied, 'This is where it all began!' I went on to tell her, 'This is where I first played with Bob Scobey and where I met my friends for the first time. Scobey, Mielke, Murphy . I was only fifteen at the time.

"My feelings about Bob Scobey are so wrapped up in memories and musical experiences that the best thing I might say is that my first experience with music and the influence that got me started as a jazz clarinetist, was my career with 'Bob Scobey'. That will stay with me the rest of my life! . . . ."

Bob took great, personal pleasure in helping other musicians get a start. He liked to talk with young cats and point out things to improve their playing and give them encouragement. Perhaps, this is how he picked up the name 'Papa' Scobey.

Papa was the kind of man who went out of his way for others. It was done without thought, totally unselfishly. He thoroughly enjoyed one-to-one contact. The effect of his passage, like ripples on the surface of a pond, left lasting impressions with others with whom he had this kind of exchange.

BOB SCOBEY'S FRISCO BAND
Left to right: Ernie Lewis, Bob Scobey, Dick Lammi, Clancy Hayes, Jack Buck, Earl Watkins, Bill Napier

Courtesy of Duncan P. Schiedt

BOB HELM
Courtesy of Shortie Short

TURK MURPHY
Courtesy of Marilyn Napier McGwynn

Dick Rippey was a college kid when this happened, but it made such a lasting impression, that he remembers it fondly today.

".... I was going to school in Wisconsin and was interested in 'pop' music at the time. My brother Bob, long-time associate with straight jazz music took me to a 'Gene Mayle' concert in Milwaukee. From that time on I was hooked on traditional jazz. Turk-Watters-Helm-Rose-Short-Clancy and of course the greatest of the horn men 'Scobey'.

"He had versatility unequaled with the ability to do the somewhat 'modern' thing he did with 'Kessel-Manne-Austin' on Contemporary, to 'Raiding the Juke Box' and the

Courtesy of Heidi Swetina

MARVIN NELSON and BOB SCOBEY
SAN FRANCISCO CHRONICLE

great trad stuff he did. Happenings and personality run hand in hand. Let me relate a story which is indicative of the great man 'Scobey' was!

"Bob came to play at the University of Illinois while I was a grad student. I had taken a group with me and a gal I especially wanted to impress. I was sitting near grandstand when the waitress came up and said, 'Bob would like to buy a beer for all of you and his good friend 'Dick Rippey'. Well, Jan, if you don't think I thought I was big stuff!!! Cripes, I was just a dumb college kid. I had met Bob in Chicago when he played at Bourbon Street, gone in several times, probably never paid for the chair I sat in on Army pay, but Bob remembered me. What a guy! . . . ."

In 1956, when the San Francisco Symphony presented

Rolf Lievermann's Concerto for Jazz Band and Orchestra, the conductor Enrique Jorda asked Bob Scobey to augment his band for the occasion.

". . . . It was a breathtaking performance! Aura filled the chambers!" wrote Alexander Fried of the San Francisco Examiner.

"I enjoyed the unusual performance so much, Jazz raised it's barbaric yamp as a climax to the San Francisco Symphony Concert and the effect was literally sensational. Jumps and boogie-woogie battered the ear drums. Blues soothed the shattered nerves. The youthful sell-out crowd was truly delighted. Listeners of older spirit and years simply looked strickened. For my part, I had a grand time of it . . . ."

BLACK HAWK CLUB
(Jazz Center of the West Coast)

San Francisco Symphony Orchestra
ENRIQUE JORDÁ, Conductor

DIXIELAND RAGTIME JAMBOREE

PROGRAM
MASTER OF CEREMONIES — HAWTHORNE

THE SAN FRANCISCO SYMPHONY ORCHESTRA
EARL MURRAY, Associate Conductor

Dances from "Fancy Free" .... Leonard Bernstein

The composer demonstrates in vivid fashion, the influence of jazz music on a symphonic composition

WALLY ROSE'S DIXIELAND BAND
ALLIE LORRAINE, Vocalist

Dixieland One Step — Dippermouth Blues
Tin Roof Blues — Black and White Rag

RAGTIME PIANIST BURT BALES
PHILIP KARP, Bass
LLOYD DAVIS, Percussion } Symphony Members

King Porter Stomp — Blues by Burt Bales
Maple Leaf Rag

EARL "FATHA" HINES AND THE ALL STARS
The World Is Waiting for the Sunrise
Honeysuckle Rose — St. Louis Blues
Darktown Strutters Ball

INTERMISSION

BAY CITY JAZZ BAND
SANFORD NEWBAUER, Director
Yerba Buena Strut — Alligator Blues
Come Back Sweet Papa — Yerba Buena Blues

PIANIST JOE SULLIVAN
Little Rock Get Away — That's A-Plenty
Gin Mill Blues

KID ORY'S CREOLE JAZZ BAND
MARVIN NELSON, Trumpet
PHILIP KARP, Bass } Symphony Members
LLOYD DAVIS, Percussion
Muskrat Ramble — High Society
Savoy Blues

BOB SCOBEY'S FRISCO JAZZ BAND
Augmented by
MARVIN NELSON, Trumpet
PHILIP KARP, Bass } Symphony Members
PHILIP LASPINA, Trombone
CLANCY HAYES, Vocalist and RALPH SUTTON, Pianist
Waiting for the Robert E. Lee — When the Saints Come Marchin In
Canadian Capers — Ace in the Hole
New Orleans — Hobson Street Blues

THE SAN FRANCISCO SYMPHONY ORCHESTRA
ENRIQUE JORDA, Conductor
Rhapsody In Blue .... George Gershwin
WALLY ROSE, Pianist

The jazz musicians will take their places in key solo positions within the Symphony Orchestra

Baldwin Pianos

The San Francisco Symphony Association extends its sincere appreciation to all who have so generously contributed to the success of this unique presentation.

Courtesy of Sanford Newbauer

Billboard, a weekly-trade publication of the music business, on June 11, 1955 wrote:

"*. . . . Bob Scobey must have been a little leery bringing his Frisco Dixielanders to Gotham for the first time in a house that featured arch modernists 'Gerry Mulligan', and 'Chet Baker' on the same bill. However, the freshly minted sound of Scobey's trumpet and the singing of his vocalist 'Clancy Hayes' falls winningly on the ears of two-beat and cool partisans alike!*

"*New York still does not often hear bands of Scobey's caliber, and the audience let's him know how much they appreciate his work . . . .*"

I think it even surprised Bob to be so successful on his first ventures away from San Francisco. He didn't realize the effect his records had, preceding his appearances.

Yes, Bob Scobey played for the people. He had request cards on the tables so the customers would call the tunes they wanted to hear and this would compile most of the show. Bob knew them all and what could be better than giving your audience exactly what they requested. He was out to please them with their favorites.

After a little stay out of town and across the nation, Bob returned to his home base in San Francisco.

By the mid-fifties Bob was into TV specials. A summer TV show called 'Jazz Session' was put together by Dr. Benjamin Draper, the executive producer of the series. Dr. Draper was a pioneer in broadcasting and at one time headed the Television Department of the California Academy of Sciences.

THE JAZZ SESSION
Courtesy of Moss Photography

Jesse Tiny Crump

JAZZ SESSION - KRON - TV
LIZZIE MILES, DR. BENJAMIN DRAPER,
JUNE CHRISTY
Courtesy of Moss Photography

Squire Girsback

Freddie Higuera

Jack Buck

Bill Napier

Bob Scobey

Clancy Hayes

They invited guest stars: 'Duke Ellington', 'Earl 'Fatha' Hines', 'Louis Armstrong', 'June Christy', 'Andre Previn', 'Cab Calloway', 'Jeri Southern' and 'Carmen McRae'. 'Marty Marsala's' band and 'The Rampart Street Paraders', including 'Stan Wrightsman' at the keyboard, 'Matty Matlock', clarinet, 'Nick Fatool' on drums, 'Abe Lincoln' on trombone, and 'Hal McCormick' bass, all sat in with Scobey's band. Wish I could have heard that session. The enthusiasm with having such traditional, exciting musicians all together for one show must have been one big ball. These men have lead bands themselves, but to have them jamming in one session . . .Wow!

These shows were primarily improvizational. Everyone just sang and played the way they felt. Jazz at its very best! Vern Louden directed the show and Bonnie Keever was the musical hostess. Ernie Rook, who was the assistant director at the time, felt the show was a great success and gathered all of the scripts and bound a book entitled the "Jazz Session'.

The series was quite a treat for Bob. He finally had a little socializing time with his musical buddies. Taping a television show, including rehearsal and camera time, runs considerably shorter than, say, a gig in a night club, which runs 6 hours. With the extra hours there was more time to really get to know each other.

Left to right: BOB SCOBEY, DUKE ELLINGTON, ERNIE ROOK, VERN LOUDEN
Courtesy of Moss Photography

**CLANCY HAYES
BOB SCOBEY**
Courtesy of Moss Photography

Left to right: Stan Wrightsman, Matty Matlock,
Bob Scobey, Nick Fatool, Abe Lincoln, Squires Girsback
Courtesy of Moss Photography

One of the shows featured Lizzie Miles performing and singing many selections from the Golden Era of the Blues. She was quite a powerhouse, and no one can hold a candle to her renditions of the Blues.

This series was an extraordinary showcase for Bob and his band, as well as an opportunity to talk with the other musicians. Some of the talks went so well they decided to use them on the show. One show featuring 'Duke Ellington', 'Earl Fatha Hines' and 'Scobey', caught the early beginings of music for these men . . .

Bob Scobey: *"Say, Duke, how did you start in the business?"*
Duke Ellington: *"Well, if you go back far enough, you'd find me in Washington, D.C., my home town. Before coming to New York, forming the band and developing my ideas, I played ragtime piano with small groups in D.C. You see, the East Coast was piano country. There were many fine men who played with a full left hand and conceived beautiful melodic ideas without ever breaking rhythm. The pianists, the fiddle players, the men who played banjo and guitars, they used to play pretty; jazz used to be real pretty."*

Scobey: *"It's easy to see where some of the foundation was being laid for the taste and elegance you brought to the jazz scene. We usually hear about New Orleans' Jazz, but Dixieland music was developing throughout the South. Before radio, there wasn't the exchange of ideas we have now. Different schools of jazz developed in each city.*

Duke: *"By the time I arrived on the New York scene, the east and west or New Orleans Jazz had met and were blending into the music we know today."*

Earl 'Fatha' Hines: *"It wasn't like that in Chicago. We never heard the word Dixieland, that term came much later. We were kept real busy playing the best way we knew how. Chicago really was something in those days. Musicians came from everywhere to play our kind of music. And the spenders came too. It was like a gold-rush and everybody had a good time. 'Louis Armstrong', 'Zutty Singleton' and I worked together a lot. It was the great jazz age of the 20's. You know what I mean, Scobey. Give us a chorus on your horn, something from the 20's. We'll back you up!"* . . . and the roaring jazz session began.

When Duke Ellington sat in playing Royal Garden Blues,

BOB SCOBEY
CLANCY HAYES
EARL FATHA HINES
Courtesy of Moss Photography

the speed was on and these fellows really drove that number home, home to all the audience in and around San Francisco who were tuned in.

Bob Short, a tuba player, was on four or five albums Bob made, and he toured with his band on some of the out of town dates, as well as playing with him in San Francisco.

"... My time of being under the 'impression' of 'Scobey' started even before I met him, from the legends surrounding the 'YBJB', and of course the records. Then, when I really came in contact, personally, with him, it must have been in 1947 when he was at the Melody Club in Oakland. I was on a vacation trip and on my way from Portland to Los Angeles.

"That was in his earliest days as bandleader on his own. His commanding style had already 'taken hold' but was to develop on and until he reached the 'pinnacle' which I felt was in the period between 1959 until his illness overtook him and robbed him of the needed strength to play such swinging powerful leads.

"While we were appearing in Vegas, Bob wanted to learn to fly and I got to be closer to him during that period and could see his natural talents in other areas than music. His unusually strong competence in the period while I was his flight instructor was demonstrated to me in that he hardly needed an 'instructor'. He seemed to grasp the principles of handling the airplane so easily.

"So it was with his trumpet. I'm sure when he was a boy he never had too much trouble accomplishing the mechanics of the instrument. His superb taste in what not to play and his knack for implying notes that he did not play was the basis of his "style."

"While in Vegas he would get into bull sessions with other entertainers and end up joining someone for tennis or golf. The next morning, even when he hadn't had time to stay up on either game, he would overwhelm and devastate his opponents one by one and always seemed to be able to do it without effort. And he looked so good, always in form as though he had been doing it everyday. It was, no doubt, part of his great confidence that he had arrived at during this high period of his life.

"During the time Lizzie Miles was with the band, Bob made a special effort to do everything for her best interest. No matter how hard he tried, she had her 'upbringing' which had taught her 'never to trust no white man' cause they's liable to 'steal her stuff'.

"Once at Storyville in San Francisco, Bob was doing some experiments with 'balance' of the band's volume prepatory to a recording session, and when an extra, strange *microphone appeared on the stage, Lizzie stomped off and went back to her hotel room, and had to be sweet talked into returning to sing again . . . ."*

I had the pleasure of meeting Professor Hayakawa in Mill Valley, California, in 1960, when Bob and I went to visit him at his home and met with his lovely wife and family. He and Bob had quite a discussion of semantics and politics, and renewing of old acquaintances.

Since that time Professor Hayakawa is now Sen. Hayakawa and President Emeritus of San Francisco State University. He is one of our greatest, living semantics experts. Humanitarian in nature, he is also a public figure of increasing importance. His book 'Our Language and Our World' in the chapter, 'Popular Songs and the Facts of Life' draws a masterful and wonderfully, lucid comparison of the bed rock basic honesty of Jazz and the illusions, delusions, myths and conceptions reflected in some modern music lyrics.

Bob appeared in Concert at the San Francisco State College. His band musically illustrated the lecture given by Dr. S.I. Hayakawa, who at the time was Professor of Language Arts at San Francisco College.

The band featured 'Scobey' on trumpet; 'Clancy Hayes', banjo and vocals; 'Bill Napier', clarinet; 'Jesse Tiny Crump', piano; 'Bob Short', tuba; 'Hal McCormick', bass; 'Freddie Higuera', drums. An album by Good Time Jazz, L-12023 was issued and Professor Hayakawa wrote the liner notes, recalling these lecture-concerts.

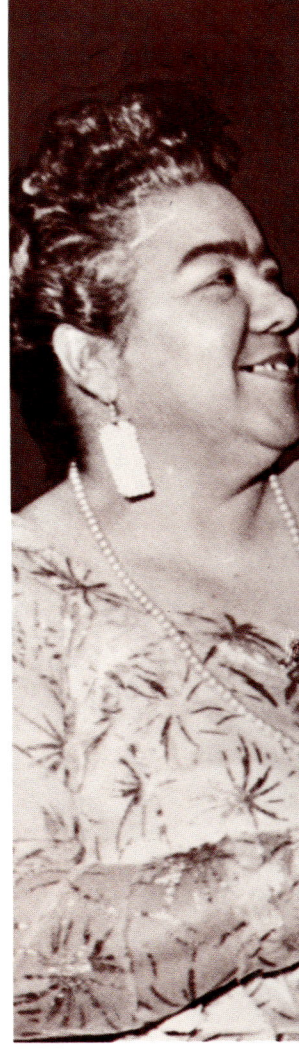

". . . . The program consisted first of the lecture 'The Meaning of Jazz' published under the title 'Popular Songs vs. the Facts of Life', in 'Language and Our World', with musical illustrations by 'Bob Scobey Frisco Band' and the singers, 'Clancy Hayes' and a robust, creole jazz singer from New Orleans, 'Lizzie Miles'. Following the intermission the program ended with a one-hour, wide-open swinging jazz concert, uninterrupted by the lecturer.

"These lecture-concert programs were polished at San Jose College, University of California at Davis, Mills College in Oakland, in preparation for a future tour of the Universities throughout the States in the early part of 1956.

"I was deeply indebted to all the gifted performers for their sympathetic understanding of the argument of this paper: Some of the selections like a 'Closer Walk With Thee', 'Jazz Me Blues', 'Doctor Jazz', 'Indiana' and 'Jada' exemplified the height of the Dixieland tradition and related to my writing.

"The important reason for calling this lecture-concert

BOB SHORT
Courtesy of Ed Lawless

LIZZIE MILES, BOB SCOBEY, DR. S. I. HAYAKAWA
Courtesy of Dr. Hayakawa

tour is that the music is exactly the sort of thing the musicians performed and upon which the main argument of the lecture was based. What the musicians were doing for the college audiences in our tour was, in its own peculiar way, impeccably academic: they were acquainting young people with tradition—Blues and Dixieland—trying to interpret that tradition afresh so that their audiences would gain (as they say in humanities courses) a deeper historical perspective by means of which to understand the developments of today.

"And in my lecture, I tried to show how the unaffected, realistic emotional content of the blues contrasted with the sick sentimentality of much of popular music. A high point in the evening was when 'Clancy Hayes' would sing satirically, in illustrations of my argument about the retreat into schizophrenia that results from such unrealistic views of love

as are so often celebrated in Popular song, 'I'd Rather Have a Paper Doll to Call My Own' . . .

"*Today, as I listen again to Bob's recordings—the vivid, exclamatory attack of 'Bob Scobey' and 'Jack Buck's' horns, the profoundly traditional jazz piano of 'Tiny Crump' (who was Ida Cox's accompanist in the 1920's) and the firm, joyous cursive beat of 'Freddie Higuera's' drums, 'Hal McCormack's' bass, and 'Clancy Hayes' banjo (all firmed up in this instance with 'Bob Short's' tuba)—I cannot help recalling, with amusement, the faces of the youthful cats in our college audiences. These young people, who had been musically brought up in the recent tradition of bearded undertake . . . playing hushed-tone poems in chamber-music solemnity, had never before been introduced to the idea that jazz could be fun! . . . .*"

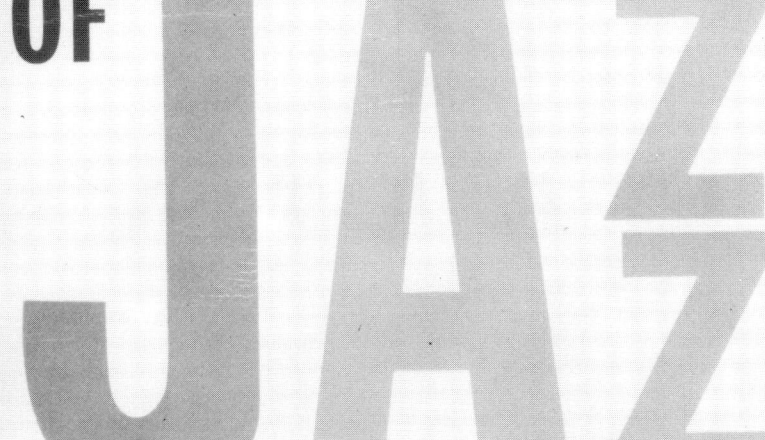

7 "FOR EVERY SOMETHIN' THERE'S ANOTHER SOMETHIN'"

WHILE JAZZ WAS GETTING ITS START IN NEW Orleans, in the final hours of the 19th century, a future blues singer was born. Lizzie Miles was the archetype of the red-hot mamas of jazz!

Lizzie grew up next door to 'Sidney Bechet', the extraordinary jazz clarinetist (later soprano sax), and she remembered hearing him play his nickel flute. That's all he had to play on then.

Lizzie's interest in music grew because of Bechet. They would gather on the corner, in the evening, (the curbstone were their musicians' chairs), and sing and play together.

I can picture Lizzie, a baby, soothed and serenaded to sleep by the music beneath her window. It is a little wonder she had to sing, for the sounds of jazz and the blues were in her blood, and a deep-rooted part of her life, from earliest childhood. She started very early, singing at the age of five, in her Catholic catechism classes. Lizzie often said with a broad smile, *"I just love to sing, and I hope I can continue until I'm 100 years old!"*

Her career started out, as most entertainers of the day, doing circuit theatres and stage performances across the country. She had issued many records with 'Tony Almerico's' band before joining Scobey's group.

She traveled with the Cole Bros. Circus from 1914 through 1918, doing hundreds of one night stands. In 1919, she appeared at the Dreamland in Chicago with 'King Oliver' and 'Louis Armstrong'. In 1924, she was featured in Europe as the 'Black Rose'. In New Orleans she sang with 'Tony Almerico's' band in the Parisian Room.

While she was still young, Lizzie teamed up with music writer 'Clarence Williams', who wrote 'I Ain't Gonna Give Nobody None of This Jelly Roll', 'Michigan Water Blues', and many others. Early sheet music was sold, with the aid of a vocalist and piano man, face to face with the buying public. More often than not, they were stopped at the doorway of the music stores, so they took their music directly to the people. The pair wore out shoe leather on the streets and sidewalks of Chicago, peddling Williams' tunes and charts for ten cents a piece. They would knock on doors, and if they were invited in, they would sing and play (if the folks had a piano) on the spot, to sell a few more tunes. Once in a while, they were able to get a congregation together, a big gathering of

LIZZIE MILES
©Jan Scobey 1976

LIZZIE MILES and BOB SCOBEY
Courtesy of EBONY MAGAZINE

appreciative listeners, and make a real killing. It was hard work, but it helped toughen Lizzie.

Dear Lizzie's philosophies and observations of people, like the lyrics of jazz tunes, always cut right to the heart of the truth, and she saw the reality without illusions.

One day, she was traveling to a job with 'Bob Scobey' and a few musicians in his band. They pulled to a stop light and Lizzie noticed a really, drunken man, tattered and shabby, roaming the streets, swaying to and fro, and looking quite forlorn and lonely. All of a sudden, a lady, almost in the very same condition, came running toward that man and affectionately took his arm.

Lizzie exclaimed . . . *"Doesn't that go to show you! For every somethin' there's another somethin'!"* All the guys laughed—'Lizzie Miles' saw life how it really was.

She was an authentic, Creole jazz singer, whose robust

Courtesy of Shortie Short

LIZZIE MILES
©Jan Scobey 1976

sound sparked audiences everywhere. Her endowment of French, Spanish and Negro heritage was reflected in her singing and combined these rich cultures into a new sound—'Creole Jazz'.

CLANCY HAYES—LIZZIE MILES—BOB SCOBEY

Courtesy of Ebony Magazine

Lizzie and Bob met through the friendships they both had with 'Sidney Bechet'. Lizzie had stopped singing for awhile, but Bob knew she had a lot more to give to her audiences. He persuaded her to join forces. Bob was still at Club Storyville in San Francisco, and they also played a lot of Vegas and Tahoe dates together. Scobey helped re-establish her as the 'Great Blues Singer' she always was.

BOB SCOBEY
Courtesy of Shortie Short

LIZZIE MILES

©Jan Scobey 1976

When Lizzie performed, she donned the costumes, jewelry, and gay shawls that were so fashionable in New Orleans in the thirties era. After becoming associated with Bob Scobey's band she had resurrected all of her finery from stored trunks. Lizzie appeared with Bob in Concert, on records, and lecture tours across the United States, from about 1954 through 1957.

". . . . Jazz hasn't changed but few musicians play it with the feeling of the oldtimers," Lizzie remarked to an 'Ebony Magazine' interviewer. *"Bob Scobey is one of those few!"* The news reporter watched her comeback:

LIZZIE MILES
©Jan Scobey 1976

". . . . BLUES SINGER MAKES COMEBACK . . .
'Lizzie Miles' is a new jazz sensation at 60 . . . A Veteran 60-year-old songstress of the ragtime era whom promoters considered 'washed up' and 'too old' to perform, has staged the most remarkable comeback in show business history. She is 'Lizzie Miles', her full name is 'Elizabeth Mary Landreaux Miles', a hefty, husky-voiced, blues shouter who discounted the odds against her return and launched a triumphal new career as star vocalist with 'Bob Scobey's renowned Dixieland band. She has become a solid attraction in jazz by demonstrating that she still can entertain at her advanced age.

"Jewel-studded shoes and gown sparkling, 'Red-Hot-Mama' Lizzie Miles goes into a lively dance step at the 'Blue Note' in Chicago. Alabama and Virginia minstrel shows were her training ground.

"Singing in a ragtime style she calls 'coon shouting', Lizzie naturally appeals strongest to the Dixieland set. She draws well with the modern, progressive crowd too. Steeped in Dixieland tradition, she first blossomed as singer about 46 years ago in New Orleans (1909), hails from bygone era of 'Bessie Smith', 'King Oliver', 'Ma Rainey' and 'Big Eye Louis Nelson'.

"It upset her that the youngsters had no chance to see 'real talent in minstrels'. She insisted people are different, 'not as happy and carefree' as they were years ago . . . ."

In later years, when I saw Lizzie and Bob embrace each other, during a visit to New Orleans, I could see they were tight, close friends. She wished she could have traveled again and join the band, but she preferred to stay in New Orleans. She was 67 now, and getting older. When she was asked if she would return to the stage—she answered with her broad smile, *"I've done it all, and its good to spend my last days at home!"*

LIZZIE MILES
©Jan Scobey 1976

8 TRAVELIN' SHOES

MUSICIANS LIVE A DIFFERENT KIND OF LIFE than the 'nine-to-fiver'. Most people get up with their kids, have a little morning conversation over breakfast, go to work and return in the evening for supper, a round up of the family's day, television and bed.

It's not the same for entertainers. They are night people. After dark, it is a different world entirely! Most persons are asleep while the entertainer works. When the jobs do come, they may be a string of one-nighters, sometimes hundreds of miles apart. They may have to travel in weather that is icy cold or baking hot, just to make a buck.

During the early years of Scobey's career, he experienced all the ups and downs of every struggling, young entertainer. Bob Scobey did it all. In the early days, as he led his band in clubs across America, the unexpected was always around the corner.

Most musicians play a lot of one-night jobs. It's a difficult part of the business and there is no way to avoid them. It's all part of paying your dues. The one nighter means just that, you contract to give a one night performance. Then, as soon as the gig is over, and with hardly time for a little late night relaxation over a drink or coffee, even a shower, everyone packs their instruments, jumps into a car or bus, and they are off to the next town, 300 to 600 miles away, even further today.

Have you ever tried changing your clothes in a car while someone else was driving and then you must take the wheel so they can change? Sometimes they slept more in the bus then in a bed.

You got there any way you could. Not many musicians were flying then. Just long hours of traveling by bus, car or train. These long jaunts were handled in less than 24 hours, and musicians were still dragging and beat from the last show.

If they were lucky enough to pick up several gigs in a row, and all in one town or club, that was great for then they could establish a semblance of permanent housekeeping. When the group was on the road, it was hectic. Band practice was often held in the back seat of a car, as it rolled along the highway; speeding with one eye on the clock to make the date on time, and the other in the rear view mirror to look out for the small town, speed traps.

There were highway mishaps—blowouts, boiling radiators and frozen motors. There were frustrating delays

BOB SCOBEY
MISSISSIPPI RIVERBOAT
Courtesy of Robert Bordeaux

in the boondocks, while some broken part had to be replaced. There was a time or two when half the group would be stuck in a snowdrift, in the middle of nowhere, while the rest of the guys; a hundred miles farther up the road, were on stage, trying to sound like a complete ensemble. And Scobey would, too! He had a spark and drive that would make his melodic horn sound like an entire brass section. Scobey had a good way with audiences. His big, happy smile, his easy manner, his happy music—the audience loved it!

Imagine this! Fifteen degrees below freezing, eight shivering musicians, all trying, at the same time and frantically, to warm up and get into their outfits, in a dressing room the size of a john—playing nearly frozen instruments—and still they knocked out the listeners every time, with four or five swinging sets of great dixieland jazz.

Or picture this! Finally they drove up to the front door of the club where they were to play that evening, only to find it padlocked with a big sign: 'Closed' (by order of the liquor commissioner, or I.R.S.). Even when the club was doing business, the club owner's checks would often bounce. This all spelled out 'no paychecks' for that night or week. If the next gig was a couple of days off, it would make things even tougher.

It was not all misery. Visiting new cities, making friends, being exposed to interesting people and business, all added to the plus side of the profession. Some jobs were very prestigious and often, country club dates included an opportunity to get on the golf course.

The boys loved to cut-up when they could. Bob had one guy in the band that could spot marijuana growing along side the road in the middle of the night! I don't know how he did it, but he would suddenly yell, *"Stop the car, we just passed some weed!"*

Sure enough, when they turned the car around, there in the headlights would be a stand of wild marijuana, crossing the country in Iowa, Kentucky, or Illinois. The boys would all pile out of the car and with whoops of joy, like children at Christmas, they would rake in the free, unexpected harvest.

One time, Bob recalled, the second auto drove up to an amazing spectacle. The guys had discovered a field of wild pot. They had taken all of their gear out of the car and had the highway strewn with instruments, suitcases and clothing! They were trying to make room for the marijuana plants and they were in the frantic process of redistributing the load before they were discovered.

As they traveled from town to town, they told tall tales and jokes and kidded one another. After a while, the guys got really tight. They developed a camaraderie and a closeness that was hard to beat in any other profession. They fought and argued too! When a whole band of ten or fifteen people (counting wives, girlfriends and sometimes the kids) shared their ups and downs, it was close company. If the money was low and the jobs were lean or scarce, it was easy to get short-tempered. Some musicians had wives and children back home. They would worry about them and that didn't help their disposition, either. On the bandstand, they forgot everything except their music. The sounds were swinging and strong and they played their souls out. That's professionalism!

Liquor and drugs were easy to get. Customers enjoyed buying drinks for the musicians and of course the guys disliked refusing them. Besides, it helped to ease the pressure. For some, it was drugs. I don't mean pot. I'm speaking of the harder stuff like cocaine, bennies and pills. The stress-ridden entertainer was ready-made for the pusher. You would be surprised at some of their sources. Respectable doctors, truck drivers, druggists, any profession of people who could be right there, offering anything the musician might want and for free! It happened to me more than once so I know it's so.

When someone was feeling 'down' (and there were a million reasons for getting that way), it was easy to want to unload their troubles for a while, to feel good so they wouldn't care so much about some bad scene going on for them. Of course, most of the guys abstained from many of these enticements.

Ulcers! That's another thing. The menus were all short-order, rancid, greasy and a grab-it-on-the-run, style. It truly amazes me that more musicians didn't develop ulcers, become dope addicts or alcoholics!

Very few did, but occasionally someone in the band couldn't even stand up or didn't show for the gig. Bob was easy going on most things but he wouldn't stand for this sort of jive. When it happened, he went looking for a substitute, and on short notice, it would present more problems. 'Clancy Hayes', his vocalist, was Bob's right arm, long-time friend and the exception to Bob's rule. Clancy loved his Early Times. He would be stewed to the gills and he could still reach the mike and belt out a beautiful rendition of 'Bill Bailey' or 'Cake Walking Baby', with a voice as clear and mellow as a bell, and rhythm that could rock a room full of people. Clancy was a 'pro' when it came time to be 'on', but later on, once at an all important booking (The Flamingo in Vegas), he totally lost control and actually fell off the bandstand and Bob and his band were cancelled.

It was all Scobey could do to act in the various roles of peacemaker, father confessor, short term loan broker and all-around supervisor . . . besides finding work, week after week, to put bread on the table for five or six families, including his own. He had to do this without losing sight of his own personal dreams.

But they got by. They played their music . . . and how they played! Perhaps that's why 'The Blues' always came off so well. They surely had them from time to time. Yes, that's the way it was on the road.

'RALPH SUTTON':

". . . . When I came out from New York, in the early fifties, I played at the Hangover Club in San Francisco for a month in the summer, it was the first time I met Bob. I didn't really get to know him until he came east on a tour. He and 'Clancy Hayes' and I became good friends. I mentioned to Bob that I would like to leave New York and move to San Francisco. He told me he might be opening a club there sometime in the future, and if he did, would I be interested in coming out and play solo - intermission piano. I told him 'yes'!

"The next time I saw him was in Chicago where I was playing at the London House. He and his band were playing in town too, and Bob and Clancy came in to see me. Scobey told me he was opening a club called Storyville on the edge of Chinatown in San Francisco around May and would I still be interested. I said, yes, so I left New York, with my family, in June, and started playing solo at Storyville.

"After a few months at the club, Bob and the band were going on the road. 'Tiny Crump', who was playing piano in

Courtesy of Marilyn Napier McGwynn

RALPH SUTTON

RALPH SUTTON, TINY CRUMP, LIZZIE MILES
Courtesy of Moss Photography

the band, didn't want to go, so Bob asked me if I would make the tour. I told Bob I didn't want to either since I loved the Bay Area. I longed to stay relaxed at the home base. He finally twisted my arm hard enough with the dollar sign and so I made the tour. The band consisted of 'Jack Buck', 'Clancy', 'Bill Napier', 'Dave Black', 'Bob Short', 'Lizzie Miles' and myself.

"I was with Bob for a year to the exact day, and I called it the year of the 'vests', because of the band's costume. We were good friends and got along fine. Bob could get a little nervous at times, but all in all, we had a lot of laughs together...."

**LIZZIE MILES
CLANCY HAYES**
Courtesy of Moss Photography

Bob was acquainted and friendly to thousands. Bob was a friend to dozens. But 'Dave Black' was also, as Bob often remarked, *"My right hand!"*

Black was billed as 'Ace Drummer' with 'Bob Scobey's Frisco Jazz Band'. For years, before he joined the band, he had played with 'Duke Ellington' and 'Lena Horne', and when he became part of Bob's group, he stayed for six years, until the end.

Black was on most of the later recordings and his tempo control is reflected in the powerful rhythmic drive for which Scobey is famous. They understood each other musically.

DAVE BLACK

JESSE TINY CRUMP
Courtesy of Shortie Short

When 'Dave Black' played, it was a strong 4/4 time, using two bass drums and he sounded like a man with ten feet and six arms! Every couple of sets, Bob had Dave present many of his famous drum solos. (One of his masterpieces is called "Drummer's Blues', recorded on Jansco).

Dave sent me a tape recalling these days working with Papa Scobey. As I listened to his voice, I wish I could have duplicated his feelings and emotions which could only come across on the recorded sound. Here it is, 14 years later, and when Dave spoke of Bob's illness and the loss of a good friend, it was still a tough chore for Dave to relate it to me. You could hear that he was only doing it to honor Bob and for history.

Dave Black met Bob Scobey around 1956 in San Francisco. He worked a casual one night with a saxophone player who had done some bookings for Bob around the Bay Area.

". . . . When Bob came in town, he was looking for a drummer and this agent told Scobey about me. He called me for a 'casual' that was at the Claremont Country Club.

"I remember very well that I was there early and we were suppose to start at 9:00 p.m. sharp. The band didn't show up until about 9:30 p.m., driving up late from Los Angeles, because they had recorded the Bing Crosby album the day before. I regret having just missed doing the Crosby job with Bob.

"Bob liked my playing a lot. I was a good, heavy drummer. Clancy liked it too, because I gave all the special drum-affects to Clancy's material like 'Parson Kansas Blues' that Clancy wrote. I used to do a train beat on it with brushes and stuff like that. In the beginning I played with them, doing 'casuals' around San Francisco, here and there. Eventually I got in tighter with Bob and we became friends. Bob was one great man and a great musician.

"Most of the people that worked with him, including myself, made way over scale. He paid us a salary, whether we worked the full week or not, and it was a good salary for the week's work. When he did get extra jobs like an extra casual, or recording on a day off, he would always pay the guys even for that. He didn't have to, it wasn't necessary. When someone is playing on salary, you're supposed to work five, six, or seven days a week and collect the same pay. Nobody's obligated to pay you extra, which is what Bob did. He was very, very considerate that way. He would give us sixty or seventy dollars for a casual job and extra for the week's work.

"He was demanding about what he wanted but in a nice

way. He wanted a good swinging band, especially a gay, cheerful attitude in order to create that happy, dixieland feeling. He was a stickler for that, I remember well!

"He didn't like any wild faces or cut-ups on the job. He thought monkeying around would be generated to his audience. Playing that particular kind of music, you had to be happy, feel good and look good. That was one of his main demands.

"Unlike most dixieland musicians, Bob was very open minded to every other kind of music. He listened to everything and never put anything or anyone down. He was never a downer when it came to other people's music. He often mentioned the great respect he had for 'Dizzie Gillespie', and what a great trumpet player he thought he was, even through they played different bags. He enjoyed listening to Dizzie. So, Bob kept his ears up to everything, all kinds of music. He got a kick out of it all and never knocked anything to my knowledge! . . . ."

A long time ago, when Mrs. Short married the bassist, 'Bob Short', she acquired the name 'Shortie'. She didn't like her given, first name (which will not be mentioned here) and forever after she was, and will be, 'Shortie' to her friends. She is an aquarianly, warm gal, she is my friend and she loves jazz.

". . . . Bob Scobey was a brilliant player and extremely personable. He had a quick mind and a great sense of humor. He always carried out his plans no matter what they were—to have a club, move to Chicago, go to Europe, or whatever.

"He was so friendly - he brought many, many people together who, because of him, remain friends today. When another musician friend was in trouble, he found ways to help them—many, many times!

"Bob Scobey had other interests too! In Las Vegas once, he took us on a gem hunting expedition. That was fun! He opened up a whole new world of adventure in nature for us.

"Once, when his band still headquartered in Chicago, we dropped by Scobey's house, unexpectedly. He was not awake because it was early in the day, and the children brought us to the bedroom. After serving tea, the kids stayed with him on the bed during our whole visit, listening and playing. He was a warm father, and took the children to the jobs whenever he could . . . ."

In 1957, Scobey was getting eager for a bigger slice of the pie of success. A larger record company could get him the hit record he was after. It was the one thing he felt was so

LIZZIE MILES - FLOYD BEAN - BOB SCOBEY
THE FLAMINGO - LAS VEGAS

BOB SCOBEY
Courtesy of Shortie Short

necessary for popularity and success. It appeared, with only one record or hit, the public would remember a personality and be dedicated, seemingly, forever. So Bob Scobey signed with Verve.

Bob always admired the two-trumpet team of 'Oliver and Armstrong' back in the early Storyville Days of New Orleans. He enjoyed a lot of dynamics during his performances, a term he further explained by remarking often,

"Dynamics are the most essential elements in music of any kind". Jelly Roll Morton's classic advice, *"You've got to be able to come down in order to go up",* tells it like it should be.

Bob Scobey played in the New Orleans mood, but modified it with his own special techniques and tastes. He was not out to imitate anybody . . .

"We don't want to escape our obvious association with Dixieland, but we do want our efforts judged individually and not described as either good or bad Dixie. It's bad for everyone to think in terms of classifications. No matter what anyone else chooses to call it, music is only as good as it sounds to you".

The same year, Bob recorded for Norm Granz's Verve Label. For the recording date he decided to augment the band to get a larger sound and he sought out noted arranger-musician Leon C. Radsliff. Leon played clarinet and bass clarinet, as well as arranged music. His graphic and detailed

LEON C. RADSLIFF

LEON C. RADSLIFF
FRANK SNOW
JENNY LIND HALL
Courtesy of Shortie Short

SHOWBOAT - OAKLAND - 1954
Left to right: Bob Scobey, Freddie Higuera, Bill Napier,
Hal McCormick, Clancy Hayes, Jessy Tiny Crump
Courtesy of Shortie Short

account provides you with a nice description of some of the particulars of putting an album together.

"... Bob Scobey approached me with an idea for an album to be written by me and recorded in the San Francisco area, with local musicians to be added to his regular dixieland group.

"Always the straight-ahead gentlemen, business details were quickly and equitably settled and the work began. Bob picked the tunes and provided me with his lead sheets for the material I did not have.

"I knew of him, of course, for some time but had always thought of his work in the context of a rather small, standard-dixieland band. His idea was to use his regular group, adding enough horns to give a 'big' sound while still retaining much of the individual style-freedom that made Bob Scobey instantly recognizable as a musician.

"During the gestation period, I caught the small group several times at the 'Show Boat', then anchored at Jack London Square in Oakland. From these hearings and conferences with Bob—the shape of the album took form. We were able to make decisions as to who would take solos and when—utilizing well established routines for the most part.

"The writing progressed as I had a good idea of the individuals who would be soloing and contributing to the ensembles. Between us, we had settled on the added local players and insisted that the writing be 'comfortable' for all—leaving room for that individuality that he prized so highly. In this respect, I was reminded very much of 'Jack Teagarden' for whom I really had cut my writing teeth in the 1940's.

"Everything just seemed to pour out and Bob never did set a deadline. With copyists Marshall and Virginia Wright and nearly finished with the charts, Bob set a first session date at Jenny Lind Hall.

"It was very live, soundwise. He liked the acoustics of the place, the authentic 'distemper' of the house piano, and the people who ran it. The hall was operated by a fraternal group; more family than typical landlord and they took a great interest in the session proceedings—even to providing some 'mysterious' refreshments dipped out of a large glass bowl at appropriate times.

"The album was cut in two or three sessions. A couple of happenings have stayed with me through the years and might bear re-telling.

"Tiny Crump - the pianist was so used to talking while playing. He finally had to tie a hankerchief around his mouth so he would be reminded not to talk on the 'ring out'. If that

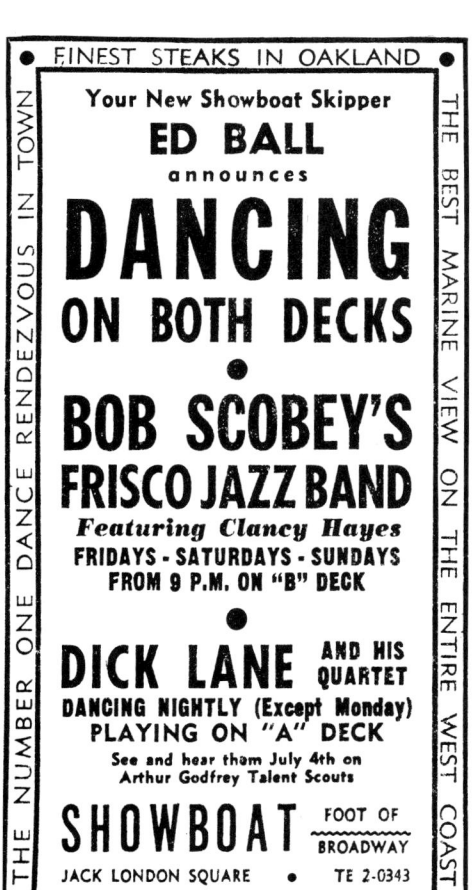

BOB SCOBEY - LEON C. RADSLIFF
Courtesy of Shortie Short

CLANCY HAYES
Courtesy of Shortie Short

BOB SHORT
Courtesy of Shortie Short

FRANK SNOW
BOB SCOBEY
FREDDIE HIGUERA
Courtesy of Shortie Short

BOB SCOBEY
Courtesy of Shortie Short

BOB SCOBEY - JACK BUCK - BILL NAPIER
Courtesy of Shortie Short

wasn't a sight? Big 'Tiny' Crump—a burglar in reverse polarity!

"The total group had never played together before (or since) and if there was any tension about the outcome——it fled after the first tune. Bob was always calm and what came out of his horn was the 'Rock of Gibraltar' and just as monumental!

"A couple of tunes have also stuck with me, one was the 'Crave'. I had never heard of it, but Bob wanted it, and as the orchestration progressed, I could hear why! I couldn't wait to hear it played! When Bob wanted 'Star Dust' with the verse, I had some misgivings in the context of it, particularly when he insisted that I play some bass clarinet on that track. Of course, no Scobey album would have been complete without 'Swingin' Doors' by Clancy Hayes.

"All of us thought the effort came out well, we had a ball doing it, and there isn't much more you can ask than that. In times after that, I returned to the studios and Bob had gone another way . . . taking part of my heart with him . . . ."

Scobey's band, recording Leon's arrangements were a hit and led to two more recordings for Verve. One of these was with Lizzie Miles entitled Bourbon Street. On the Miles recording, Lizzie comes on strong with tunes like 'Make Me Pallet On The Floor' and 'Baby Won't You Please Come Home'. By 1957, while in the later years of her life, Lizzie had given up the stage. As related to me personally, she had prayed for a favor, (never revealed), and having it answered, she never sang professionally, on stage again.

With Bob traveling to all the colleges and universities, it was inevitable an album would be issued with collegiate favorites. Using the same musicians as the previous albums, Bob recorded in New York, in 1958, some great sing-a-long arrangements by 'Bill Stegmeyer'. With selections such as 'Whiffenpoof Song', 'Let the Rest of The World Go By', and 'Shine on Harvest Moon', the album 'College Classics' was a hit.

BILL NAPIER
JACK BUCK
BOB SCOBEY
Courtesy of Shortie Short

The decade was nearing its end. Bob's star was never brighter. His plans were growing more ambitious, he was laying the groundwork for international concert tours and multi-media exposure. Everything was coming up roses!

JESSE TINY CRUMP - BOB SCOBEY
Courtesy of Shortie Short

BOB SCOBEY - RCA RECORD SESSION
Courtesy of RCA

9   I NEED A HIT RECORD!

ROM VERVE RECORDS TO RCA VICTOR... Fred Reynolds, originally a Disc Jockey for Station WGN in Chicago, later to become Music Editor of the Monthly magazine 'Music at Home', was very instrumental in Bob's career.

Fred connected Bob with his East Coast audiences, by preceding his arrival with a good deal of air play of Scobey's band on records. Some of the selections, 'Battle Hymn of The Republic', 'Peoria', 'I Want To Go Back To Michigan', 'Ace in the Hole' and 'Strange Blues', truly captured the Scobey sound exactly as if at a night club performance, the way the fans had heard it.

".... Bob can talk intelligently about the latest outburst in the UN, the political philosophies of Abe Lincoln, or what's happening with the commercial trend of TV.

"I first heard of 'Bob Scobey's Frisco Jazz Band' when his earliest Good Time Jazz records were sent to me for review in my Chicago Tribune column, Platter Chatter, for possible use on my various disc jockey programs. I fell in love with them immediately, gave them very favorable reviews, and played them often on WGN. Apparently they made quite a hit with my audience, for it wasn't too long after I introduced them on the air, that I was able to talk Frank Holzfiend, the manager of Chicago's Blue Note (the

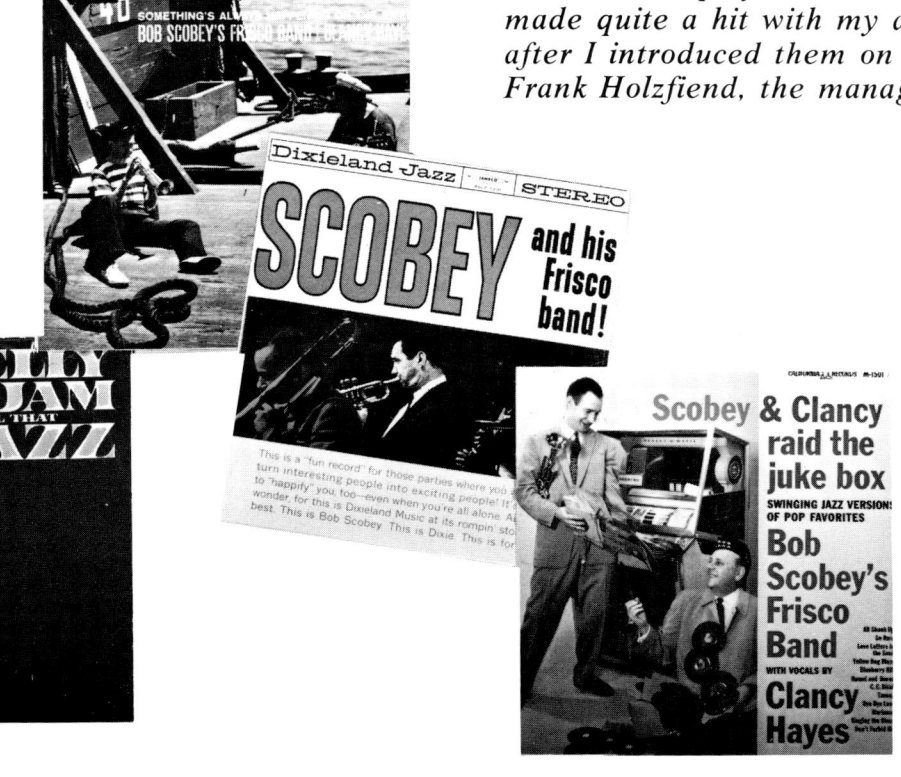
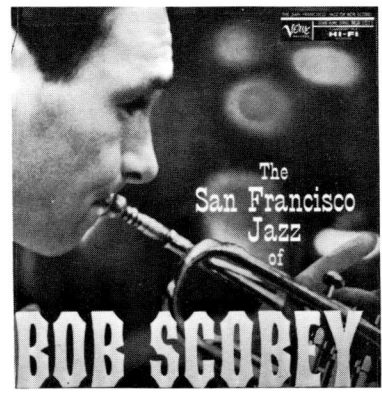

Courtesy of Duncan P. Schiedt

BING CROSBY - BOB SCOBEY
Recording Bing With A Beat
Courtesy of RCA Victor Records

outstanding Jazz Joint of the Windy City), to sign up Bob and his band for a two week engagement.

"Naturally, I plugged this fact on the air, both before and during the engagement. The band was an instant hit amongst the jazz buffs of Chicago, and I believe that Bob and company broke every attendance record at the Blue Note!

"After leaving WGN I became an Artist and Repertoire director for RCA records. Through that capacity I was able to sign the 'Frisco Jazz Band' to an exclusive RCA recording contract . . . ."

Scobey recorded the first of five albums with R.C.A., 'Beauty And The Beat'. On it the boys and Clancy chopped out then popular tunes such as 'Linda' in a fast dance step rhythm. It was a sound that, to my mind, lacked the jazz spontaneity, that was so synonymous with Bob. However, it was what R.C.A. wanted and everyone was happy.

Then Fred Reynolds thought up a swinging combination—'Scobey and Crosby'!

NICK FATOOL
Courtesy of Shortie Short

". . . . Surely, one of the most exciting albums came after I had persuaded Bing Crosby to sign up with RCA for the one album to be made with 'Bob Scobey's Frisco Jazz Band', 'Bing with a Beat'! I know that Bob and Company got a terrific kick out of making that particular recording, for working with Crosby is an entirely exhilerating experience. I was always baffled as to how Bob kept up his spirits during the many, many hours of recording. He was always UP! . . . ."

They had big ideas for Bob and the next disc, featured Scobey and Crosby. This was an unusually exciting recording session. The band was augmented to get the big sound. Bing's voice was smooth and mellow then, and still is; being the most easily, recognized voice in the world. I asked Bing to recall the session.

". . . . I remember Bob very well. He was a marvelous jazz musician, had great taste, great judgement of pace, and of routining an arrangement.

Jack Kapp thought we'd be a good pair to put together. He wanted to get a good jazz record and he thought Bob's group would be super - and they turned out so, too. Because he was a big hit around San Francisco at the time and I was in Los Angeles, there wasn't much problem getting us together.

That's how the record date came about and that's how I first met Bob, although I knew all about him and his work long before that. He had great ability - no question about it.

MANNIE KLEIN
Courtesy of the Los Angeles Public Library

WARREN SMITH - MATTY MATLOCK - CLANCY HAYES
Recording Session Conference   Courtesy of Helen Coronado

CLANCY HAYES
Recording in a sound proof booth.
Courtesy of Shortie Short

Left to right: SAMMY GOLDSTEIN, RALPH SUTTON, CLANCY HAYES, RED CALLENDER
Courtesy of Shortie Short

CLANCY HAYES
Courtesy of Shortie Short

MANNIE KLEIN - BOB SCOBEY
Courtesy of Shortie Short

JACK BUCK
ABE LINCOLN
␣ARREN SMITH
BILL NAPIER
␣urtesy of Shortie Short

LET'S TAKE IT FROM THE TOP, FELLAS

Courtesy of Shortie Short . . . . capturing the artistic movements of a leader.

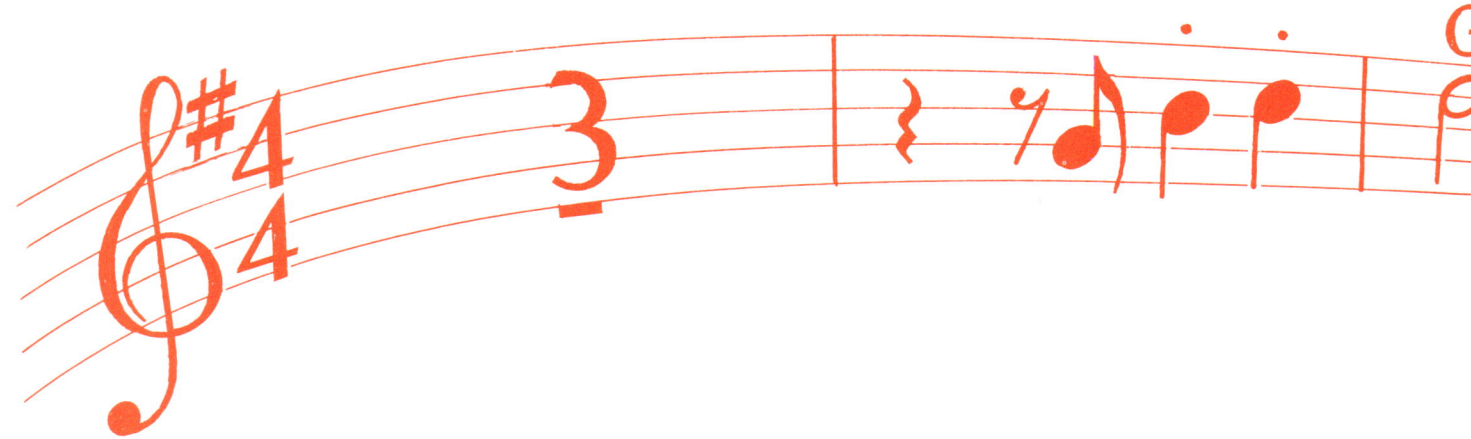

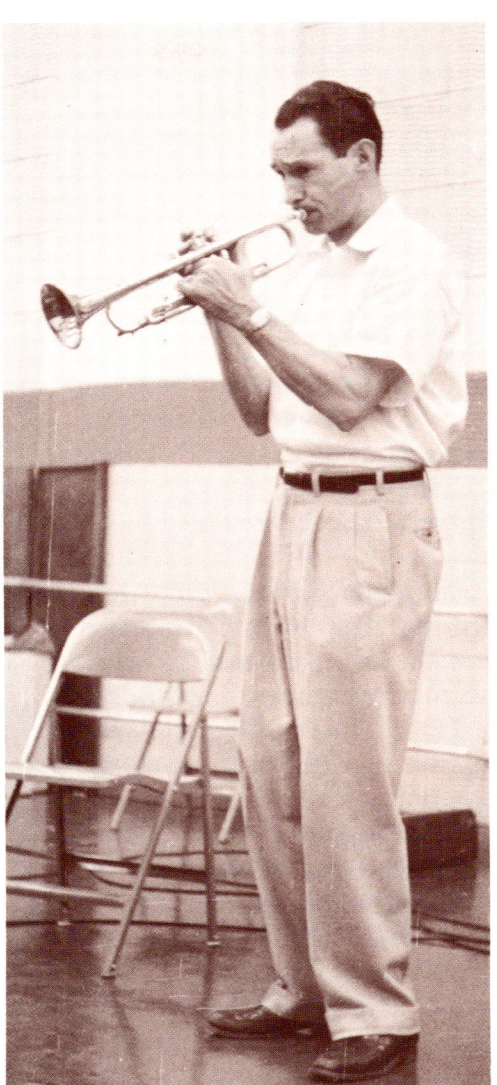

YEAH! A GOOD TAKE

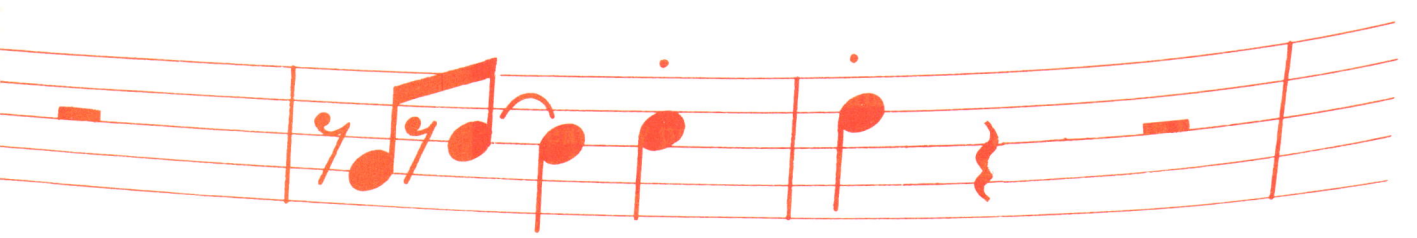

Clyde Pound, a pianist was on several recordings with Papa Scobey. He saw the band from the inside, looking out. His appraisal of most of the RCA recordings is impartial and, I believe, keenly accurate.

"*. . . . Bob seemed to be always looking for a magic gimmick—vocalists, two trombones, arrangements, commercial albums. I always felt, and told Bob, he should record the band the way it really played! The band was good. He played with a lot of fire and balls, but the records were charts which didn't come off anywhere near the capability the group had. It wasn't really jazz except for the solos, and Bob would insist that the solos be built around the melody. I believed the band created, on its own, the best, without being hung up by the charts of an arranger who knew very little about the creative potential of the band. They just turned out a slick kind of product with commercial potential, but it wasn't good enough!*

"*Bob was very creative, I don't think he realized the arrangements for the recordings really stiffled him and kept him from playing to his full capability. Sometimes, on a gig, the band would cook it's ass off, but it never got recorded that way . . . .*"

ABE LINCOLN
Courtesy of Ed Lawless

'Clyde Pound' was just out of his teens when he replaced 'Ralph Sutton' at the keyboard. Ralph was a brilliant 'stride pianist' but, from the start, he never wanted to leave California. He only came with Bob after some heavy, money-type, arm twisting. As time passed, Sutton grew more weary of the road trips, so, after a year, he returned happily to Belvidere and his family. His departure gave young Clyde one of the best breaks of his budding career. He successfully auditioned for the Piano Chair and started with the group at Lafayette's Pioneer Village in 1957.

". . . . *I was in a kid's dixieland band and my dad was a dixie music fan, when I first met and heard Bob play at the ripe age of 14. He took me to Hambone Kelly's in El Cerrito for Sunday Jams. Later on, we went to Victor & Roxie's in Oakland, when Bob, Clancy, Burt Bales and Jack Buck were playing. I was trying to play piano and they let me sit in a couple of times. They were very tolerant.*

"*Five or six years later, around 1958, Ralph Sutton left Bob and I got the job mainly through the recommendation of 'Pete Dovidio' who was working with Bob at the time. It was a weird scene, because Clancy and Bob would put me on about being that 14 year old kid who used to hang out at Victor and Roxie's.*

"*Bob was really fun. He smoked a lot (marijuana) and drank Metaxa and no matter how late anyone was to a gig,*

CLANCY HAYES, TONI LEE SCOTT, BOB SCOBEY,
PETE DOVIDIO, JACK BUCK, DOUG SKINNER

Courtesy of Clyde Pound

he would be later! He always got lost going somewhere...."

In later years, when I knew Bob, he was a stickler for punctuality and didn't allow smoking or drinking on stage, or if it affected your playing. He even fined musicians when they were late for rehearsals, but then again, this is a little later on in his career when he got wise to the values of discipline and punctuality. Clyde continued . . .

where I should have kept on trying to build myself up. The guy was a real inspiration!

"I saw him and his band every time they would come into our town and, one band that really impressed me was the one that had 'Jim Beebe' and 'Brian Shanley', 'Clancy' and 'Toni' in the group. They really swung. 'Toni Lee Scott' told me herself, Bob had inspired her, too, because she had the problem with her artificial limb. He got her to really get out there and pitch. She had a very lasting, fond memory of Bob . . . ."

'Abe Lincoln', Bob's trombonist, like most of his co-patriot musicians, had fun with him and the band.

". . . . I had one heck of a wonderful time with Bob. In my book of trumpet players, Bob was one of the top ranking men in the business, with a fine style of playing.

When we closed in Frisco, he gave us a 'Big Italian' dinner, which he served with generous helpings. It sure was good! . . . ."

At a new high-water mark in Bob's career, Sesac recorded Scobey's band. In the recording industry they provided piped-in music for shopping centers, office buildings, dental offices, and everywhere that continuous, canned 'musak' is needed.

Scobey's recordings for the Sesac Transcribed Library (about 12 were issued) are rare since these selections were never recorded on any other label available to the buying public. Fortunately, every so often, on a jet over Kansas, leaning back in a barber's chair, or having your teeth drilled at the dentist's, you will suddenly, out of the blue, hear the Happy Sounds of Scobey's dixieland music—'Memories of Bunk' or 'Sudan'! Sesac wrote:

". . . . Bob Scobey is one of the major forces responsible for the revival of the traditional ensemble style of New Orleans jazz, now dubbed the San Francisco Style.

"The particular art of New Orleans ensemble playing, as developed by such early jazz pace-setters as 'King Oliver' and 'Jelly Roll Morton', was considered dead and forgotten. Scobey joined forces with Watters and Murphy to form this dedicated band in the late nineteen thirties. Because of these efforts some of our finest early jazz pieces have been notated and preserved, including many early rags, blues, stomps, and other tunes which existed, for the most part, only on old phonograph records or hastily scrawled copyright lead sheets—yellow with age. In studying and performing, these old forms of 'Traditional Ensemble Style' became a living

THE PREVIEW LOUNGE - CHICAGO
Courtesy of Clyde Pound

entity once again.

"The dedication and fervor, which inspired this movement, soon caught on like wildfire and ironically proved to have a very steady commercial value. These men were not re-creators of old styles or imitators, they were a devoted group, avidly determined to bring new life to a living tradition, and to find new audiences for this music. This they have accomplished with phenomenal success.

"The Scobey sound, which he calls the 'Happy Sound' is less formal and attracts a wide range of enthusiasts . . . ."

Bob was approaching a rendezvous with his particular destiny. I, 'Jeannette Marie Ursula Dona van Castile' was just around the corner. Our paths were about to cross . . . and the beat goes on!!!

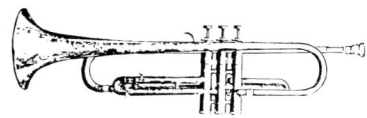

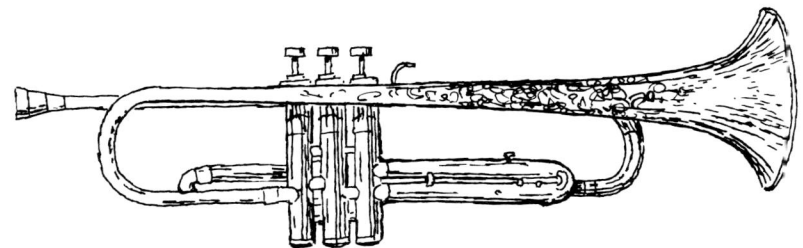

PART TWO

10   A GOOD MAN IS HARD TO FIND

MET MY DEAR ROBERT, AS I OFTEN CALLED him, when I was 24 and he was 43. It was 1958, and a whole year would pass before we began a steady relationship. I was a waitress, in a fast-moving and glamorous key-club, and it is not surprising I ignored his early overtures.

At the Gaslight Club, in Chicago, the life was up and jet-like. The entertainment was top-notch, the waitresses were picked for poise and attractiveness, and dressed to accentuate the positive. Youth, good figures, and beauty attracted an avalanche of men who would constantly 'hit' on the girls. As a result, the management tried hard to protect their investment in pretty and well-trained gals. It was an ultra-strict rule of the house . . . Waitresses could not date the customers. If they did, they were immediately fired. I handled gentlemen's advances by not allowing any familiarity from the very start. This would also void any temptations I might have to accept dates on the sneak. It was a great position for a girl. The tips were big, and there was always lots of excitement. It was too good a spot to risk losing it. Besides, you couldn't possibly offend good customers by refusing to date everyone—when it was a house rule. Waitresses moved around so quickly, rushing for drinks, that individuals seldom stood out in our minds. Big tippers were common-place so that wouldn't make an impression. Anyway, that is the biggest reason Bob and I didn't get to know one another until nearly a year later. For now, he was just another customer of the key club.

I remember a lot of good, exciting times at the Gaslight. The Gaslight Club had the atmosphere of the Gay Nineties—the era in American History when life was easy going and much happier. The world was sleeping. It was between wars, and in America at least, everyone had a place and a hope for the future. It was gay! The women dressed in great ball dresses or butterfly colored costumes. Men walked on quiet Sundays, in pink and green-striped, ice-cream shirts. It was a much happier, peaceful world, and the rich decorations and happy, alive, playtime atmosphere of the club reflected this. It attracted fine customers.

There were white, marbled statues, beautiful, warm paintings of nude women; brilliant, hued stained-glass; lovely Tiffany lamps reflecting diamond rainbows everywhere. There was a walnut-paneled room with the atmosphere of the good times. It melted imperceptibly into the naughty and exciting era of the roaring '20's and its speakeasys.

The red and white checked tablecloths covered the tables, and large bowls of freshly popped corn were teasers for more drinks. They had an oyster bar, and finger sandwiches were made with turkey, ham and cheese, and served on silver trays. The brevity of our costumes completed an atmosphere of elegance and excitement. The waitresses, management, bartenders and entertainers, all enjoyed our positions to the hilt, and we were digging our jobs.

Our costumes were exquisitely designed. They enhanced our feminine charms to the best, possible advantage, and they were still tasteful and sophisticated. Mrs. Brown, the wardrobe mistress saw to that. A new girl's view of the variety of materials (surely my first visit to the dressmaker), was a kaleidoscope of color. It was exciting to see bolts and bolts of velvet; soft powder blue, Irish Kelly green, vibrant gold, brilliant red and vermilions.

The seamstress would carefully tailor each of our costumes to our individual measurements. The costumes were studded with gleaming beads and sparkling sequins. There was material in front that draped around the curve of our hips, and was gathered into a big bustle that gave us the stature of an open-feathered peacock. The black-mesh opera hose didn't keep our legs very warm, but the colorful garter that graced our legs was often exchanged for $5.00 from a benevolent patron.

Oh yeah! It was a fun job, and one of the nicest I have ever had.

The club had many small rooms and in every one something different was happening—old time movies, ragtime piano, jazz trios, gals dancing the frenetic Charleston! We joined right in on sing-a-longs, or a boop-boop-de-boop. You could hear old favorites—'Sweet Georgia Brown', and 'Yes, Sir That's My Baby' ringing loud and clear . . . Happy Times!

It all rolled by quickly at the Gaslight. I had been saving a bankroll, and one day I quit my job and headed for Las Vegas for a vacation. After several months in Vegas and watching my money disappear, I decided to get back home to Chicago and go to work again.

I went job-hunting and soon discovered the top spot for waitressing now was the ''Cafe Continental'. This club was the newest in-spot (you wouldn't believe how quickly the 'in-spots' in a vast city like Chicago can change around). The club was on Walton Place, in the Gold Coast area, near Rush Street.

Appearing there, at that time, was a Dixieland band from

San Francisco. They were drawing a record number of fans and conventioneers. Everyone on the Gold Coast, the waitresses and bartenders especially, were talking about the great business the Cafe was doing. The tips were the biggest in town and naturally, after I had picked up on the street talk, I tried to get a job at the club. It was rough. There were no openings, the manager was cold, and he gave me no hope of a spot in the foreseeable future.

To get the good jobs in any club, you must be a part of the clique every business seems to have. I have found life is full of them; at every level of business and society, there is the magic circle. Well, I left my name and phone number, anyway, just in case.

Some time passed, and lo and behold, I was called in to work! I thought my experience at the Gaslight club might have helped. However, when I went to work, I found, to my disappointment, the spot opened for me was as hostess. This meant I would only seat customers, making a mere ninety dollars a week. Worse still, I wouldn't be noticed. Cocktail waitresses; with their cute, frilly, scanty, eye-catching costumes; got the big tips! I thought, however, it was a way to break into that inner circle, so I accepted it gladly. My hostess job, luckily, lasted only a week.

When the next opening for a waitress came up, I was first to be offered the job. Then I donned my costume and the big hellos came in loud and clear from every direction!!!

I had a great figure and actually won bets on the size of my waist. Having the good fortune to be so well endowed with an hour-glass figure, I wanted to be noticed. With the help of a waist cincher, I could bring my waist in to 17 inches. It was quite dramatic, because my hips were 36. So in my little waitressing tights I became a star of the Continental.

Bob Scobey was the leader of the Dixieland Band from San Francisco. He quickly spotted me and wouldn't give up coaxing me to date. My barriers were truly down. I felt we were meeting for the first time and I learned from him of his fruitless attempts to date me a year earlier, at the Gaslight Club. So began my life with Bob Scobey.

You could count on always seeing Bob, in those days, with an egg-milkshake in his hand. He had two or three a day. I never suspected he had an ulcer because he never mentioned it. Later, I found out the purpose of the milkshake, was to nurse his bothersome stomach problems.

All I knew of Bob was that he was cheery, exciting and busy. I remember those qualities about him more than anything . . . He had vitality . . . He was able to turn even the toughest situations into something funny or happy. He was always putting together a deal, a one nighter, or a T.V.

appearance. He loved to talk to people and he was filled with a contageous enthusiasm that made everyone around him feel good. Bob had a zest for life that wouldn't quit, and it put many a man, 20 years his junior, to shame.

I knew I was in love and could only see the glow and the smile in his magical brown eyes. As I look back to that time, I think Bob must have been trying very hard to find the right combination for success. He almost tried too many things.

Scobey was working on this steady gig at the Cafe Continental on Walton Place, a side street off of Rush Street. He was successful and he assumed he was all set. Business was booming and there was a full house every night of the week. Nonetheless he still had to scuffle for his bread. At first, his arrangement with the owners was on a percentage basis. Before too long, he could see the people he was dealing with were not on the honor system. With all the money he and his band were bringing into the Continental, he still had to fight to get paid. Some weeks, it was worse than pulling teeth to get his take from the management.

I remember some of my dates with Bob were most unusual. I would find myself waiting in a car across the street from the Devonshire Hotel while Bob was inside with the 'boys' who appeared to own the club. This was at 4:30 in the morning, and we were tired from the long nights' work. The 'Devonshire Hotel Coffee Shop' became the 'meet' place when payday came around each Saturday night.

Bob would go in to talk to the syndicate bunch. It was the only way to count on getting his pay. After Bob and I grew tighter, and I was his steady companion, he would take me into the hotel with him. We would sit down together, over coffee, with several of these silk-suited Caesars of the underworld and work at getting Bob's money.

The dialogue between these toughies and Bob was straight out of a 'George Raft' or 'Edward G. Robinson' gangland movie.

Bob was truly prodigious. He could communicate with everyone he met, and on their level. It didn't matter who they were, from hoodlum to high society, nor did it matter what they had to talk about. Bob was well versed on many subjects. He certainly had the capability of moving these characters every time and to get them to peel off the money he had coming. They reached right into their pockets and would come up with $3,000 cash. It soon became obvious to Bob, not to continue working there on a percentage basis. He got a guarantee from them of $2600 a week, which was still $400 a week less than the percentage basis he anticipated. He had no proof of the rip-off, although he would use the figure his host, Gary, would give him. He could trust Gary for an honest account. In later months, the guarantee turned out to be better, for at times, when a convention was not in town, and it was tax time for the residents of Chicago, business did fall off a bit.

It always completely baffled me to see Jimmy A. and Irv R. hold back bread from the very people who brought in the crowds and made bundles of money for them. Sometimes, it appeared, they made $20,000 in one week, for not only would the club be packed, but a line would form outside that went clear around a block. I can only guess that the gutter rules of survival that kept them out of prison and nearer the top of the heap in the rackets, bred in them an instinct for always trying to get the best of the other guy.

Then, too, perhaps a lot of people they dealt with might have been weaker and wouldn't want to bother with the hassle, or muscles, so out of habit of getting away with things, their powers grew stronger. When dealing with Bob though, they laughed and seemingly had a great respect for him, still hating to part with any dollar they didn't have to.

On the other hand, these same people, I can recall, were completely different in the environment of the home, with their families around them or at special gatherings for birthdays, etc. They could be warm, kind, considerate and generous. At family parties and get-to-gethers, even funerals (Bob and I were invited to attend), they demonstrated great love and devotion for their children, wives and other members of their family. I have heard priests (the night pastor of Rush Street) exclaim over the larger donations and good they would do for charity. At the parties, there was always a lot of red wine, spaghetti and other fine Italian dishes, cooked to spicy perfection and everybody had a grand time together. How does one figure such a mixed bag?

Bob had played to big audiences and full houses at the Cafe Continental for a solid year. He was internationally known now and the number of devoted fans were increasing, constantly. He also played scattered, one nighters like Playboy parties, TV shows, radio shows and recording dates. After a year of steady work he decided that he had earned a vacation of some kind, at least a change of scene. You don't get too many planned vacations in the music business.

The Stardust Hotel in Las Vegas had offered 'Bob Scobey and his Frisco Band' three weeks of work in the Lounge, and at twice the pay. Now he had an opportunity to visit his old San Francisco stomping grounds with setting up appearances at Facks II on Bush Street right after the Vegas engagement. Bob would still keep his home base in Chicago, at the Cafe Continental, and maybe with this trip away, the 'boys' would appreciate the business he drew in, a bit more. This was to be a super-working vacation and he eagerly

PLAYBOY PENTHOUSE
HUGH HEFNER—BOB SCOBEY—CLANCY HAYES

"©PLAYBOY"

looked forward to it. So in December of '59 he accepted these engagements.

Bob's wife, (he was still married) and his three children had traveled on ahead, by car, to Vegas. Bob didn't invite me along, because his family would be on the trip. I was pushed out about it, I'll admit, but I can't remember the exact chain of events that excluded me from going. I guess we were only seeing each other occasionally at the time.

Well, the last night, before he left for Las Vegas, he invited me to spend the night at his home and see him off at the airport, which was just a few miles from his residence.

At first, I didn't want to go. I felt it was deceitful to stay overnight in a married man's home while his family was away. My feminine vanity was also pinched to think that he had not invited me to join him and share the good times.

Bob gave me repeated assurances that all was okay. He said his maid, Ethel, who was also a close, personal friend and really a mother to the children, would be there and she understood Bob's marital situation, which was failing daily.

Late that afternoon, we traveled to his home on Telegraph Road, in Bannockburn, Illinois. It was a big, stately mansion. When I first approached it, the view was breathtaking as the home was on what appeared to be two

PLAYBOY TV SHOW
Left to right: Bob Scobey, Dave Black, Jim Beebe,
Brian Shanley, Clancy Hayes

"©PLAYBOY"

acres of greenery although it was wintertime. I was glad I had decided to come along because now I would see the mysterious side of Bob.

The very first room I entered was the kitchen. There, Ethel the maid was preparing something for Bob to eat. I relaxed immediately. She was a kindly woman. My first impressions were memorable for she was a lady who had seen more joy and misery than most people ever hear about. She was a large woman, six feet tall, and with large bones rather than fat. She had a big smile on her face and was so happy to see 'Mr. Scobey', as she affectionately called him. Her voice was warm and pleasant and I quickly felt at home and at ease.

Soon, Bob was off to the telephone and making the numerous phone calls that were habitual with him. Often, people would remark how Bob would come into their homes, say a quick hello, and ask to use the phone. It was surely no different here at his own pad. This time he had to tie all loose ends for the job following the Stardust engagement, at Facks II, in San Francisco.

Before long, Ethel's easy manner and quality of inspiring confidence had me talking freely to her about my dilemma, staying overnight at his house. She quickly backed up Bob and assured me it was okay. It was at this time, some of the reasons for Bob's indifferences came to light. Ethel revealed that Bob and his wife had been estranged for a long time.

I was starting to feel shocked at Bob's apparent tolerance until I began to realize he had long since given up on his marriage and simply let things drift because he was just too busy to face the destructive showdown of a major family change at the time. The children, all very young, may have influenced postponing the inevitable decision of divorce. Bob really idolized his children. I watched their relationships in later months, when we would all go out together and I could see the deep love and concern he had for them.

Ethel was a spiritual woman, a sister in her neighborhood church. As our conversation continued, she started eulogizing 'Mr.' Scobey and told me what a good and kind person he has always been to her. She felt toward him as though he were her son. He was always helping others, never too busy. Yet, he would be putting up with 'a hellish situation in his own home'. She said *"Mr. Scobey's marriage isn't going too well, but as long as he can find a bed in the house, he seems to rise above the sordid state of his marital relationship."*

A close friend of Bob and his children, Mimi Chesrow, whose family lived next door, wrote:

". . . . Bob was the most wonderful neighbor and friend we ever had. Bob said, 'Mimi, you can just walk in my house whenever you like - you don't have to knock'. I nearly fell over! No one, before that time or since, has ever treated me with such kindness. I was in my early teens then. I have never met another man as generous, kind and good as Bob Scobey. While Bob was traveling, my mom provided food for Ethel and the children . . . ."

Ethel understood a lot about life. She attended church regularly, several times a week. She loved to sing and testify and give forth with her share of hallelujahs. Even though she was a live-in maid, she would go home to the south side of Chicago, where she kept a flat, for periodic visits with her family. Her husbands (several of them were long gone), left her with two daughters. As she revealed herself to me, I found her present religious ways were not always with her.

In her younger days, on the South side of Chicago, she was in the 'numbers game' . . . later referred to as the 'rackets'. She spoke of her many beaux. She had been married three times, twice to 'colored' men as she called them, and once to a white man. She was a good looking woman that favored her Spanish ancestory. Her black heritage may well have been that of some African Queen, or Spanish Princess, for her bearing was regal. She told me she had often been mistaken for white and was able to pass over the color line quite easily. She described some of the advantages and pitfalls this unique look had given her while she was young. Her boyfriends showered her with gifts, furs, and cars.

In Ethel's heyday, she sparkled and glittered. Although much of her life was lived with an uptown, racy crowd, Ethel was originally from the deep South. She was the first person to make me truly aware of the biggotry and prejudice that caused her race so much tragedy and had held them down so long.

But all of that was behind her now, and her *"life belonged to Jesus, Hallelujah!"* She would do a dance everytime the spirit moved her and it was often, I tell you. I looked and listened intently; awed and thoroughly fascinated by her enthusiastic stories.

Later on, when we were friends, I would go with her to church on occasion. Everyone would be in a festive mood; all the brothers and sisters would jump with joy . . . when they gathered, for Sunday services. Being raised in a catholic orphanage, we did not have so much fun in church.

Well, Ethel went on to tell me about the home scene at Bob's house. *"Many nights, Bob has to find a place to sleep in one of his children's beds, because when he gets home, tired after a nights' work, there are no beds available! Soon the children are off to school since Bob gets home about 5:30 a.m., and then he can fall asleep in peace."*

As Ethel talked I became more compassionate toward Bob and his situation. I knew I was falling more and more in love with him as she continued to justify Bob dating me. I, too, was justifying the fact I was going out with a married man, so I listened, quite eagerly, indeed.

After our talk, I toured the stately place only to find bare rooms and very little furniture. That was a big, empty, stately mansion. The children rode bicycles through the living room. I became even angrier with the wife I had not met. Poor management I thought!

The next morning, I rode with Bob to the airport, kissed him goodbye, and off he flew to Vegas—leaving me very much alone!

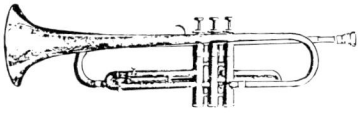

11   TROUBLE IN MIND

RETURNING TO MY TINY APARTMENT, I FELT empty inside, and full of regret. It wasn't long before my mind took over, checking out ways of arriving in Las Vegas and surprising Bob. When he called, I mentioned someone else I knew, had a private airplane and we were going to New York.

"This will stir up some jealousy," I thought, *"and offset my loneliness. Perhaps Bob will respond with, 'Well, if you can get away, why don't you come here?'"* It didn't seem to work at all, and Bob instead said,

"I'm glad you will be busy and having fun. I'm just working late hours and it's all business here."

We said our goodbyes, and as I put down the phone, I could no longer contain the ache inside me. I picked it up again, dialed the airport for reservations, called a cab, took a quick shower, and groped around for some kind of wardrobe. I was still locking my suitcase, as I reached the cab.

We rushed to the airport, and in hours I was seated, somewhat calmly, at a table in the Stardust Lounge, with stars in my eyes. I had tried to keep my composure. I gazed at the stage and 'Bob Scobey and His Frisco Band'. There they were, appearing in all their magical splendor. Then our eyes met. Instantly, I knew I had made the right decision. He appeared so happy, he could hardly wait 'til the set was over! Bob put on a spirited show. It seemed to be directed only to me!

The Stardust Lounge is vast, seating more than 200, but the people quickly faded into darkness and as soon as the set was over, Bob rushed downstage to embrace me.

"What are you doing here?", he said.

"I just couldn't stay away."

We locked into a tight embrace. After a few moments, when calm filled the air, we realized I was a problem and what to do with me became a puzzle.

I decided to rent a room in a small hotel. Bob visited me every chance he could and I frequented the Stardust to watch him perform. His wife soon found out I was in town. She was unable to identify me until New Year's Eve. At the stroke of midnight, Bob came down from the stage and gave me a kiss! I didn't know she was in the room then. Maybe he didn't either. She could easily see everyone, including the whole band, already knew about me and what was going on so, she decided to split Las Vegas.

I won!!! I felt so good about it. Bob had a day off and we drove to Los Angeles, where 'Ben Blue' and company were appearing in Blue's club. Bob wanted to hire 'Freddy

Morgan and the Idiots', 'Mack Pearson' and 'Elaine Evans', for the Cafe Continental, so he could build a better act and get to Vegas more often. I was excited just because I could tag along. It was a totally new experience for me. We returned to the Stardust for another week or so and this time I was more in touch with the band. I was able to pay more attention to them individually and I began to thoroughly appreciate their fine musicianship.

'Clancy Hayes' was on banjo and vocals; 'Toni Lee Scott' was the female vocalist; 'Dave Black' was cooking with his two-bass drums; 'Rich Matteson', on an old Helicon tuba (that's a beautiful instrument); 'Ronny Di Phillips', piano; 'Brian Shanley', clarinet; and 'Jim Beebe' tailgated the trombone. Jim, you'll note is not only an outstanding musician, but also a very perceptive and observing person. His recollections and views helped complete and fill in several gaps in the band's history, in many sections in this biography.

One night, at the Stardust, a fan of Bob's came in from San Diego. Sam was a prosperous car dealer, and spent lots of time at the dice tables. During an intermission conversation, Sam drew us to the crap table. He held the dice that time for an hour and a half! Sam played the game, primarily, on the numbers coming out, between trying to make his point. He would also take the odds after the number came out. Oh, it was Sam's lucky night! His chips were twenty-five and a hundred dollars—and mountain high! His profits were mounting into the thousands of

CLANCY—TONI—BOB
© Jan Scobey 1976

JEANNETTE
©Jan Scobey 1976

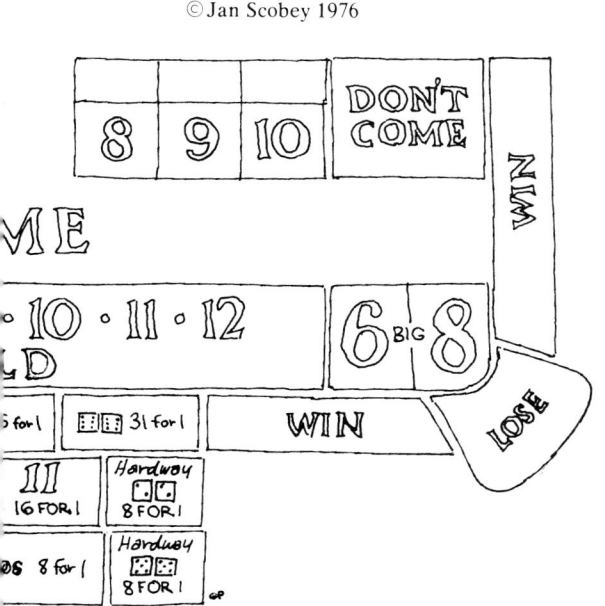

dollars!

Bob had to leave to play another set, but Sam insisted I stay with him, for he felt I was his good luck charm.

"You can still see Bob on stage from this spot," Sam coaxed me.

Sam kept giving me a couple of twenty-five dollar chips everytime he won. I kept looking at Bob on stage, and he kept watching me at the tables, during his performance.

It turned out to be quite a windfall for me, as well as Sam, and I was able to afford my very first, mink cape!

Courtesy of Marilyn Napier McGwynn

From the Stardust, we went to Facks II, on Bush Street, in San Francisco. After the crowds in Vegas I felt things would be much more calm in Frisco. So many people talked to Bob during intermission in Las Vegas I could hardly enjoy the breaks with him. Well, the same thing happened at Facks II—even more crowds! This was Bob's home base. What a following he had. The days of the famous 'Yerba Buena Jazz Band' were coming back to his audiences. Friends and fans came to the club to hear 'Bob Scobey and His Frisco Band', from miles away. The Facks II crowd gave Bob standing ovations and applause every set, for his whole stay at the club.

It was a good deal for Bob, too. The owner didn't want to

pay the going rate for the band, which was $3500 a week for an out of town gig. Instead, the management agreed on a concession-type arrangement. Bob was to receive 100% of the door charge of $2.50, plus 15 percent of the money from the bar business. I bet the owner wished he had agreed to the $3500 a week contract because business was so good, people had to wait outside for the next show, and the owners pleaded with Bob to stay on, a few extra days.

Here is where I met some of Bob's closest friends. Several nights, or should I say, in the wee small hours of the morning, after the show, we would go to the Fairmont Hotel for breakfast and talk hours and hours . . .

Things were looking pretty rosy for Scobey, but several things happened all at once when he returned to Chicago. I found Bob had regrouped his whole band and added the comedy show. Underneath the success of weeks of good business at the Stardust and then Facks II, something sad and ominous was brewing about Scobey's band. Something turned out to be a near catastrophe to Bob's ambitions and plans.

His entire band was about to disintegrate! Every one of his musicians, with the exception of 'Dave Black', was to leave him or be replaced. Not until years later, while I was researching this material did the whole mix-up unravel, for Bob never spoke of this and acted then as though everything was coming up roses! Situations like this must have eaten away at him and accelerated his severe ulcer condition.

As the pieces began to fit, I learned the details of the difficulty, from letters and conversations with people close to him, and members of his band. I'll give you my insight into the fiercely competitive world of the entertainment business.

Bob decided early in his career to handle his own bookings because of mishaps with agents, in the past. Bob sold his band to the Marlboro cigarette people for a television commercial. His band was featured and the commercial was televised all over the world. He had won out over several other top name entertainers and bands, including 'Louis Armstrong' and the 'Dukes of Dixieland'! There was no question about it, some big money was involved in the television contract. Well, human nature what it is, someone was bound to be jealous of Bob's success if they felt they weren't getting a big enough cut. This was true of some of the members of Bob's band. They had big egos and felt they should receive more than their regular, agreed upon salary.

Bob had always allowed and even encouraged everyone to have their spotlight, even if it seemed to place himself in the background. He recognized that by doing so, it not only satisfied the musician's need for exposure, but by starring everyone, he would satisfy the public and be successful. In

BOB SCOBEY—TONI LEE SCOTT
BRIAN SHANLEY—CLANCY HAY
Courtesy of Marilyn Napier McGwynn

the predicament which existed in the atmosphere of Bob's band, the members were allowed to develop their individual personalities and gain greater, personal popularity.

However, they failed to empathize—a leader accepts all the heavy responsibilities of getting jobs, paying high salaries, doing the bookwork, coordinating all the hundreds of necessary, business details which make a band come off, in addition to being a strong, sparkling leader. After paying his employees a more than fair wage (Bob always did pay well, even when the money was tight), every nickel he received of the net, above expenses and wages, should have been his without question! Bob would spend as much time working hours offstage and he did onstage, and that ended up totaling many a 16-hour day, seven days a week.

I always thought the singers, Clancy and Toni, left Bob's band when they were lured away by gossip, jealousy and anger, for they felt they did not receive part of Bob's profit on the Marlboro commercial contract. They were paid highly for doing the job, plus they received residuals, because Clancy and Toni spoke or sang. Bob did not receive extra for his part, except the initially agreed upon price. This might have been the reason for that band's dissolution, shortly after the commercial, but I discovered the reasons were more complicated. Joe Glaser of Associated Booking was probably instrumental in the loss to Bob of his employees.

Joe Glaser was a big time booking agent who handled contracts for people like 'Armstrong' and the 'Dukes'. He was probably upset because the Marlboro people insisted on having 'Bob Scobey' do the commercial. The contracts had to be executed by Glaser and he had been campaigning to get the job for one of his own properties. Failing to do so, he tried to sign Bob with his agency. Bob had been very suspicious of agents' promises because he had been burned before. It appeared then, Glaser set out to replace Bob at the Cafe Continental Club. First 'Rich Matteson' was offered more money by the 'Dukes of Dixieland', Glaser's property. Then, somehow, Clancy and Toni found out the total price of the commercial and only Marlboro, Bob and Glaser had known that. Finally, the other musicians left for equally cloudy reasons. One day, Bob, with none of the original musicians left except 'Dave Black', the drummer—was replaced at the club, with another band that backed up Clancy and Toni.

'Jim Beebe', who played trombone with Bob's band for a couple of years, threw some light on this merky situation. Jim described the times of that part of Bob's life and related the colorful background of some of the people who were involved with him.

BOB SCOBEY—FLOYD BEAN
Courtesy of George Hulme

".... Now you want to know what happened when Clancy and Toni left, and Bob came back with 'Freddy Morgan', etc. I'll give you my viewpoint. It was a series of things, not just the Marlboro Commercial. That band, with Clancy, Toni, Black, Rich, Di Phillips, Brian and myself, was one of the very best that Bob ever had. It was together for about two years, and was really tight. We had a repertoire, a presentation, and a swing, that few, if any bands had. We had everything from old trad tunes such as 'Sidewalk Blues' to Clancy's vocals. The Marlboro commercial was quite a coup for Bob. The Marlboro people wanted Bob and the band, but the contract had to go through Associated Booking, who did their best to talk them out of Bob and into their own contracted artists.

"Marlboro stuck with their original intention and got Bob. We all got paid for recording and filming it—about $300. Clancy and Toni probably got a lot more because they sang it. Then, word got out, Bob had received $15,000. for it.

"Now, Bob had, kind of, promised everyone a good taste when he got some good dollars. I can't verify whether he got that much, but I think, in particular, Clancy and Toni were ticked off about it.

"Building up along with these factors, there were others. Joe Glaser, who was really, in fact, Associated Booking, had a campaign going to get Bob to sign with him. He made all sorts of promises, such as concert tours in Europe, etc., but wouldn't put the promises down on paper. Bob wouldn't sign because he had been stung by agents with promises before. Then Glaser came on with some threats. He threatened to 'put Armstrong across the street'. Bob said, 'Fine, it will be good for our business'. Then Glaser went after Clancy. I think that some of Clancy's friends had been pushing him to go out on his own and when he was offered a contract with Audio Fidelity records, he split.

"'Rich Matteson' was not the trigger by any means, but it was coincidental that the band started to deteriorate somewhat when he left. He was a pain in the ass when he first joined the band, as he was quite pushy. He was going to have us singing like the four Freshmen and some other bullshit ideas he had, plus he was out to make a name for himself.

"He had a fancy autograph and he said that you had to have a nickname to make it. His was the 'Professor' and the sooner we started calling him that, the better! Nobody ever called him that. He hustled people to vote for him in the Downbeat polls. He stuck in everyone's craw, except Bob, who didn't pay much attention to it. Beyond that, Rich was one hell of a musician. He played a swinging, modern bass line on the tuba which was quite unusual, plus playing the

RICH MATTESON

MACK PEARSON—ELAINE EVANS—FREDDY MORGAN
Courtesy of Cliff Riddle of Hollywood

hell out of the bass trumpet.

"He was a very good arranger too. He would come in with an elaborate arrangement, quite good, but overly arranged. We would rehearse it and Bob would very deftly edit it down to a workable chart that didn't sound overblown for our style band.

"I want to mention one arrangement that Rich wrote. He came in one day with a chart for us on 'Slaughter on Tenth Avenue'. Now, this is a difficult piece for a Symphony to bring off let alone a 7 piece band. We didn't want to do it at *first and struggled with it during rehearsal until it began to make sense and we could see that it would be unusual for our type of band to do something like this. It was built around and featured a great drum solo by 'Dave Black'. It knocked audiences out when we came on with this piece following something like 'Ace In The Hole'. We recorded it for RCA, but they never released it.*

"Frank Assunto from the 'Dukes of Dixieland' offered Rich more money than I guess Bob could pay. Rich didn't want to leave and Bob didn't want him to, but off he went with the 'Dukes of Dixieland'. Bob hired a guy from the Chicago local on string bass. He wanted someone from Chicago so that he wouldn't have to pay the exhorbitant, traveling, union tax. This guy he hired had bad time and thoroughly upset the tight rhythm section we had going. This bugged everyone, but Bob wouldn't get rid of him.

"Brian and I were getting unhappy and we were entertaining vague notions about getting a band together with 'George Zack'. So, the band kind of lost the feel it had with the loss of Rich.

"When Rich left to join the Dukes, we had a lot of laughs speculating on the reaction within the Dukes when pushy Rich starts coming on. Particularly with 'Papa Jac Assunto', who was rather notoriously grumpy. We tried to envision him with Rich on the band. Dave Black has a very subtle, dry, deadpan sense of humor. One day, we were having a rehearsal and Dave was waiting for each of us as we came in.

'Did you hear what happened to 'Papa Jac' of the 'Dukes of Dixieland'?'

'No, what?'

'He tried to commit suicide!'

Well, no one fell for it until Bob came in. Dave was there, deadpan, with this newspaper.

'Say, Bob, did you hear what happened to Papa Jac?' *Dave exclaimed with concern.*

'No, What?', *Bob bit and asked.*

'He tried to commit suicide', *Dave replied.*

"Bob grabbed the paper, searching with frantic curiosity, to read the nonexistent story. We all got a hell of a laugh out of that.

"The pianist, 'Floyd Bean', deserves a mention. He worked with Bob for two or three years preceding 'Ronny DiPhillips'. He was a great stride pianist and added commercially to the band. Bob called him, 'Judge Bean' as he looked like a movie, western judge, with string-tie and all. Floyd played a swinging, Chicago style, dixieland jazz piano and behind Clancy, played some of the most beautiful accompaniments that I have ever heard any pianist play.

"Clancy was enticed away. I'm not sure about Toni. She

**DUKES OF DIXIELAND
FRED, FRANK, AND PAPA JAC ASSUNTO**
Courtesy of Frank Assunto

was getting offers and had an interest in a hair salon in Chicago. She and Clancy left at the same time and Bob let Brian and I go. We had become kind of antagonistic and looking back on it, I'm surprised that he didn't let us go sooner. He said that with losing Clancy, he had to come up with something and had hired 'Freddy Morgan and the Idiots'. Also, he was trying to get into Vegas on a more permanent basis, and felt that having more of a lounge act would help him do that. This of course turned out to be a big disaster.

"Vegas acts, with the exception of 'Louis Prima', notoriously bombed in the midwest. People in the midwest liked good, honest, swinging music, which of course is Bob Scobey. So, here he came back to Chicago with a half-assed comedy act. His fans couldn't believe it. Eventually, he dropped this and went back to having a good band.

"Clancy bombed on his own. The problem was that Clancy was no leader . . . ."

Somehow, and this is a minor tragedy, for all Clancy had to offer, he missed being exposed during the heyday revival of folk singing in the '60's. He was poorly managed after leaving Scobey. This happens very often in show business. There are thousands of fine talents who have everything together, but, because they miss the right breaks, or because of mismanagement, or a lack of it, their star never rises and we are all the losers for it. It's really tough to become and remain a fine artist, spending hours polishing or adding new material to your act, and to try and find gigs too.

Scobey was the leader and booked his own band, but this is most unusual in show biz. Clancy left Bob to go on his own. He never achieved greater fame and recognition that he deserved other than his long association with Bob. I am sure his music library and style has been an inspiration for many younger folk singers. Well, this break-up broke Bob's heart. Jim Beebe gave me his point of view.

". . . . Clancy and Bob went together like ham and eggs. Bob's driving, powerful trumpet and Clancy's warm and swinging vocals. Neither were quite the same or as effective musically without the other. Bob was a leader and Clancy wasn't. Besides being a great musician, Clancy was a warm, fun guy, but just wanted to show up and do his thing with the band. Bob had the guts and intention of leading a band and was able to bear the pressures of keeping it going. It's a shame they split because together they made some great music.

"I worked some of Clancy's jobs. Each one had rather a different pickup band and Clancy was unhappy and none of it

worked out well. The Continental hired Clancy and Toni with 'Art Hodes' Band'. Brian and I got the off nights in a band with George Zack. Zack, when he is 'on', is a great pianist and can really spark a band. He was on when we first got the job and our band came on strong. The club and Clancy really dug our group so they let Hodes go and hired us full time. Rehearsals were great but the first week turned out to be a mess! Zack was off on a toot again, and we had to fire him. That lasted a month and I guess Clancy went back to Frisco.

"*When Bob came back with Freddy Morgan—Clancy, Toni, Brian and I were gone. I don't know how much the Marlboro had to do with it. Looking at it now, whatever Bob made on that or anything else was his business. Bob was a great leader, easygoing, pleasant to work with, open to anyone's ideas or things they wanted to do. He was honest, worked very hard and went to great pains to keep the band and the payroll going . . . .*"

12   LOVE ME OR LEAVE ME

UPON MY RETURN TO CHICAGO FROM LAS Vegas, two shockers were awaiting me. Bob and his wife must have had a big argument when he got home and his wife called me on the phone. I guess some ill-meaning acquaintance of Bob's (I really knew who it was) gave her my phone number, told her who I was, and about Bob and my relationship.

She seemed fairly calm when she called. She was rather overly polite and spoke with a forced, false graciousness.

"You can expect Bob to be over soon and be kind to him. You know, his poor tummy," she told me, and hung up!

When Bob did reach me, he told me of the argument and I told him of the phone call. All he did was laugh. I became upset that his wife was trying to bug me. Then, Bob told me she asked for a divorce, and I felt better about it.

The other shocker had to do with my apartment. The gals that were sharing my apartment, did not want to alarm me while I was away and waited until I got home to tell me of the calamity. The police had raided the apartment! That one really bewildered me and threw me off guard. These girls were truly square and I had known them for two years. They could never be part of the slightest evil or wrong doing to anyone. Nonetheless, because one of the gals had dated a mysterious character from Rush Street (she only had the one date), we were all suspect. Twelve policemen had invaded our tiny, three room apartment. They had literally forced their way in, without a search warrant.

Holding the girls to one side, while they tore up the apartment, they searched for contraband. The police gave them absolutely no reason for their terrifying behaviour. They even hatcheted some furniture in their cruel haste.

When they were finally through, they hauled the girls off to the police station! It was only then, my friends were told the reason for the bust. The fellow, one of the girls had dated, was wanted in connection with a murder! WOW-WOW-WOW! The girls shuddered to think this was happening to them. Well, with all that hull-a-ba-loo, we were evicted from our apartment. The lease was in my name and no excuse could convince the management that I, at least, should keep the apartment. I had to find new lodging soon, so I presented my problem to Bob, hoping he could come up with a solution, something like . . .

"Jeannette, don't worry, we'll find another place."

Then, he and I could live together and the result of the whole fiasco would have a happy ending. However, he

Chicago Aerial View
Courtesy of the Los Angeles Public Library

offered no solution, so I decided to split town and go back to Vegas.

It was a threat to our relationship, but I had to take the chance. Everyone at the club knew I was leaving. The other waitresses had a mini-party for me and gave me a fabulous purse and hat to enjoy while reclining poolside in the Nevada sunshine.

The hour for my departure was approaching and Bob hadn't given me the offer I was hoping for. That evening, he played 'Love Me Or Leave Me', as a farewell song. Brilliant, sweet tones poured out from his golden trumpet . . . but no words for me to stop my leave.

That's the way it had to be. I finally took off. Within hours I had melted into the hustling, bustling excitement of 'Fun-City'.

I drifted to the Stardust's Chemin-de-fer table. Chemin-de-fer is played like Bacarat, except the house does not keep the 'Bank'. The 'bank' or 'shoe', contains ten decks of cards, shuffled by the croupier, and rotates between the players. Once in possession of the 'shoe', the player-banker stands a chance of making a big win.

There I was, seated at the table with ten other players. I was down to my last twenty dollars. Then the 'shoe' passed to me and I became the 'bank'!

As long as I kept betting the pot and winning I could keep it. My twenty dollars lay in the bank and one of the ten players were quick to bet with me. I drew a few cards, two each, and quickly I shouted, *"Chemin-de-fer"*, for I had an eight—I won that round. Pretty soon, with many anxious moments in between bets, I kept doubling the pot until it reached $1,000 which was the maximum bet. Oh wow, was I nervous, happy, excited . . . but with only a starter of twenty dollars, I enjoyed more bravery and willingness to take a chance with the $1,000, that for a moment, I just assumed it was the twenty I had started with. I drew my cards again. *"Chemin-de-fer!"* this time I had nine. I was saying Chemin-de-fer a lot. I had really caught a good 'bank'. After winning the second thousand, I just stayed with it until my luck ran out. The house rule of a maximum bet of $1,000 allowed me to pull back a thousand everytime I won. Now the 'bank' was on the fifth thousand—before I finally lost the bet. But I still was ahead four thousand dollars!!!

"Yippee!" I screamed with joy and excitement—as I passed on the 'shoe'. My happy outburst was so loud that it filled the factory-sized room of the Stardust. It brought the management from the lounge to find out what the excitement was about. It was Tommy McDonnell, the host of the lounge, who had been my friend, that came to my assistance. He was

introduced to me by another acquaintance from Chicago. When he came over, he tried to calm me down a bit. He told me to put the money with the cashier for the night. I was nervous. Imagine, little Jeannette being a big winner! I went away from the table with $4,000 gigantic dollars!

It was tough to sleep that night, so I was off again, this time to the Tropicana, to try my hand at black jack. You might have guessed it. I started losing my dress, almost. That morning, before I stopped playing I lost 600 dollars, but in a way, it was worth it. I had the money and the experience of having beckoning power for the first time, on such a large scale. The feeling was overwhelming.

During the game, when I showed them my receipt of money I had at the Stardust, they were quick to give me markers. When it came time to settle my markers, I ordered my money from the Stardust. That was almost worth losing the $600 for. After the come-down from cloud 99, I remembered my other loss, the big one, the break-up with

Tommy McDonnell—Jeannette
©Jan Scobey 1976

Mack Pearson—Jack Wiggins—Freddy Morgan—
Dave Black—Bob Scobey—Ricky Nelson—Tommy Smoot

Courtesy of Chicago Photographers

Toni Lee Scott—Freddy Morgan—Elaine Evans—
Mack Pearson—Bob Scobey

Courtesy of Chicago Photographers

Bob. What could I do about that?

Brainstorm . . . stars flashing . . . *"I'll fly back to Chicago after I pay my rent for a month. Get a round trip ticket to Chi and back. Buy some fancy duds, a few presents for Robert—Hmmmm!"* I rushed to one of the fancy men's stores in the hotel and bought fine clothing for a couple of hundred dollars.

I showed up at the Cafe Continental in Chicago. Everyone was overjoyed to see me looking so fine. I had a beautiful tan; and I wore a white dress that vibrated sensuously when I swayed; a stunning, beauty parlor coiffure, and a classy mink jacket. I felt I was the queen of the evening!

Bob was playing onstage when I arrived. Two weeks had gone by since we had last seen each other. As our eyes met, he stood frozen in his spot, wondering if I was a mirage. He looked perplexed and must have thought, *"Gee, it looks like Jeannette, but she's in Vegas, and she never looked that good before!"* I was vibrant and full of life. My success was beaming from my eyes. I was happy to see him while my spirits were on Mount Everest! During the intermission, he rushed over to talk to me.

"Well Bob," I said, *"How is it going for you?"*

"When did you get back in town?" Bob wondered. *"I thought you were still in Vegas."*

"I just wanted to say hello!", I laughed. *"I won't have time to visit with you, I have to fly right back to Vegas."* *"I left a few surprises for you in the band room. Wish I could stay to see you open them, but I don't have time."*

I remember his face vividly, as I left the club. The scene truly flabbergasted him totally. It was a cruel thing to do, but I had to give it one more go—my best shot—before quitting him for good. He was still married and he wasn't moving about our relationship. I imagined a quick hello and exit would get him to thinking about me again.

Well, it worked! I was in Vegas but a few hours and headed for the Stardust Hotel. There was a page for me in the Stardust Lounge. At first I tried to ignore it and then rushed to answer the page. Bob was on the other end talking from Chicago. He told me how much he cared for me and quickly proceeded to tell me of all the personal problems he was running into and that is why he didn't try to reach me earlier. Whether that was it or not, I fell for it.

Bob truly did have problems! His band was in complete disarray—one by one his people had left him. And the Idiots, the comedy group he had hired to bolster his act, were a complete fiasco—causing him to lose his dixieland fans, which lowered his take, but he was still required to pay all that heavy bread, whether he could afford it or not. The contract with the Idiots lasted for fourteen weeks.

BOB SCOBEY—Jazz at the University
Courtesy of Dyann Rivkin

bass; 'Dave Black', drums. They did some recording, too—one for Sesac, primarily for their music system.

During the fall and winter of 1960, Bob played one week concerts and one nighters, totaling more than 40 separate engagements, with all the headaches and traveling that goes with it.

In July, the band appeared in Wisconsin Dells with the Tommy Bartlett Water Show, and it gave *"Dad"* his first opportunity to visit privately with his three children. The Bartlett shows went on during the day, and a carnival was in town with all the rides and chance booths at night, before show time. It was fun when we all got together. I recall how Bob tried to put up a tent show to house the band and draw some dixieland fans, but unfortunately, the city council wouldn't give him a license.

Bob had a major accident on the lake during one of his waterskiing trips. He broke a couple of fingers on his right hand, his playing hand! It was a severe accident, especially for a trumpet man.

We were in a motor boat and someone was water-skiing at the time. Now it appeared, this person, when he had fallen, was in danger of being caught by the motor, so Bob grabbed at the spinning motor and broke his fingers trying to jam it to stop! He saved the swimmer, but his hand needed to have a cast put on it—that very night.

Bob showed up for his performance, and without a stand-by trumpet player to help out. He played the whole date, and a few more later, with his left hand. It amazed everyone who saw him but mostly the guys in the band. He never lost a note, and if your eyes were closed you would never have thought he had just had a severe injury to his

Buddy Leet—Dickie Phillips
Bill Napier—Bob Scobey
Ricky Nelson—Tommy Smoot
Dave Black

Courtesy of Norman Goldberg

hand. This kind of quick agility, and adjustment to bad situations, doing what had to be done, never reflecting on whether it was difficult or not, was one of Bob's finest attributes.

A photo taken while he was playing with his remaining, good hand gave rise to an interesting article in a European jazz periodical, 'Swingtime'. They included photos of Bob. The editor wrote to me to find out if Bob Scobey was a left handed trumpet player or if the photograph had been reversed so that Bob appeared left handed . . . . And I told him of this accident. Bob regularly played with his right hand. Columnist Gerald Kloss wrote:

". . . . At the Blue Dahlia, where Bob Scobey septet opened a nine day run of neo-Dixieland jazz, Bob showed up with his right hand in a cast, the result of a motor boat accident at Lake Geneva, Thursday. A sterling example of 'the show must go on' spirit! . . . ."

Bob had learned to handle his instrument so well that he could play with either hand! The habit of one handed playing and with such p-zazz, was Scobey's trademark!

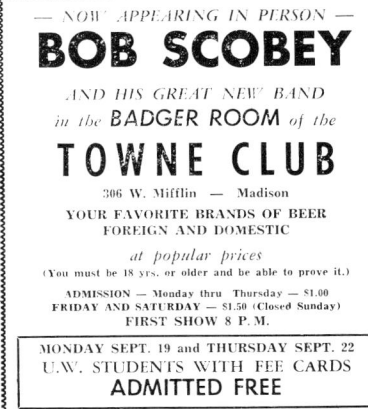

BOB SCOBEY

Courtesy of Marilyn Napier McGwynn

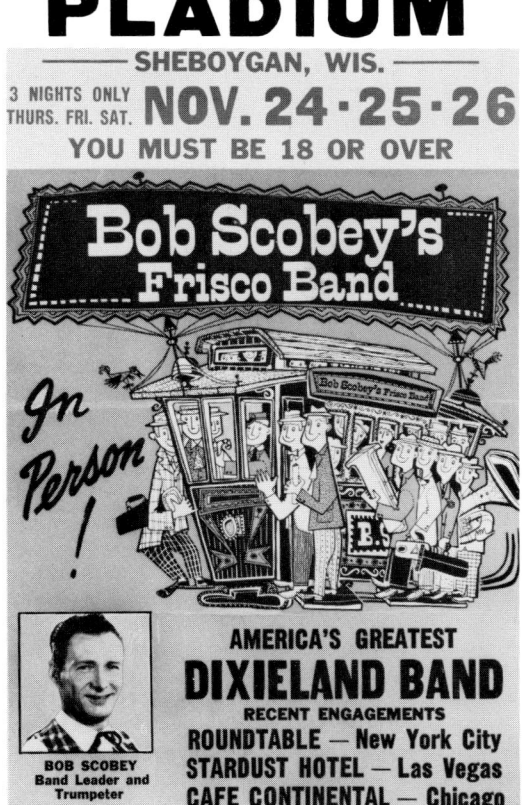

Dyann Rivkin—Bill Napier—Bob Scobey—Buddy Leet
Courtesy of Dyann Rivkin

Dyann Rivkin, a student in Journalism at the University of Wisconsin boosted the Scobey name around Madison. Dyann was such a fan and friend that, later when the band had returned to Chicago and she couldn't leave the University to go see them, she brought the band back to Madison by booking and promoting two one-nighters. Both performances were to standing-room-only crowds.

That year, for his 43rd birthday, she had a golden trumpet made and when Bob unravelled the scroll in the bell listing several hundred names of his admirers, Bob Scobey just beamed! . . .

Later on in the year, at the Towne Club, he had another welcomed, lengthy visit with his children, young Bob, Kyle and Adrienne. The band played at the Towne Club in Madison, Wisconsin, for nearly a month, but unfortunately the wages at that time depended on the crowds. It was a full house alright, however, it turned out to be more of a beer joint than a night club atmosphere. The cover charge was considerably less and the drink orders went down from two dollars a drink, to between 75 cents and a dollar.

Bob continued to pay the same high wages, and it wasn't long before he started borrowing from me to pay the band. Luckily, we still had lots of fun in this popular resort area. Bob was quite a golfer, he liked to waterski, his children and Ethel were all with us, and we caught plenty of perch for bonfire cooking.

I was quickly growing into the habit of taking care of Bob better than anyone ever did before. I guess it was apparent to others. Norman Goldberg, a dixieland fan and photographer was at the Towne Club in 1960 and he still vividly remembered Bob's, one in a lifetime, style of horn playing.

". . . . My only recollection of you comes from the night I spent photographing and taping Bob's music. I believe we were introduced briefly. I remember you as a dark-haired beauty, dressed in a long, black dress with spaghetti straps, hair swept up, and being very attentive to Bob.

"I don't know when I first became a Scobey fan, but being a trumpet player myself, I admired his unique style. I don't believe he has been recognized by the taste-making 'authorities' for the excitement and urgency his style conveyed. He seemed to me, to have personified the whip-hand, driving leadership sound the trumpet should have in Dixie music. His technique of often being a quarter beat behind the tempo when picking up on a solo, is one of the things that set him apart, giving the command to listen when he played. Jazz being a personal thing, my own explanation of what set Bob's playing apart from others may be wide of the mark, but for me, Scobey's horn was as easy to recognize as Louis' was.

"Bob and Clancy recorded "For All The Wrongs" many years ago, and I've played my old 78 rpm recording of it so often, it's mostly a hiss now. But that recording remains one of Bob's best, in my opinion. In it, he plays off in the distance, in counterpoint to Clancy's mournful singing. Bob's equally lamenting horn in the background, phrasing just right, a sob wringing off some of the notes, brilliant improvization throughout, makes me happy-sad every time I hear it. No one else got those sounds, only Bob! . . . ."

More than anything, Papa Scobey wanted a club of his own. He went back to the Cafe Continental and drew up a lease with the people who were running it, in November, 1960. It didn't work out, but you can see how much Bob had to scuffle.

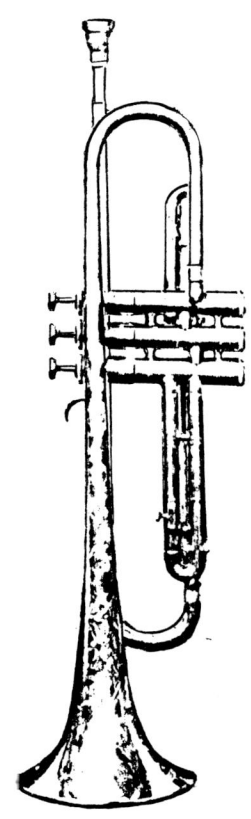

JEANNETTE
Courtesy of Norman Goldberg

BOB SCOBEY
© Jan Scobey 1976

JIM BEEBE
Courtesy of Cilento Studios

"After I got out of the service, about a month later and out of the blue, I got a call from Bob, 'Would I work with him in Las Vegas?'

"This, to me, was the thrill of a lifetime! Bob had left his regular band with Clancy Hayes in Frisco at his club, 'Storyville'. He assembled a different, but powerful band for Vegas—two trombones, 'Warren Smith' and myself; 'Bob Short', Tuba; 'Bill Campbell', piano; and 'Lizzie Miles' from New Orleans on vocals. 'Warren Smith' was one of my favorite trombonists and playing with him, Bob and Lizzie was a heady experience. I learned plenty just by osmosis.

"I had my first 'pot' experience here. Some local musician turned me on to it and I figured, 'what the hell, I'll try it'. So one night I did. Well, we got into 'All The Wrongs You've Done To Me' which featured Bob. At the end, the trombones hit some chords while Bob played an obligato, ending on them. Well, in the middle of the tune, the 'pot thing' hit me. My sense of time got scrambled and I thought

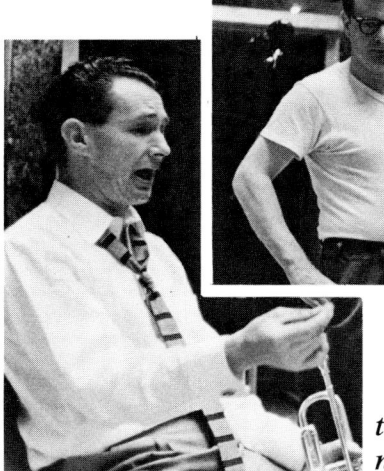

Bob Scobey—Dave Black—Rich Matteson—Jim Beebe
Courtesy of RCA Records

BRIAN SHANLEY
Courtesy of Ed Lawless

that we were at the end of the tune and I came in and hit my note—double forte. Bob figured out what was happening and just laughed. Bob went back with his regular band, and I returned to the University of Wisconsin.

"Scobey began playing around the midwest with great success. I had been at the University about two years. 'Brian Shanley' and I had a good little band with Bobby Lewis in a club in Madison, Wisconsin.

I had a call from Bob that he had four nights to fill. 'Say Jim, can you find us any gigs in Madison?' Well, he came into our club—the Shuffle Inn. Our band played too, and I'll never forget it. I have never seen a club that packed before or since. People were jammed in like sardines and Bob had a dynamite band together. 'Clancy' of course and 'Toni', a fantastic singer and a show stopper; a drummer, 'Dave Black' - a solid band which featured two trombones—'Jack Buck' and 'Doug Skinner'.

"Shortly afterward, Bob asked 'Brian Shanley', clarinet; and myself to join him, which we did. He had two trombones for a while, 'Ralph Hutchinson' and myself. When Ralph left we settled down to one trombone. 'Rich Matteson' came on and played tuba and bass trumpet and Brian Shanley wrote out some traditional things, like 'Jelly Roll Morton', tunes which pleased the trad fans.

"We had a repertoire no other group could match - traditional things - mainstream Dixieland - contemporary tunes. It was a powerful arrangement. Of course, the whole thing was sparked by Scobey's driving, forceful trumpet and his leadership.

"When I joined Bob this time, he taught me something I consider the most important thing I ever learned pertaining

time. His records sound better than ever today. He still has legions of fans around. A week doesn't go by that I don't run into someone who tells me how much they loved and missed Scobey....''

In 1958, Bob was the very first to revive and bring in Dixieland Jazz into the cold and windy city. By 1960 jazz bands and clubs were springing up like mushrooms after rain. The Clarite Lounge on Clark Street starred 'Jack Ivert and his Riverboat Five'; 'Doc Evans' was at the Downbeat; Jazz limited on Grand Avenue featured 'Bill Rhinehardt's Band', and there were many others. Bob, I believe, single handedly started a brand new jazz revival in Chicago.

Trumpet man, Bobby Lewis and his band, the Dixielanders, were playing at the Shuffle Inn:

BOBBY LEWIS
Courtesy of Richard Faverty

''.... When Bob Scobey's band was brought in, every performance was S.R.O. - Standing Room Only! He was the "JAZZ KING" of Madison! The success of the first engagement with Bob Scobey led to other jobs for me— 'Jack Teagarden', the 'Harmonicats', the 'Dukes of Dixieland' and all because of Scobey. So you can see the direct reflection in my life from meeting and knowing Bob Scobey.

'''Bobbyloo' he used to call me, and always had a handshake and a smile. He was quite a guy!....''

Roger Stillman, who played bass on several gigs in Madison remembered:

''.... I first got acquainted with the Scobey band through his recordings. The guys I ran with up in Madison, Wisconsin would get together in music stores and go through the record department for Scobey records, for his arrangements so we could transpose them on our own charts.

"I thought of Bob the way all the guys thought. He was a hell of a nice guy, easy to work with (if you played right), and musically, he was a tireless worker. His style was easily recognizable and still is. When his band kicked off, something happened. We all knew Scobey was giving his all.

"My biggest pleasure, though, was introducing him to 'Bobby Hackett', because he dug his playing and never had a chance to meet him during all those years. When I introduced Hackett to Scobey, he was all smiles and the conflab flowed between them so, they did get on together!....''

ROGER STILLMAN

Bob had an uncanny sense of time. I remember when he rehearsed for his own recording session on Ragtime Records, the guys in the band would remark about it. No matter how many starts there were to a tune, it would always be counted off to the exact metronome Bob had, going in his head, and it always stayed there. This amazed the engineers too. If there would have to be any splicing, with someone who had perfect timing like Bob, it made their job considerably easier.

'Doc Evans', an internationally known jazz trumpeter; a professional since 1929, now conducts the Bloomington Civic Orchestra and has from it's formation back in 1963. On occasion, he travels across the states playing jazz. Doc is a top man, respected in music and among the Dixieland jazz devotees, his opinion would have been valued by Bob.

DOC EVANS

". . . . I was much impressed, musically, by Bob's integrity, the way he organized his group and by his clean, uncluttered and inventive style of playing. I felt that here was a man who was completely honest, musically.

"He was not afraid to use a new approach on an old tune if it pleased his taste, but he never lost sight of the values in the old music. As to his playing, he was lyrical, economical of notes and was constantly developing an individual style which I much admired. It seemed to me he was trying to steer away from the stiff, self conscious approach of so many revivalist bands. I admired the clean tone and attack of his horn and the way he really led the band with the trumpet. Technique on the trumpet is common, but the taste and musical integrity that Bob possessed are exceedingly rare . . . ."

So many columnists have written about Bob. Much of it, simply ground out, without much genuine concern for an in depth, sincere review of his work. But Bob Fallstrom didn't take that approach when he was borrowed from the sports section of the Herald and Review in Decatur. A byline to Fallstrom's story, written by his editor, is special.

"Quiet, slow-moving, slow-talking Bob Fallstrom, who has an extensive collection of jazz records too says he is 'rocked to the socks' by Scobey, and we find credence in the assertion that 'jazz makes even the silent sing . . . ." Bob Fallstrom wrote:

BOB FALLSTROM

". . . . Have money troubles? Is Junior lagging in his schoolwork? Worried about that leaky roof? Don't fret. Go see Bob Scobey's Jazz Band the next time it returns to the St. Nicholas Hotel!

"Scobey and Co. specialize in 'happy music'——the kind that is guaranteed to put a smile on your face. It is a different sort of music, a combination of Dixieland, New Orleans and Chicago jazz styles with a heavy dash of showmanship, the driving trumpet of Scobey, the rollicking vocals of banjo player Clancy Hayes and the solid beat of drummer Dave

Ricky Nelson—Bob Scobey—Dave Black—Bill Napier—
Dickie Phillips—Tommy Smoot—Buddy Leet

Courtesy of Norman Goldberg

Black.
"Once you listen to a Scobey record or, better yet, see him in person, the reason for the band's increasing popularity is evident. The foot-tapping, cheerful music with a jazz beat is easy to take. I'm prejudiced and I admit it. Scobey and Clancy rock me down to the socks and have since their first record went on the market. It's nice to know some 300 who packed in the club, had the same idea! . . . ."

At last the old year grew enfeebled, a young 1961 New Year Baby toddled eagerly just around the corner and in Traverse City, after the New Year's night gig, Bob and I totaled up the year's receipts.

He had taken in $62,000, and his payroll was $79,000. Some year!

Schedule of Engagements
Bob Scobey Band 1960

Jan 1–17	Stardust Hotel, Las Vegas, Nev.
Jan 11	Santa Monica Auditorium
Jan 18–23	Facks II, San Francisco, Caly.
Jan 28–29	Towne Club, Madison, Wis. (Ladies)
Jan 30–Feb 7	Boat Show, Chicago, Ill.
Feb 8–June 25	Cafe Continental, Chi.
June 26	Geo Bells, Chi.
June 27	Sky Club, Aurora, Ill.
June 28	Saloon Room, Bradley, Ill.
June 29–30	Towne Club, Madison, Wis.
July 1–10	Wharf Bar, Wis. Dells, Wis.
July 11–17	Mickelberry's, Chi. Hieghts, Ill.
July 22–Aug 7	Blue Dahlia, Milw. Wis.
Aug 9–20	New Lakeview Club, Spring Park, Minn.
Aug 22–Oct 1	Towne Club, Madison, Wis.
Oct 4–23	Blue Dahlia, Milw, Wis.
Oct 26	Maple Bluff C.C. Madison Wis.
Oct 27–29	Towne Club, Madison, Wis.
Oct 30–31	Orchard Twin Bowl
Nov 3–5	Towne Club, Madison Wis
Nov 7–8	Geo Bells, Chi. Ill.
Nov 9	Libertyville H.S., Ill.
Nov 10	Grand Rapids Pantlind Hotel
Nov 11	Traverse City C.C.
Nov 12	Muskegon, Mich Jazz Club
Nov 14	The Rail, Oshkosh, Wis.
Nov 15	Marquette Univ, Milw, Wis
Nov 16	Crystal Lake, Ill.
Nov 17–19	Towne Club, Madison Wis.
Nov 20–21	Orchard Twin Bowl
Nov 23	North Hills C.C. Milw, Wis
Nov 24–26	Sheboygan, Wis.
Nov 29–Dec 3	Kendelos, Dayton, Ohio
Dec 5–10	Geo Bells, Chi. Ill.
Dec 12–17	Berghoff Gardens, Ft Wayne, Ind.
Dec 18	Mickelberry, Chi Heights, Ill.
Dec 19–27	Vacation
Dec 28	Chi. Club Date (Par Attraction)
Dec 29–30	Oasis, Grand Rapids, Mich.
Dec 31	Traverse City C.C. Mich.

14 BLUE SKIES

> Noticing the days hurrying by,
> When your in Love,
> My, My how they fly.
>
>   . . . Irving Berlin

HAVE YOU EVER HAD HARD TIMES FOR A really long time, like a draining series of gray days, full of drizzle and rain; . . . . and then, like the warm sun, suddenly breaking through the clouds, everything started going good for you again? You were so happy your heart could burst? Imagine a wonderful, exciting future ahead and a person beside you that you loved and with whom you could share all the joys?

It was like that for Bob and me in the spring of 1961. For a year, after Bob's band and his hopes had fallen away from him (The Cafe Continental break-up with 'Clancy Hayes' and the members of his band) we tried to rebuild. It wasn't the same happy combination. It went from one short gig to another, many of them in beer joints and always on short pay. Then, as he and I saved our money, we began to think once more of going into our own club.

At one time, Bob and I wanted to buy the 'Chez Paree' on Wabash Avenue in Chicago. During the Chez Paree's hey day, it was the most popular club in all of Chicago, but now it was defunct. Bob's ex-wife's attorney had now come around to Bob's side (undoubtedly thinking there was money around) and was going to help us put a deal together with whomever owned the building. When Bob and I saw the Chez Paree, it was closed up, drab, dark and almost eerie . . . It had many possibilities and certainly could hold the crowds we were anticipating. It had been a haven for entertainment for many years, and people could identify with it. By the time we were into the paperwork, we realized the undertaking was a bit too big for us. We didn't have nearly enough money for such a big operation. We were certain of our objectives though, and determined somehow to get our own, permanent base of operations, so we continued to search for a club of our own.

A few blocks over on State Street, in Chicago, was an area just beginning to be known as 'Old Town'. Many cities have an 'old town'. It is a section of the city which has the oldest buildings, and unless they are restored, it becomes a shabby, low rent district.

Old town, in Chicago has moved closer to Wells Street as of this writing and is fully restored, rebuilt and prosperous. However, in 1961, it was not. Bob reasoned that the street

BOB SCOBEY
Courtesy of RCA Records

It was Opening Night! June 9, 1961, at the new 'Bourbon Street'. All of Chicago came out to see us and listen to Bob's music. It was a glittering, glorious, festive night and I will never forget it!

It was like an old-time Hollywood Premier! The house was packed with many sophisticated, bejeweled, mink-draped ladies and tuxedoed gentlemen. All of the great Chicago columnists and nite-life historians were there. Will Leonard, Irv 'Kup' Kupcinet, Herb Lyon, Tony Weitzel, Bentley Stegner, Len Harris, and on and one. It was a Blast!

Walking into the club, you entered up a wide stairway to a diamond lit palace of filigreed fanciness. You floated on through the splendor and were greeted by a resplendent maitre-de. Underfoot were soft-cushioned, thick wine-colored carpets! Red velvet, crystal chandeliers, and a fairyland beauty of a fantasy world was all around you. It was truly gorgeous! Seated at your table in the intimate, dim-lit interior, your eyes were irresistibly attracted to center stage and the band.

Bob had a toe-touch system for lights and the band came brightly into view as the spotlights were raised. There they were, 'Bob Scobey', trumpet; 'Bill Hanck', trombone; 'Bill Napier', clarinet; 'Tommy Smoot', piano; 'Buddy Leet', banjo; 'Connie Milano', bass; and 'Dave Black', drums.

That evening was special and while the music poured the people roared. The band was electric! Bob's stage system of adding lights and special microphoned gadgetries all worked to perfection.

Business was so good that night, I personally made $140.00 in tips. I helped as cocktail waitress and I also managed the *"26"* table (dice game) that night. Super! Super! Good times were back. Bob was now on a payroll system and his checks wouldn't bounce. As we were into several weeks of business the word got out . . . it was now an Internationally—World Renowned Club. Jazz musicians started frequenting the place. 'Jonah Jones', 'Doc Evans', 'Clark Terry', 'Frank Assunto', 'Louis Armstrong', any group appearing in town for a few weeks would stop in.

One trumpet player, 'Bobby Lewis', who used to come in the club, sat-in with the band. Scobey always missed the old days, music of the '40's and early '50's. He also really enjoyed the '20's duo-trumpet team of 'King Oliver and Louis Armstrong'. When 'Bobby Lewis' came in, they would capture much of that part of traditional dixieland sound and the patrons jumped and danced with joy. 'Bob Lewis' was the only one who would actually play these parts with Bob. I asked him what it was like:

". . . . Bob Scobey as a trumpet player was unorthodox.

BILL HANCK
Courtesy of George Fletcher

BILL NAPIER
Courtesy of George Fletcher

CONNIE MILANO
Courtesy of George Fletcher

JEANNETTE
© Jan Scobey 1976

Big sounds, fair technique, mostly in the staff (he never liked the high register), terrible embouchure (by legitimate standards), tremendous jazz feel and an incredible knowledge of traditional jazz literature.

"*He knew, not only all the tunes, but all the verses, choruses and changes. Bob also had a drive that very few trumpet players possessed, much like 'Louis'. Bob and I always got along well. We respected each other as people and trumpet players. I knew how to play a second trumpet part. Thus we would be reminiscent of 'King Oliver and Louis'. . . .*"

When Bobby refers to Scobey's embouchure, I feel I know a little about what he means because I started to play trumpet after Bob was gone and did it for five years. I, too, had it rough developing an embouchure. Remember Louis, with the hankerchief? What you didn't see was the blood he was wiping from his lips. I found, when I was studying and

BOB SCOBEY—
    LOUIS (SATCHMO) ARMSTRONG

DAVE BLACK
Courtesy of Jim Schoenmann

TOMMY SMOOT
Courtesy of Jim Schoenmann

BUDDY LEET
Courtesy of George Fletcher

having to play a job the same day, I would end up switching and messing up my embouchure too. I feel you have to be a legitimate (symphony type) player to develop the higher register-type embouchure . . . which means discipline, discipline, discipline! When it comes to playing jazz, especially full time, your head is totally turned around because jazz means . . . freedom, freedom, freedom!

The club owner, Ron, soon became a true friend to Bob and me. His affection for Bob was genuine and we felt the same way about Ron. I asked his wife, Gloria, to write to me about those days. I appreciated her candor in describing her very personal feelings. I think other peoples' observations and opinions, good or bad of me (because I was so close to Bob and I certainly affected Bob's life in many ways) will give you an extra dimensional view of the total unique person that made up all the facets of Bob's personality. A prime example of the way first meetings can be deceptive is told.

". . . . I first met Bob at the little club on State Street before Ron redecorated Bourbon Street for him. It was certainly no earthshattering meeting. Please remember, Jan, as I recount these years when I first met Bob, I was sixteen. Our first exchange was rather formal. I remember telling Bob that I did not care for Dixieland (a statement that we talked of in later years because I credited him with introducing me to and teaching me to enjoy Dixieland.)

"On first meeting I thought Bob was too "musician", you know, the popular language and the entertainer talk. I am sure he would have dismissed me as an underage, unsophisticated Lolita, had I not been Ron's wife, so it was not a mutual admiration society.

"Because Ron was spending so much time on Bourbon Street, getting it ready for the opening, I got my nose out of joint and really started on a pouting campaign. I think that is the reason Ron opened on June 9th, my birthday was the 8th and he was trying to pacify me. I was starting to like Bob more and more, every time I met and talked with him. He was "different", vibrant and very unaffected.

"I don't remember how long I had known Bob before I met you, but I certainly remember meeting you. Ron and I met you and Bob downtown at a Cantonese restaurant in some hotel. I took one look at you and decided I didn't like you! Here was obviously the typical "show-girl" type; cold, shallow, everything on looks, only interested in money or a 'name' performer. You were certainly beautiful enough, and at that time in a glamourous, show-girl way, to make any other female dislike you without further cause.

"That evening you really did perform in such a way as to

give credence to my first opinion. You kept interrupting the business talk between Bob and Ron to have Bob light your cigarette. This seemed very important to you that night. You even talked of it. The importance of a man not ignoring his date and lighting her cigarette. You, for the most part, totally ignored me that night and all your conversation was aimed at Bob or my husband.

"Needless to say, when we left and on the way home that night, I had plenty to say about 'Miss Jan', who-ever-she is? Ron at first had a similar impression of you, mainly I think from the cigarette interruptions and of course my influence. He didn't like your seeming interference with their 'men talk' and 'business plans'.

"The next meeting that I recall vividly was when Ron and I came to your apartment on Lake Shore Drive for dinner. By this time I had decided that I liked Bob—but certainly, I did not like the idea of spending an evening with you. You were too pretty, your figure far too good and I was jealous as hell! My only comfortable feeling was that you were shallow . . . and would not therefore appeal to my husband (I hoped).

"Well that night was really an eye opener . . . Your apartment was beautiful and especially outstanding were the velvet draperies (which I found out you had made) and the floors shone like polished mirrors (which I found out you had polished on hands and knees).

"Then you proceeded to cook a delicious meal, dressed to the teeth and wearing high heels, and you served it on a perfectly appointed table set with linen and crystal.

"Well . . . . that really knocked the props out from under me. As the saying goes: give the devil her due! I couldn't help but admire your versatility, though at first, grudgingly. Ron and I discussed this on the way home. It was a new (and growing) experience to compliment a beautiful woman that I had wanted so badly to have reason to discredit.

"After that awakening, our friendship seemed to grow steadily. The relationship between the four of us was close. Bob became dear to me because of his honesty and that special excitement about living that you felt around him. I know that Ron truly liked Bob. As you know Ron gives his friendships very, very sparingly . . . ."

Scobey and Company were leading a busy period performing at his new club, doing radio shows, and recording on the Ragtime label. Bob was always doing charitable affairs, the Red Cross, Veterans shows, telethons.

Television had become 'King Media' now. It was so powerful and influential, that the TV screen could make an international star almost overnight.

In 1961, that autumn, Bob was doing more commercials for KRAFT JAM'S AND JELLIES, KLEENEX, and MILLER HIGH LIFE BEER. It was one of several methods Bob was already using that would have, I believe, catapulted him toward his ultimate goal . . . that of bringing music to the whole world.

In December, with all this going on, Bob made a TV pilot, filmed at Bourbon Street with guest star 'Jonah Jones'. The idea was to put on a talk show around the performing stars. Perhaps 15 minutes would be spent 'Jonah Jones' playing his horn with Bob's band and then they would offer discussion between them of music, and other interests. It was a fine idea. Well Bob was sitting very pretty, and I was too, except for one little irritation. I still wasn't Bob's wife.

That was soon remedied, not through my plotting, because I figured that it was up to Bob, not me. Ron made the decision for us, at least his encouragement helped. He liked to catch us off-guard with unexpected remarks. Ron introduced the subject suddenly one day, out of the blue, by stopping Bob cold with:

"Say, Bob when are you going to marry that gal?" But Bob kept his cool and the conversation kept on going in another direction . . . Ron persisted,

"If you don't, someone else will grab her. I'll take care of everything."

Ron even suggested where to go for blood tests and cheerfully volunteered to set-up the total nuptial arrangements right then and there.

Somehow it all happened just that quickly. He had his friend drive us around and later we went to City Hall for our license. He knew the judge who performed the ceremony not too far away in Berwyn and he took care of all the *"fix-in's"*; flowers, champagne and all.

I guess Bob was really ready, he just needed that extra shove. I know I was and so Bob and I were united in matrimony on December 26, 1961.

The pre-publicity news-releases of the European tours described Bob's band . . . .

"Abe Saperstein is bringing from America, as his added No. 1 Attraction, 'Bob Scobey's Frisco Band', one of the foremost of its kind in all the world. With Bob's talent, a trumpeter classified as near-genius, and a knowledge of what it takes to lead and select good musicians, Bob Scobey long ago became a success specializing in what he called 'Happy Music'. A relaxed, cheerful sound that falls somewhere between New Orleans Style, San Francisco Style, Chicago Style Dixieland and modern jazz interpretations, and actually none of these."

So now we were going to tour Europe. It was the chance of a lifetime for Bob, and a wonderful adventure for me. Bob had two goals. They included having a hit record, and to be internationally well known. He hoped some day to be famous, for his musical offerings, all over the world. This was his big chance to work toward one of his objectives which was so important to him. We would tour nine countries, in a three month span, and he could spread his special brand of 'Happy Music', all across the face of the earth! He could sense the welcome that the young, new-world-spirit of American Jazz would receive in old Europe and he looked forward to it, eagerly and joyfully.

It was still March though, and we were living for today with an eye to the future, and enjoying the big business at Bourbon Street. I stopped working at the club for awhile. I wanted to do something on my own. I went to work at the LaSalle Hotel to try my hand at singing.

I wanted to sing with Bob's band after his singer left the group. Bob didn't take me seriously at all. In fact he laughed about it. Finally, when he realized I was mighty serious, he conceded, *"give it one shot"*.

He told me about an extra-ordinary vocal coach that charged ten dollars a half hour.

"If you are any good she will accept you as a student, otherwise forget it", he informed me. *"Don't feel badly if she refuses to teach you because it's not as easy to sing as you think."*

I didn't drive at the time, so Bob had to take me to her studio. He waited for me in the car and when I met him after my interview with the coach, he could see I was beaming from ear to ear. The coach felt I would be a good student even though she was critical of my vocal range. After just a few weeks of lessons, I answered an ad in the paper for a singer. I know I wasn't perfectly ready, but I had to have a go at it.

My first job was hilarious. Bob came to see me, and after the show he couldn't help but laugh. Seeing me working with

MEADOWLARK
ABE SAPERSTEIN

Courtesy of Abe Saperstein

JEANNETTE
Courtesy of Chicago Photographers

the *"Birdie man"*, as he called him (I sang with a trained bird act), was probably pretty funny to Bob! He shook my hand and gave me five for trying.

Whenever you are about to embark on a long journey, one of the most important items to be attended to is to check out your health. Being sick, away from home, is miserable and hazardous. Bob went into the Caldwell Hospital for a thorough, complete, five-day checkup.

The doctors were already aware that Bob had a troublesome stomach ulcer, and allowing for that, after tests, x-rays and a review of his condition, he was checked out as fine and in fairly good health.

The particularly interesting fact to be noted here is that they told him his ulcer was benign. What a relief! Our minds say...

"Hey, Tiger Lil, where's your hat box?"

That's how I got in the game too! Just one of the boys!

Without exception, all the members of Saperstein's troup were happy, lovely people. They were tremendous company, cutting up whenever they could, and everything we saw and did together became more fun because of all the sharing of these experiences.

Charles 'Tex' Harrison, Meadowlark Lemon, Murphy Summons, J.C. Gipson, Abe Saperstein, Hubert Ausbie, Willie Thomas, Melvin Davis, Ernest Jones

Jim Ciol, Ron Ellis, Mike Pascale, Ken Peterson, Bob Wilkinson, Ned Randall, Millard Harris, Bob Mivky

Courtesy of Abe Saperstein

'Bob Scobey and His Frisco Band' were the intermission act between the Globetrotters basketball half-time. They were a smash! A big hit! Bob was tall and handsome in his gold lamé jacket and the other musicians in the band wore striking, deep-red jackets. They were dazzling, a group that looked as great as they played. The music brought standing ovations! Everybody loved his 'Happy Music'.

In England we wandered through the Soho district and Picadilly Square. There were trips to jazz clubs in every city. In a few clubs we visited, the patrons actually reclined on the floor during the performance and some would come planning to spend the whole night there.

Bob was interviewed everywhere he traveled. In England, Max Jones, Editor of Melody Magazine, questioned Scobey on audiences and other entertainers:

Courtesy of Melody Maker

Jazz collectors in this country, mindful of the volume of records he made in California with Lu Watters, Turk Murphy and bands of his own, still think of BOB SCOBEY as a West Coast trumpet man.

In fact, Scobey moved to Chicago four years ago and hasn't been back to San Francisco since.

"*It just was too difficult to make a living out there.*" he explained over dinner at Wembley's Empire Pool Arena, where his band—still known as the Frisco Band—plays nightly (until tomorrow) between stints of basketball.

"*When I moved, in January, 1958, most of the guys stayed on the Coast—they had families, kids in school and so forth. Only Clancy Hayes came with me.*

"*I decided that in order to keep a band of the calibre I was used to, it was necessary to move east. I made Chicago my base. That's my home now, and I have an interest in a club, on Rush Street there, named Bourbon Street.*

"*We operate there most of the time, except when we're out on the road.*"

I asked Scobey about the kind of customers he played to in Chicago.

"*A lot of transient clientele,*" he said. "*If we had to depend on regular citizens, our business would be cut in half. A good part of the clientele consists of business men passing through Chicago or in town for a week for some convention.*

"*Chicago is unique in that respect. We have an enormous number of conventions and trade fairs, with as many as 200,000 visitors in town at one time.*

"*These are the people who go out. They're in a party mood and want to go out and see something, not stay home with television. This is important, mind you.*"

Obviously, then, the American audience for traditional

early white players—all of 'em. He had a pretty sad end didn't he? Or so I heard, I know Miff's old partner Red Nichols quite well. He works in Los Angeles most of the time, has been out there for years. Picks up a lot of work through his old friends such as Bing Crosby. Does a lot of studio work. That picture brought him out a bit, great publicity for him. I would say he never played as well as they do on this record. His trumpet is too contrived for me—all those solos were written out beforehand. But he gave something to jazz; all those oldtimers did. I took my style from Louis of course—he has always been the trumpet player for me, ever since I first heard a record of his when I was at High School. Power, feeling and everything—he is the most captivating musician I have ever heard."

"Louis Armstrong-Duke Ellington, Well there's that man again. What a trumpet player and what an entertainer! He just makes people feel good! You know there is a certain school of musicians today who don't try to get with their audiences. They seem to feel that the object of their playing is merely to play something screwy that will change the whole course of jazz. They don't know what entertainment is, and I don't think they understand very much about jazz. I like the people who come and hear me to like what I play for them, and understand what I play, and to go away happy, not depressed. Like Louis. Some people in America say Louis is finished. I don't get that, just listen to him there—he's still playing great. The giant of jazz! How many years has he been on tour? much too long. But vacations present a problem; he must keep that lip in trim, or else it's murder. And Duke there on piano—he's great. I saw him just recently and thought he looked wonderful. Some of the boys, Clark Terry and Johnny Hodges, came in my club recently; we had a good night I can tell you. I know Duke would like to have my drummer back in his band. Duke's had some good drummers, but my boy Dave Black is pretty hard to beat. He left Duke because he had a light case of polio. So when he came out of hospital he came out to the Coast and decided he had better take it easy for a spell. He played with Lena Horne for a time and then settled down in 'Frisco. He was recommended to me for some outside job I had one night and so I took him on. I knew nothing about him, didn't know he'd been with Duke or anything, but directly I heard him I knew he was the best drummer I had ever played with. He has nothing less than an uncanny feeling for time—the tempo is always just right, and he's in there all the time. He can in fact do it all. There is no one who has so much technique, excepting his friend Buddy Rich. Buddy has more self confidence, but that's the only thing he has over Dave in my opinion."

Sometimes, too much for my liking, females gathered around Bob. Once, a girl who admired Bob, while he was performing in Paris, brought a present of a large box of french chocolates to the locker room (dressing room). Bob accepted the candy gladly, and shared it with the rest of the guys in the band.

When I walked in, I noticed all the guys smirking a bit. It was apparent to me they were trying to keep some kind of secret. Bob looked guiltiest of all!

Finally, I think it was Buddy Leet, broke the silence and said,

"Jeannette, why don't you have a piece of these lovely chocolates." chuckle! chuckle!

"What's going on here?" I said. *"You guys are all cracking up about a box of candy."*

Then Buddy said, *"It's special candy from a special person, right Bob?"*

I marched over to Bob and icily inquired, *"Robert, where did this candy come from?"*

Bob airily brushed it off.

"Some girl brought it to the band." chuckled Buddy Leet.

The band chorused a couple of *"yeas"* and *"Ho-Ho's"*.

Bob, all the while, just sat grinning from ear to ear, like a satisfied, canary-eating cat.

"Oh, Bob, tell her what actually happened." Buddy Leet snickered.

Then I realized what was going on.

"Well", I said. *"Let me tell you Bob, she is probably some pigeon looking for a free ticket to the States"*. With that I angrily hurled the candy into the wastebasket and stomped out of the locker room!

I could hear the boys in the band cracking up over Bob's discomfort, but, I felt mistreated and insulted, very put out . . . I never stayed angry long and fortunately Bob was easygoing and tolerant, so he simply laughed it off.

One more mishap happened in Paris. Maybe it was my time of the month or something. We had a devastating fuss, the first night in Paris, over accommodations. I was expecting the royal treatment, like a Queen, at least in Paris. When we got to our hotel room, during the height of the tourist season, we found cramped, dark quarters, with the toilet all the way down the end of a narrow hallway. They didn't even have a bed in the room. They told us one would be coming soon.

Of course, I had an imagination that wouldn't quit when I was younger, and dreamt of Paris being the peak city of grandeur and this scene threw me off, considerably. I walked out to the little balcony, while they were assembling the bed,

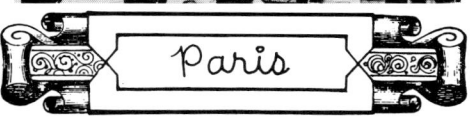

Courtesy of Los Angeles Public Library

Courtesy of Abe Saperstein

Courtesy of Abe Saperstein

Courtesy of Abe Saperstein

Courtesy of the Los Angeles Public Library

In Venice we visited St. Mark's square and later took a boat to a gambling casino. The casino was a small room by Vegas standards, but it was elegant. However, everyone in the room kept a straight face, devoid of any expressions or emotions—most of all, the stone-faced croupier. Women weren't allowed to gamble, only the men——I couldn't stand the freezing atmosphere. Even though millions of lire were flowing, I had to leave. It was not our style or type of excitement, so familiar to us, after being to Reno and Las Vegas.

We had a wonderful time in Rotterdam and Amsterdam. My Aunt Tina lives there and she greeted us with flowers and presents and she had prepared a lovely Dutch dinner especially for us. Aunt Tina adored Bob and our visit was a big moment in her life and ours. I still take out my beautiful Delft candles we acquired on a family trip to DeHaag, whenever I have a special dinner.

BOB SCOBEY in ROME
©Jan Scobey 1976

Bob was a curious person. In Brussels we visited the lace factory and he wanted to know all about the manufacturing of lace. No detail was too small for Bob to ask about.

We visited the cameo and glass factories in Milano. Bob's sincere appreciation, and curiosity over every detail, endeared him to the managers. Such a *"famous American Entertainer"*, who took so much time to admire and appreciate the fine workmanship and their labor was warmly welcomed everywhere we went!

Down to the catacombs in Rome—up to the art museums—then the ruins in Pompeii, seeing Naples and the smoking splendor of Mount Vesevius, all added to an exciting vacation. So much was going on every day.

Bob wanted to know about the mechanics and workings of it all and I soon became interested in that part too. It was one of the reasons why Bob's band was so successful. He paid great attention to small details. His insatiable curiosity brought him quickly to understand all the work of any job and his professional pride forced him to do the job the way it should be done.

I recall, when we went sightseeing, Bob was always energetic and ready to go exploring. Some of our adventures describe the kind of traveling companion he was. Sometimes, so much, that I would beg leave and stay home on several occasions.

He was always happy and good to be with. Bob would laugh at everything. I soon asked him how he could stay so cheerful all the time.

"When I was just starting in the music business", he told me, *"I was naturally, excessively shy. When I was in the 'Yerba Buena Jazz Band', Watters would leave the stand after the set, and go back into the musicians' room, or in the kitchen, and avoid talking to the people. I asked Lu,*

"Why do you always leave the fans?"

"I dislike talking with people", Lu told him.

"I saw early in life", Bob continued, *"that you cannot stay in the music business and avoid conversations with your fans. I was determined to change my own personality habits, from a rather shy entertainer who seldom smiled, to one who was almost always, naturally, sincerely happy.*

"I spent time reading a lot so I could converse intelligently with people, and I did! Finally, smiling became second nature to me . . . ."

In Germany, several of the jazz houses were really huge, like a stadium with different rooms that were sectioned off. Five bands would appear adjacent to one another, yet separated sound-wise, so they wouldn't interfere with the other bands.

We traveled through all of Europe - even East Berlin.

BOB SCOBEY in ROME

©Jan Scobey 1976

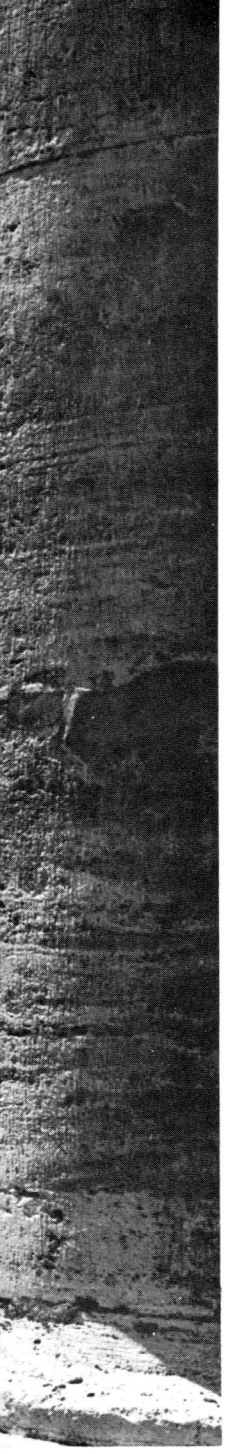

Abe had carefully planned a grand tour. He sought a complete itinerary of places to see at all of our stops. I might have mentioned earlier the performance part of our trip, at the most, only took an hour or two each day.

To tour nine countries in three months took extra flights, and often we bused. With all the one nighters, quick stops, interviews, publicity shots and a compulsion to see the sights when we could, Bob's ulcer started acting up again. We searched, often in vain, for at least an omelet, milk or something that would be easy on his stomach. He was forced to eat what was available and often the diet interferred with his ulcerous condition. I noticed more hamburgers being sold in Europe, than in the United States. Bob couldn't find cold milk in London, and the warm milk wasn't too appetizing.

French and German wines were world renowned, but wine was taboo for Bob's diet and it was chancy to drink the water. In Spain, we could find no fresh eggs, and we seldom had time or the place to prepare foods ourselves. When Bob was ill, and that was becoming more frequent, he still smiled and forged ahead. Eating became a problem as he was back again to quickly prepared foods, eaten in a hurry, and under tension. Bob didn't complain, but since he had trouble later on and I knew what kind of foods we were both getting, as I reviewed our trip, I realized he had to be suffering more than anyone realized.

I recall, one time, we were in a German restaurant. We had a cool reception from the waitress. She probably was nervous to see 50 Americans, all hungry and eager to be waited on. Sometimes we traveled through small towns and this was one of them. I became angry with the waitress because she couldn't get the milk Bob wanted to cool his pain. Finally, just before the bus was leaving, she came along with it.

Situations like this were coming up all the time. There were many fine restaurants and Abe would periodically take us to them or we would search them out ourselves, but, usually, late at night. Bob needed something in his stomach five and six times a day, minimum. By the time our trip was over, Bob was totally exhausted, we were all happy just to set foot on American soil once more. Hurrah for the good old U.S.A.!

BOB SCOBEY in ROME

© Jan Scobey 1976

was pale and drawn, his eyes were closed, and he seemed to be scarcely breathing. I had a sudden, strong sense of depression about his condition. I don't know what it was, but I had the intuitive feeling this was more than just an ulcer operation.

There was just too much activity around him. The nurses and aides seemed exceptionally eager to attend Bob and they seemed especially tender and careful as they shifted his limp, sleeping body into the hospital bed. I followed them into the room, trying to catch a glimpse, some sign or signal, that would assure me he was going to be alright. Engrossed in what I was seeing, I felt a touch at my shoulder. The doctor gently led me into the corridor, just outside his room. *"Mrs. Scobey"*, he said.

"Your husband is gravely, gravely ill. We were lucky to be able to save his life and only time will tell us the outcome. It was a perforated ulcer, indeed!"

The surgeon went on to suggest I hire private nurses to watch Bob around the clock. *"Oh my, it is more serious than I thought."*

This service was not provided by the hospital, however, they helped me arrange it and before too long a private, registered nurse arrived. She was a kind, considerate person and she went right to Bob, and then to his chart. She checked out all vital signs and kept him cool. Knowing he had this special attention gave me a great sense of relief.

The physician was comforting as he tried his best to reassure me. How could it be any other way? Bob was too full of life and we both had so much living to do.

For six days and nights I wore out my shoes pacing the hospital corridors, smoking countless cigarettes. In and out of Bob's room—watching over him, hardly eating . . .

Bob was running a high fever, so high he was packed in ice. The fever seemed to be consuming him. Skin layers grew dry and peeled. His genitals, other sensitive parts of his body, burnt and peeled from the heat.

Then, at last, his temperature began slowly to drop! I kept busy making many phone calls and that helped pass the time. I called everyone I knew, musicians, friends, relatives, family. It helped a little to share the burden of his illness with others. It eased my fear and panic, just a little. I sat in his room a great part of the time, watching the nurses in their daily activities, as they took care of him.

Eventually the sixth day passed. Bob was getting better fast now. I thought, often, as I watched him recover before my eyes, *"How lucky we are to have a fine surgeon!"*

Soon, it was obvious, the 24 hour nurse would no longer be needed. Bob's intravenous feeding was stopped. All appeared to be going so well.

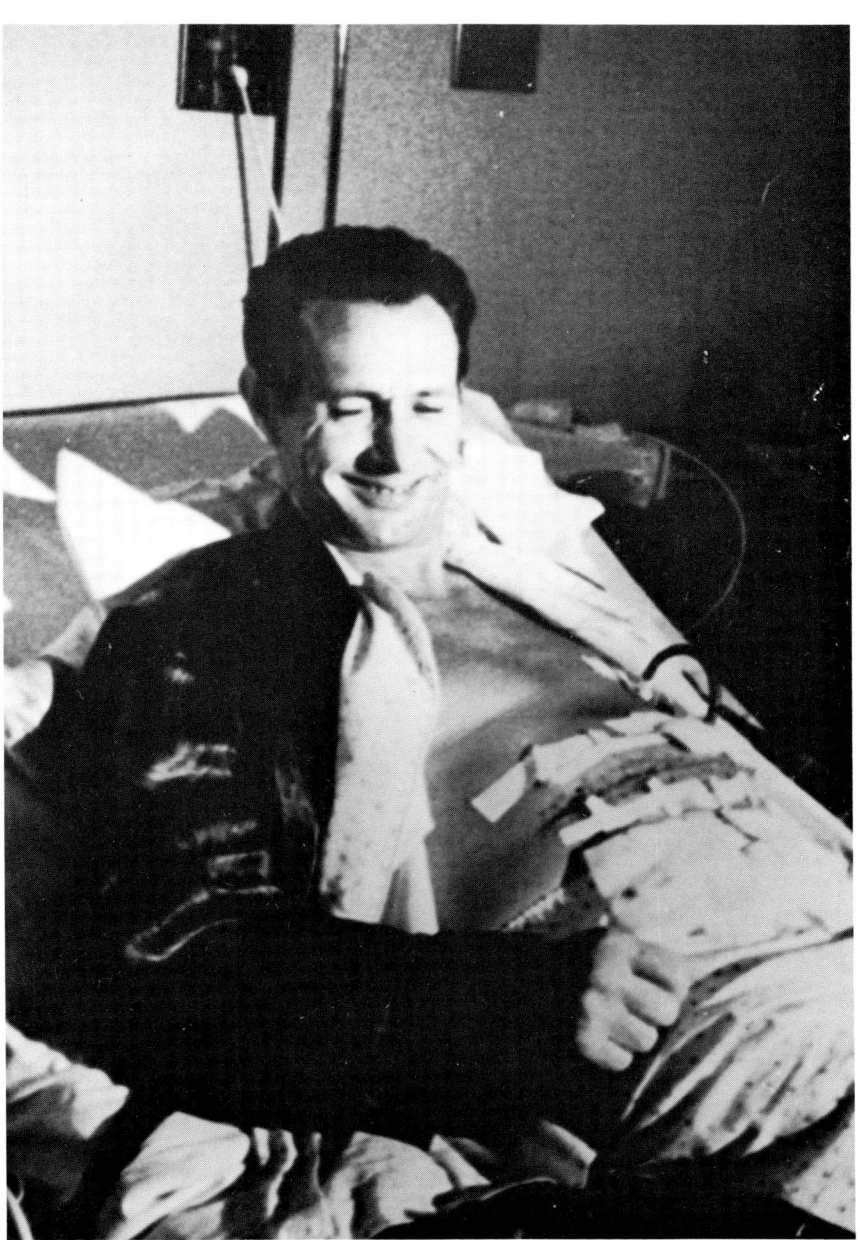

BOB SCOBEY
Courtesy of Marilyn Napier McGwynn

Someone you love is very sick and you are filled with despair, then they get well and life is beautiful once more. You feel Up! Up! I was walking in the halls, day dreaming. Bob was asleep in his room, so I thought I would take a break. I heard the paging system call my name . . . . It didn't register on my ear at first. Then I heard it again . . .

"*Paging Mrs. Bob Scobey, Paging Mrs. Bob Scobey.*"

It occurred to me that I had missed a phone call in Bob's room and the staff was just accommodating me. I only heard medical personnel paged on the system, before. I felt a little thrill of apprehension.

When I answered the page at the floor desk, I was directed to Dr. Port's office. "*Go down the hallway, around a couple of corners to his office.*" My steps hurried as I neared it. When I walked in, I was unprepared for the serious look on his face.

"*Bob's getting better,*" I thought.

Dr. Port got quickly to the point. He reminded me that their only accomplishment, during the operation, was to save Bob's life.

"*The operation only succeeded in cleaning up the perforation,*" he informed me. "*We were forced to work quickly so that the damage could be contained.*"

Then the subject of a pathology report arose, which had just come back from the lab. I didn't quite understand what he meant.

"*Mrs. Scobey,*" said Dr. Port, "*I am sorry to inform you that your husband has cancer.*"

"*CANCER, CANCER?*" "*What is that?*" I thought. "*Ridiculous! I didn't hear him right.*"

For a long time the room remained utterly still and silent. My eyes started to fill. I felt I was in a vice of shock.

I questioned the accuracy of the report and he explained, "*That is why it took so long. We are positive!*"

Then I lowered my head and began to sniffle, then cry. Tears streamed down my face. The words choked in my throat. I couldn't talk. I continued to sob. My heart was breaking. I had heard about cancer and how awful it can be, but I was totally unprepared to hear about it in relationship to my dear, Robert. After a time, Dr. Port took my hand, and began gently to reassure me.

"*Just let him get well from this operation. He is recovering fast and perhaps in a month we can operate again and try to take care of the problem.*" Dr. Port continued,

"*You know Mrs. Scobey cancer is unpredictable, and lots of people do make it after having cancer. Let's take it one day at a time.*" He patted my shoulder.

"*Come on now, stop the tears and hang in there. You can't go back to Bob's room the way you look.*"

I pulled my poor self together and started the long—trip back to Bob's room. Anyone seeing me, walk down the hall, must have wondered at the vacant stare in my eyes and my muttering.

"It's awful, it's awful," I kept saying, as I shook my head to say no! Once, I actually kicked the wall in anger and bitter frustration. I kept on thinking it couldn't be true!

"Why, we were still newlyweds! We hadn't had our first anniversary yet." I had never experienced any illness before, nor, had I known anyone close to me that had. What relationships do you have in a situation like this? Most people like me, can only feel utter shock and helplessness when they are told that they, or someone they love has cancer.

Well, I had to go back to the room. Get back quickly, or Bob would miss me and surely wonder what was wrong. I had been with Bob, constantly, when he was awake, and I was gone this time, much too long. He would soon begin to miss me. I tried to dry all my tears, and did my best to regain my composure. When I walked in, Bob knew something was wrong. I couldn't fool him.

"What's wrong, honey?", Bob cried out.

I couldn't bring myself to tell him anything, and it certainly wasn't the right moment. Besides the doctor said it was time now, just to make Bob well. I brushed Bob's question quickly aside.

"I'm getting a little run down about you and I caught a cold." "But now that you're getting better, I'm sure I'll be all right too."

That was the only thing said. I tried to act happy.

BOB SCOBEY
Courtesy of Marilyn Napier McGwynn

17 THERE'LL BE SOME CHANGES MADE

BOB WAS IN THE HOSPITAL ABOUT TWO weeks and he was stronger each day. However, the physician would not release him until we had a comfortable place to live, where he would be free of worry and work. (You'll remember, we were living at the motel in Lincolnwood when he was rushed to the hospital). The physician gave strict orders! *"No lifting! . . . No work! . . . No chores!"*

I found a sunny apartment at 5600 North Lakeshore Drive. Everything in the apartment had to be exactly right for Bob. I wanted to cheer him up. Bob had to stay in the hospital a couple of extra days until I had it all together.

We had growing concern for the medical bills. Years, before, when Bob and the band were out of work, Bob sold life insurance. I don't know how successful that short-lived career was for him, but it got him through the rough spots until the band business picked up again. One thing he did then, for which I was grateful, was to buy a small life insurance policy and medical insurance. The medical policy gave him limited coverage as most private medical plans do, and it's coverage was even more limited because it had an exclusion for any illness related to stomach disorders. Probably, even back then, the insurance examiners spotted an ulcer or mild stomach condition that would not permit him a standard insurance rating. He never bothered to try and get the rating removed.

The medical plan paid nothing at all. If he had chosen, Bob could have been treated at the Veteran's Hospital since his service record entitled him to free treatment. He had such a deep and profound respect for University hospitals, that he declined that option in favor of treatment at Caldwell. I think, because he had grown up in California, and was familiar with UCLA and Stanford, he acquired this preference for what he believed to be a superior level of professional treatment.

As the bills came in, I kept them paid and tried not to let Bob worry about the rising medical costs. The bills didn't matter because I believed he would be well soon. It's easy to pay your bills once you're well and I was sure he would beat it.

I was raised in an orphanage. It was a 'hot-house' environment. The girls and boys were very sheltered and protected. When we grew up, that sheltered conditioning carried a penalty. Among other things, like most of my friends from the orphanage, I never learned how to drive a car. Now, no bones about it, I had to learn. I knew that Bob would be sick a while longer and after the second operation he would especially need someone to run errands and drive different places. Those thirty mile, round trips for the constant medical care he needed, could no longer be handled either by ambulance or cab. Visits to Bob in the hospital were running daily. Sometimes, I visited him two or three times a day. I had to learn how to drive.

I always had a fear of driving, never being a driver before, and it was a great, great undertaking for me to submit to something that I had such fear of. I thought I might have an accident or even kill someone. All that had to be put aside. The necessity to help Bob was more important than my personal fears. So, I went to driving school.

A few times, when Bob was in the car with me, he would say, *"it's no big thing, just stay in the grooves of the road put there by other cars." "No need to move the steering wheel so much. Just coast along, evenly, in your lane."*

And the very first time I drove, after receiving my license, Bob and the kids rode along with me! Well the steering wheel was jiggling back and forth as I nervously attempted to keep the car going forward, in a perfectly straight line. It must have un-nerved Bob a bit.

Finally, poor Bob couldn't take it and again he said, *"Keep in the grooves of the road! You don't have to hang on so tightly."* The children treated it like a carnival, fun-ride and it probably was that exciting for them.

Caldwell hospital was 15 miles from home and later on, when Bob required more medical attention, I thoroughly appreciated that I learned to drive.

The day Bob came home from the hospital we had a small family party. The children greeted their daddy with unrepressed joy and love. We were all content and so glad to see him home again. Can you visualize the play-acting and game of pretense that took place on my part? I kept smiling brightly, outwardly, knowing all along, his condition. Somehow the children's happiness only served to exaggerate and magnify my internal sadness. I remembered the surgeon's terrifying diagnosis a few weeks earlier, and I was frightened by the uncertainty of the future.

In the apartment, comfortably at home, Bob was accommodating the children. Sometimes he walked around, wearing a big smile and a large white sheet. Adrienne found a wreath for his head. He was playing the part of Julius Caesar! The children loved to play games and Bob made it a festive occasion for them.

I looked on with a smile on my face but deep within my soul I was crying, but, I dared not let my grief, or secret out.

If I could have told someone, just one person, so I could have shared my burden, it would have helped relieve some of my suffering. But, I could not because the surgeon had admonished me against letting Bob know, so he would come to the second operation with the best, positive frame of mind.

During the month between operations (the first one to repair the perforation and the second to do exploratory surgery and I hoped, remove the cancer), Bob visited the doctor for post-operative care and treatment. Dr. Port reminded Bob,

"You must exercise very often and vigorously in these next few weeks and get yourself in top shape. Gain all the strength you can, because in about a month I want to go back in and complete the repairs." To my knowledge, the surgeon never explained further, and I never heard Bob ask why . . . .

Bob searched his memory for all the old callisthenics and exercises he was forced to do in the Army. Mustering all his strength and with great determination, he began to work. Push-ups, sit-ups, deep knee-bends—he would work out as often as his strength would permit. He would walk down to the Racquet Club and play handball. That is a very strenuous and fast moving game. Bob had set his mind to getting back to normal and he was succeeding.

He went back to work at Bourbon Street with high spirits, and his old energy returning. Life was becoming very pleasurable for us both in spite of the chilling knowledge of the physical diagnosis—a diagnosis that stayed in the front of my thoughts—all my waking hours.

OCTOBER 1962

Have you ever looked into the eyes of someone you loved—very deeply—into their soul . . . . a like situation, yet totally opposite, might be the time when you were first dating, and actions were more meaningful than words. You could look at your lover, your eyes would meet and your thoughts were in unison. You were both on the same plane.

This time I looked deeply into Bob's eyes, and I believe his very soul. I realized we were not on the same plane, yet we had evolved, the two of us, as one. I knew he might be on the edge of death, and there was not a damn thing I could do about it. Let me tell you, there is nothing more tragic or intimate than lovers who know that pain and even death may soon take one of them away forever. Knowing about Bob's condition did that to me . . . .

This part of my recollections, when the moment came for me to write, flowed freely, but after all this time, 14 years, it was as hard to bear as recalling his final hours. I felt this particular experience very deeply as I relived it. Tears were falling on my cheeks, on my fingers and hands, as I typed on.

Bob's true condition was always on my mind. I thought of it constantly, for nearly a month. I felt so helpless!

"What is it that is eating away at Bob?" "I can't even see it."

All my anger, all my tears, all my wishes did absolutely no good! Bob was an innocent victim. He didn't deserve to go through this pain and torture. I wanted, with all my heart and powers to help Bob, but there was absolutely nothing I could do. It seemed to be between Bob and his physician, yet, the secret of his illness, keeping it from him, just didn't seem right.

As I thought more, I felt Bob would be strong enough to hear the truth. As I stood off to the side, watching him labor at his exercises on the living room floor, I debated with myself, his right to know the full truth about his condition.

He continued performing his sit-ups and push-ups—— there was dedication in his efforts, the same way he had always worked at achieving perfection in his music . . . . at anything he did.

Finally, I could hold back no longer! With moistened eyes, the words I had to say were difficult, they choked in my throat as I confessed my secret knowledge. The tears welled up into my eyes and came streaming down my cheeks. It was a jumbled, almost incoherent deliverance and remembering it now brings many, many tears.

You see, I felt I had to do the telling, for I knew Bob as a person, a composite of a great deal more than just the isolated cancer condition which is of primary concern for many physicians towards the sufferer.

I winced as I studdered badly.

"Sweetheart", I said, *"Bob your operation is necessary because you have . . . because you have . . . cancer!"*

Bob's face froze . . . He was shocked and startled. The blood had drained from his face and he turned as white as chalk.

It took a while to really sink in, just as it had for me when the doctor first told me, back in his office. As I watched his face, I teared and then began to bawl. I felt his agony and wanted more than anything else to take the words back or take his troubles on my shoulders! I wanted, desperately, to lessen the hurt I knew he was trying to accept and to hold in. I had been torn and confused about it for weeks, wanting to tell him . . . afraid to tell him . . . now, finally, I just couldn't hold back any longer. Oh, what had I done? I was sure I had made a terrible mistake in telling him, I had terrible, instant regrets. Why hadn't I been able to hold it in?

BOB SCOBEY
©Jan Scobey 1976

BOBBY BALLARD

Soon enough, he composed himself again and held me close, comforting me and telling me that all would be okay.

When the moment was over, we both felt somehow renewed in our embrace. From then on we both always felt that somehow . . . someway . . . he would lick this cancer. We believed this almost until his dying day.

If Bob had doubts, he never mentioned it. I know I certainly had a positive and energetic approach to help him heal and hopes for his full recovery. I always felt Bob would make it.

Bob stimulated his body with exercise and fresh air; we both kept busy at our regular daily chores and we went along with the usual things that had made up our days before he became ill.

Bob took it easy, but he would go down to Bourbon Street every chance he could. He enjoyed working. He would participate and get involved any way he could. Scobey chewed the fat with the boys in the dressing room, played darts, or he would talk to friends and fans between sets. He sat in with the band when he was feeling better—more so, just before his second operation.

During his illness, his band kept working at Bourbon Street, thanks to Ron, who was forever a friend. He helped share the load. Bob hired 'Bobby Ballard' on trumpet in his place, when he realized he would have to go back into the hospital. They played together onstage, and Ballard became Bob's 'Ace In the Hole'.

Scobey started to really feel healthy and strong. It seemed, after I told him he had cancer, events moved too swiftly for either one of us to mope or brood upon the horrible thoughts one can imagine with such a dreaded disease. I was very busy with the club. I was learning the administrative details such as taking inventory and working with the bookkeeper. We had planned, before Bob's illness, to purchase the club outright.

Now, more than ever, I had to get myself together and handle all the business affairs, so Bob could relax and spend all of his time, free from worry, and devoted to making himself well again.

OCTOBER 24, 1962

Bob underwent the second operation. He was putting up a good front and never mentioned any deep feelings he might have had concerning his condition. With spirits up, he accepted his second operation.

When the surgeon had finished and Bob was coming out of the anesthesia, everything seemed calm. We didn't have the kind of feeling of crisis we had six weeks earlier. Remember, the second operation was of an exploratory nature to determine the position and extent, and hopefully, the removal of the cancer. It did not appear to be an operation of urgency and our attitudes reflected this. Bob was ready for it, and his recovery, after surgery, was normal, smooth and certainly a more calm time than the first.

After a few days, Dr. Port explained to us the results of their second operation and investigation. I remember Dr. Port's attitude seemed light and beneficial while he informed us that after going in, he decided to leave everything alone. He felt had they removed the tumour it would leave Bob disabled.

In this respect, Dr. Port knew Bob's personality and strength for his life was through his music. Without music Bob would have felt totally lost. Our fears were also disarmed when he added, there were other solutions. Dr. Port planned to eliminate the cancerous growth with chemotherapy. He said it was working well and we accepted his opinion.

I didn't question it then, but now, in retrospect, I think we should have. Perhaps because of the tumour's inaccessibility, the removal might have necessitated taking chances with other vital organs so close to this key area in the gastrointestinal tract, but it might have been the better course to take. The doctor seemed so confident that the chemotherapy way was the best way for Bob to go. At least, in my presence, there were no questions raised.

As I think back, it is conceivable that the physician knew the cancer had metastasized. I think, the surgeon believed it to be terminal from the start. In a letter I received during my research Dr. Port said, *"The surgeon would have had to remove all of his small bowel and this still would not cure the cancer."**

Perhaps, he saw no point in alarming Bob or me, or causing added agony of spending his last days with an operation which would help him to exist.

On November 12, 1962, Bob began chemotherapy shots of 5-Fluorouracil (5-FU). He had been warned to expect some hair loss common to chemotherapy. I remember, Bob had heard somewhere about the possible effectiveness of administering hormones to arrest the tumour spread. Bob was doing some creative thinking in an effort to help himself. He told the doctors of this, but they dismissed it as being a relatively new approach and they preferred to give him their own, more familiar chemotherapy program.

Bob was also told to expect an accumulation of fluid in the area of the tumour. They assured him the pressure he would feel could be relieved by tapping the tumour from time to time.

About fifteen days had gone by after the second

---

*A letter received from Dr. Port, July 2, 1976 stated the tumour metastasized, probably, before the first operation, in that it spread to the lining of the abdominal cavity. (Before Europe most likely).

operation. I noticed one area of his incision did not seem to be healing properly. There seemed to be a sharp point protruding from under the skin. I knew that couldn't be right, so I brought it to the doctor's attention. Sure enough, SOME JACKASS HAD LEFT EITHER, A SMALL TOOL OR CLAMP INSIDE HIM!

This illustrates how careless, negligent and impersonal a sufferer may be treated. It was pathetic because Bob had placed so much faith in the Caldwell Hospital. Supposedly, in a university hospital, doctors, nurses and interns, one and all come around to look at the new sufferer. It seemed reasonable that several persons must have examined Bob and viewed the incision area many times during and after the operation (or at least they should have). Imagine—no one spotted this gross error!

The physician wanted Bob in the hospital for a month because of the time required to administer the chemotherapy treatment and fully observe his reactions to the drug. It came up rather quickly, the cost would be prohibitive for us. When we added all the previous treatment, expenditures, Bob and I had accumulated up until then, without benefits from insurance, the expense became astronomical. So, the attendants decided they would do this treatment, free of charge. There were provisions, in rare cases, for this chemotherapy program to be handled through grants. I learned much later, during my present research, that this is a common procedure when the hospital physicians and researchers determine to accept a 'terminal' sufferer for experimental treatment.

Bob didn't like staying in the hospital, full time, one bit! Finally, it was agreed that at 6 p.m. he could leave the hospital if he promised to return before midnight. This gave him the opportunity to play nearly half of the night at the club, which kept Bob happy.

The affects of chemotherapy seemed to take a wrong turn and affected him differently than expected. (Doing my own research shows this to happen, frequently.) First, the thinning of his hair began. We were prepared for this, but not to the extent of what occurred. Bob had beautiful, thick, black, wavy hair which was becoming thin and grey. Eventually he had bald spots. Then Bob's appetite started to diminish and it wasn't long before he just never felt like eating.

As a result of research and similar cases, the physicians knew the final outcome—for Bob. Someone should have directed us to a nutritionist. I doubt very much, if any of the attendants knew much about holistic medicine.

In our busy, confused state of mind and without experience in matters of self-help, for Bob's illness, we needed, but never received, the necessary nutritional guidance. The physicians, had they considered Bob as a total being, who needed various treatments should have given us this advice earlier, much earlier. Instead, we had to watch Bob drop steadily from a 209, to 160 pounds. He just lacked a desire to eat any solid food. I guess we could have made use of food emulsifiers and juicers, which were available at the time. However, when you are so concerned of an illness, and kept so pre-occupied with tending to a sick person, unless someone brings a suggestion of positiveness, like nutrition, you just don't think of it yourself.

DECEMBER 1962

After the month at Caldwell, Bob came home. As his condition worsened, I saw massive physical changes in his appearance. The change must have been even more dramatic to his friends who were not with him constantly, as I was.

Now, Bob's weight dropped to 150 pounds, in just three months. The chemotherapy had drained his energy and caused him to lose most of his heavy, curly, black hair. He grew steadily weaker, especially during the daytime. At night, he seemed to summon all his reserves of strength to get up and go to the club and play like the old times.

". . . . *'SCOBEY'S JAZZ BAND CONSOLES, CHEERS, EXCITES'*, wrote Joe Boyd in the Milwaukee Sentinel.

"The foremost purveyor of dixieland jazz is horn man Bob Scobey and his band.

"Scobey tucked his trumpet under his arm Sunday and toddled from his Chicago pad to Milwaukee for a gig at Buddy Beek's. Scobey, despite his recent illness, has never been better.

"His horn is not one of those angelically pure pipes. It's frankly gutsy and low-down. When he does the blues, man, you know just how dismal it was identifying that chick's remains down in the St. James Infirmary in New Orleans.

"When Scobey and his boys are doing an up tune, urging you to 'Hold that Tiger' or hang onto 'That Old Ace Down In the Hole', you get the message.

"An appearance of the Scobey band amounts almost to a Dixieland festival. In the first set alone the boys played 18 numbers without pausing for a breath . . . ."

Yes, it appeared Bob was more active as he grew weaker. I always wished he would rest. I remember one time, a doctor, who was a Scobey fan, visited us from Pittsburg. When he arrived at our Lakeshore apartment, Bob was taking a turn for the worse. The doctor took one look at him and asked,

"Bob, what medical treatment are you getting?"

Bob answered, *"Just chemotherapy."*

"Is there anything else, like vitamins or something for your discomfort?" questioned Dr. Sundry.

"No" Bob replied.

Bob wasn't up to giving details, for he was weak.

The physician advised us he would go downstairs and get something from the drugstore. Dr. Sundry apparently was satisfied this help would be compatible with Bob's regular therapy.

"I'll be right back," Dr. Sundry reassured us.

Soon enough, he returned with his paraphanelia. He had an old fashioned hypodermic injection set that had to be boiled, (now they have throw away appliances), compazine (tranquilizer, and treatment for nausea), and Vitamin B-12.

I watched with great interest as the doctor boiled the water over our cookstove and sterilized several needles and the glass syringe for several minutes. While I was watching, Dr. Sundry told me I should be aware of all of these details. They were important for sanitary reasons.

We washed our hands, the needles were ready and the doctor disinfected the bottles with alcohol. As he drew the fluid, he explained the CC (cubic centimeters) marking on the syringe.

"We'll give him 2 cc's now, Jeanette. You must check the dosage and always compress the syringe until a little liquid comes out before administering a shot. This lets all the air out. Be very careful to do this as air bubbles, carelessly injected, could cause an embolism (air bubble blockage in a blood vessel) and even kill. So these are very important steps to follow."

With those words he handed ME the hypodermic set. I proceded to let the air out and started returning it to the doctor.

"Oh, No!" exclaimed Dr. Sundry. *"You give him this one."*

I shuddered, turned chicken and somehow could only hear, in my thoughts, the words 'a shot can even kill'.

I didn't expect to give Bob the first shot! I recoiled mentally and emotionally from the act of sticking a needle into Bob, or anyone else for that matter.

Off in the living room Bob could overhear all that was going on. In an irritated way, possibly anxiously wanting the shot, Bob yelled at me. He was really short-tempered as he said,

"It's no big deal, Jeannette, you can do it!"

Then I knew I had to do it sooner or later because we couldn't afford to go back and forth to the hospital or to have a full time nurse on hand. I also had no doubt that anyone could care as much for Bob as I, or be as gentle and thorough in treating him.

The doctor gave me a complete minicourse on 'How to give a shot'. He showed what places you give shots, like the arm and thigh. But he preferred the buttocks and upper hip area.

"You wipe the area with alcohol," he said, *"Lift up a handful of flesh and muscle tissue, again making certain there is no air in the needle. Inject, by piercing the skin about an inch, and slowly force the fluid into the tissue. This way the shot will not be painful. Lay an alcohol swab on the puncture when you remove the needle. Just hold it there a moment and don't rub. The wound from your tiny puncture will heal immediately."*

When I was finished, Bob even gave me a little smile. Then I had to do the same thing for the Vitamin B-12. This time, when I approached Bob I was light-hearted.

"Okay, Bob, remember you asked for it!"

Bob exclaimed impatiently, *"Oh, come on Jeannette, let's get it over with."*

After all his butt was exposed, and right there I let him have it!

Well, it helped him and I wondered why our personal doctors didn't tell us about this course of treatment. I wondered how much earlier Bob should have been given vitamin supplements.

That day, the first time I gave Bob his necessary injections by myself, marked the beginning of what was to be a full-time, round the clock nursing duty. I was content and dedicated to the responsibility because I loved Bob, and his illness did not bring on any shying-away, bitterness or resentment. I was still certain Bob would get better and it was a very small price to pay to help him to fully recover. I was to nurse Bob for the next seven months.

There were times ahead I had to administer his shots under unusual conditions. In a car, at the club, in the strangest of places because Bob's anxiety came on more frequently and unpredictably.

I told our own physician about the compazine and B-12 proposed by a visiting doctor. He agreed it was okay to administer these things to Bob and started writing our prescriptions necessary to keep Bob supplied with these drugs.

Bob started using the compazine only when he needed it, rather than on a regular, every three or four-hour, basis. Often, while he was at the club, during intermission, we would go into the dressing room, I would take bar alcohol, cleanse the area, and give him his shot. Sure, I felt discomfort about it, but those things must be put aside when duty calls.

Although I tried to be a sweet and calm wife and nurse,

the last few months started to work on my nerves and every once in awhile I would become the frenzied, ill-tempered wife. I didn't think about it much at the time, because I think all normal wives yell at their husbands, periodically. I should have been more tolerant. Luckily my outbursts would only last seconds, like a minor explosion, just to get Bob to move along to another idea.

JUST BEFORE CHRISTMAS, 1962

The December snow and the chill winds from Lake Michigan roared down around us bringing the deep, winter cold. Bob and I decided to get away from it all and headed to Florida for a short vacation. We looked forward to the wonderful, warm sunshine, knowing Bob would benefit greatly from it.

A tan would certainly lift his spirits and put color into his thin face. And Hialeah race track was open! Bob's favorite sport was horse racing. He loved to watch the races, gauge and figure the odds, and bet on the horses. He was pretty good at it, too! He would pour over the racing forms for hours, using volumes of paper, as he tried to figure out a winning, racing pattern.

He was quite an expert at it and he won often. Why, one of his children's hospital bills was paid by a windfall from a winning race bet.

Rick Nelson, who played trombone in Bob's band, reminded me of his own happy experience with Bob.

RICKY NELSON
Courtesy of Jim Schoenmann

"Bob took the whole band to the race track when they had a horse dedicated to him for 'Bob Scobey Day'. We all bet and sure as hell the horse came in! I believe you were there too, Jeannette."

Yes, I was there. I remember it well. We were in the Turf Club and there was a small window transom just below where we were standing to see the race. As the horses neared the finish, I carried on, screamed and yelled with such enthusiasm, that a partial bridge I had, fell right out of my mouth! Oh, was I embarrassed. It slipped through the transom and landed outside, below, near the grandstand. Luckily, Bob had to go immediately to the winner's circle for honors. So, enroute, we picked up my partial bridge in the grand stand area. I was happy to find it unbroken. My chagrin soon took a second place to my joy as we all stood in the winner's circle, happy with Bob's lucky day.

In Florida, we were greeted with clear sunny days. We knew a few people living there, who at one time, worked at Bourbon Street. They were quick to fill us in on all the high spots. Jai-Lai games, greyhound races, and of course horse-racing.

We weren't in Florida more than several days when Bob suffered a severe attack. He grew weak and became nauseous, constantly. It was very bad and I had to drive him to the nearest, Florida hospital for help and emergency treatment.

Upon arrival, the opening question was not "what's wrong" but *"Were's your $100 cash deposit?"*

We had our check book with us, but very little cash. This selfish, insensitive attitude really made me ill and caused me to have a lot of animosity toward them. They refused to honor our out-of-state checks, so I had to leave Bob outside the emergency rooms and in a waiting room, while I rushed to a friend's house to get the $100.

Recalling this incident makes my blood boil with indignation. It has generated a feeling of disgust and hatred for all the calloused people who are guilty of this type of greedy indifference.

I tried to analyze it from their point of view. I know private hospitals are businesses and must collect for services to operate. Surely, in a case of obvious, extreme emergency, the doctor's hippocratic oath and duty should take precedence over the dollar sign and personal greed! I cannot accept the fault is with management alone. There were doctors close by who could have rushed forward and treated him. Perhaps the American people are at last beginning to realize that parts of the AMA group and individual medical people are less altruistic and idealistic than we have been taught to believe.

What if Bob had not been such a popular personality, or didn't know anyone nearby? I am certain we would not have been able to raise the cash for a day or so. What would have happened to Bob? These horrendous things must happen, even more often, to the truly less fortunate and needy masses of people. This kind of criminal indifference should be investigated by those in Washington or the AMA who should have responsibility for seeing to hospital ethics.

Bob spent two days in the hospital before he had any energy to move. That was the unusual thing with his form of cancer. The effects on his body came and went. But I'm certain his mind was continually haunted by the reality of his illness. Several times, I caught him, looking in the mirror. As I watched I could almost see the activity going on in his brain, trying to absorb what was happening to his body. He would look into the mirror and see a gaunt face, that once was full and happy.

As soon as Bob felt better, we cut our vacation short and hurried back home, thoroughly exhausted. Many things were changing for Bob and me. Bob's aggresiveness and sexual expression almost came to a halt, except on rare occasions. His drive was saved for the trumpet, and even that was about all he could muster. Now that he was ill more often, I had to keep many a 'casual gig' straight.

One time, while the guys were working full time at Bourbon Street, they also had to work a casual gig at the Edgewater Beach Hotel for a political function. During intermission at Bourbon Street, I drove the band, some six miles, to the job. The fellas ran up stage and belted a few numbers out, then we rushed back to my car and drove another six miles back to Bourbon Street. Would you believe, they made it back in time for the next show. Although the guys never complained, these times had to be very rough on them too.

EVERY ENTERTAINER WORKS NEW YEAR'S EVE. AT MIDNIGHT BOB WAS ONSTAGE, SMILING AND RINGING IN 1963 WITH HIS 'HAPPY MUSIC'.

18 STORMY WEATHER

FTER OUR RETURN FROM THE VACATION in Florida, Bob had recovered his strength and we came back home. He felt much better and went to play at Bourbon Street, full time, no less! People from the media who knew of his illness and saw him continue to play with seemingly undiminished strength and style, were utterly amazed. Many news columnists were writing about his determination and persistency to lick cancer. They could not possibly know what price Bob was paying for his cool appearance.

Herb Lyon, a Chicago columnist, saw Bob on stage and spoke with him between sets. Certainly he admired his courage, but Herb Lyon went back to his typewriter to comment on another facet of Bob's character—his positive, 'up' attitude. *"Bob talks freely to everyone about his cancer surgery and proudly proclaims, 'I'm gonna beat it!'"*

The chemotherapy wasn't slowing the cancer in the least bit, but it was causing Bob to lose his hair, weight, and depleting all his strength. He was forced to ever greater effort to find the stamina and energy to play.

It was a long 30 mile round trip to the hospital or between home and the club.

Often, while I was driving, Bob would hit a low spot and I would have to pull over and give him a shot. When we arrived at the club, he would be faced with another straining, long climb up the 'Mount Everest' of two flights of stairs to the club. You couldn't stop him. He wanted more than anything to get to Bourbon Street every night. Going up the stairs, he would stop and draw from the wellsprings of his little, remaining strength—and then climb a few more steps. There would always be a stool waiting for him onstage to sit upon.

The trumpet requires enormous power and breath. You fill your lungs toward your diaphragm and stomach area with air, and slowly let it out and control your tones. It was in the very area of his greatest discomfort. But play he did! I don't know where he found the stamina to go on. He usually sat down toward the last few months. In the front line of trumpet, trombone and clarinet, Bob would be the only one sitting down.

Trumpet player, 'Bob Ballard' would carry the musical load now, and Scobey would just fill in when he was able, but most of the time Bob just sang. People that heard his horn in those days knew the feeling of melancholia and depression, for it was unavoidably coming from Scobey's horn.

As Bob's body and strength continued to fade away, I

saw his mental acuity became stronger. He was always mighty perceptive and sensitive to everything that went on and he continued to be the strong leader in every way. Larry Kostka wrote to me about that time of Bob's struggle:

". . . . *Probably the last band Bob had was the epitome of all the bands he ever had. At Bourbon Street his group included 'Ricky Nelson', 'Buddy Leet', 'Tommy Smoot', 'Bill Napier', 'Jimmy Johnson' and 'Dave Black'. The drive and push in that band was truly phenomenal. Having 'Dave Black' in the band, was probably the biggest, single, greatest thing that ever happened to Bob's sound.*

"*When 'Bob Scobey's Frisco Band' appeared at the Red Arrow in Stickney, Illinois, in 1960, I remember he had trouble with his stomach even then, and was really straining to play his horn. I guess the cancer problem that he later developed was beginning to work its way in. He was always drinking half and half or whipping cream to cool his stomach.*

"*Once I asked him how he chose the music business because I had heard he was keenly interested in science. He said, 'I wanted to study science but just didn't have the money at the time, and being in the middle of the depression, I guess I chose to stick to music because I could get work with pick-up bands'.*

"*Wally Phillips, on WGN, plugged Scobey records more than anyone. He was a disc jockey and when Bob was ill, Wally Phillips kept his audiences informed and up to date on his progress, because Bob always said he would lick and beat his illness.*

"*The last time I had seen Bob, after being in the service and away from Chicago for a year, was in December, 1962. The change was dramatic! He lost a lot of weight, but one thing, he kept playing his horn and trying. He was living his life pretty much like the inspiration he gave me eleven years before when I had to quit playing drums because of a slight paralysis. I kept practicing, took lessons from 'Dave Black' while he was still in Chicago, and in 1969 I played with a group at the Big Horn. Everyone in that group had played with 'Bob Scobey'. Only Bob was missing. It was an emotional experience playing with all the musicians when, one time, I thought I would never play again. Wish Bob Scobey could have been there!* . . . ."

LARRY KOSTKA

One of the greatest sources of Bob's strength came directly through the emotional and financial support and encouragement of Ron, the owner of Bourbon Street, who backed Bob and his band. Most club owners, faced with a band leader who looked like a skeleton and barely had the energy to stay seated on stage, much less perform, would

BOBBY BALLARD and BOB SCOBEY

Courtesy of Marilyn Napier McGwynn

baby in American music . . . . JAZZ!

It was great to drop in the many clubs in the quarter and hear all the dixieland bands, and all mighty good! There was Al Hirt's place and Pete Fountain's club. And the greatest thrill was seeing all the older players at Preservation Hall. Oh, were they cooking! Hot Jazz! The mystique of yesteryear steals up and grabs hold of you in New Orleans. It was a fast moving week for us. Bob in his 25 years of playing New Orleans type music, had never been in New Orleans! Now he was sitting in with some of the old timer musicians. He really loved it, and some of the clubs had been around in King Oliver's and Satchmo's days of yore.

While we were there, we drove to another old part of town to visit his former singer, the great 'Ms. Lizzie Miles'. Lizzie was excitedly waiting for us at the foot of her steps leading to her home, when we arrived. She was a big woman, all smiles and beaming, happy to see her old friend Bob, again.

She invited us into her home. I was deeply impressed by the very religious overtones of the pictures and decorations in her home. Lizzie had accepted Jesus some years earlier, and he ruled her life, as she was fond of telling one and all.

We weren't there very long, before an old bitterness against Bob, over royalties, came to the surface and was resentfully voiced.

"*Bob*", I heard Lizzie complain, "*What ever happened to the royalties on the 'Bourbon Street' album I recorded for Verve Records?*" Bob answered frankly and honestly,

"*You know, Lizzie, how the record companies are. I have never received any royalties from them either. They claim not enough records were sold to pay for the recording date and packaging.*"

I know Bob was telling the truth, and he went on to let her know, just that past year, he had put out an album on his own label, Ragtime. "*I was able to see a profit after the first 3,000 albums.*"

"*Lizzie,*" Bob went on, "*I've an incredible fact to tell, more records no royalties, it doesn't figure! Every single record company for whom I have recorded had failed to make enough of a profit in issuing the records to pay me royalties. Each company has issued not just one album, but up to five and seven albums in one company. Yet, year after year, they paid no royalties. Still, and this is even more illogical, they insisted and encouraged me to produce my music for records. I had to go to the bigger companies at first, because I thought it would help my career along.*

"*When there were no royalties, I put out my own album . . . I agree with you, they didn't put out all those albums at a loss to them . . . Someone was making a*

LIZZIE MILES
©Jan Scobey 1976

©Jan Scobey 1976

©Jan Scobey 1976

bundle . . . You know these larger companies excuse themselves by claiming they must give away an avalanche of freebees to radio stations and other outlets for promotional reasons. Only Good Time Jazz was able to give me a taste, and they, too, just let 15 years go by before they came up with short money. You tell me how they could keep issuing them?"

Even though Bob gave Lizzie the only explanation he knew, I don't think she could accept it. It didn't make sense to her as it didn't make sense to Bob. She still believed that others were making a bundle from her singing efforts and she included Bob in this group. Lizzie still felt prejudices.

Resigned, as we were leaving, she turned to her picture of Jesus and said, *"Bob, Jesus is my friend now and my life is in the hands of the lord. I will prove to you that I am right by outliving you."*

Bob laughed it off and we left, really happy to have visited with her. At this time Lizzie was in her late 60's and Bob was just 44. He was looking good and wasn't a bit sick at the time, and surely Lizzie had no inkling he would soon have cancer.

Well, all of February, Bob had his ups and downs. He tried to keep his spirits high but the disease was too consuming.

MARCH 1963

About March 12, 1963 Bob became gravely ill and had to be hospitalized again. His condition was aggravated by a horrible case of hiccoughs. Have you ever had the hiccoughs? A few minutes and you hope they are over. Perhaps friends jollied you along and with the paper bag trick or trying to startle you, they were gone.

Bob's case of hiccoughs turned out to be torture. They were painful and demoralizing, and prevented him from speaking clearly, eating, or nearly all normal activity. Bob had them for three days without any letup! He became weak and exhausted, his condition deteriorated, and the hospital could do nothing to stop them. First they gave him shots, to no affect. I tried scaring or startling him .... still no results. The medical staff even went back to the old paperbag trip several times and still nothing helped.*

To watch his helplessness, his weakened and pathetic condition and the racking ceaseless hiccoughs was a depressing and saddening experience. He worsened and the doctor prepared me, saying he thought Bob wouldn't make it this time. I went to the waiting room and every new intern or doctor I could corner, would be the target of my frenetic questions.

I finally recognized they could be right, and so I called everyone I knew, friends, family and fans, and told them the doctors felt this was it and Bob was dying. I told them,

"If you want to see Bob, now is the time because there will be no funeral!"

Toward Bob's ending days and lingering illness, nearly all of his friends stopped coming to see him. I remember one day, 'Jimmy Johnson', the bassist, was there and I cried as I

JIMMY JOHNSON
BASSIST
Courtesy of Cilento Studios

---

*In Volume II, Cancer? What you Can Do!, some solutions to hiccoughs are in Chapter of Conventional Treatment.

told him the physicians felt Bob would die.

There was one other true, true friend . . . the club owner, Ron. How did he do it? He had a lot of business to attend to and Caldwell Hospital was 30 miles round trip. Yet, he was always around when we asked for help. He came to see Bob too! Bob's darkest hour appeared to be nearing. A San Francisco Newspaper published that Bob had died!

I was emotionally exhausted, staying at the hospital every second. I practically pounded my poor head into the wall in anger once again, trying not to absorb and realize what was actually happening.

Suddenly and unexpectedly Bob recovered! The hiccoughs subsided and he was gaining strength from the intravenous feeding. That very day that Bob recovered, Lizzie Miles passed away in New Orleans. I sometimes wonder if she heard about Bob's illness, for it appeared in all the newspapers across the country.

As I see it, the way all this happened, she took his pain and suffering from him, through her prayers and death. This may seem ethereal to write about, but this one really happened. Perhaps, finally, Lizzie's spirit was satisfied that her friend, Bob was telling her the truth about the record royalties. Maybe someone who knew the truth, told her Bob was right. A newsman, who knew of Lizzie's and Bob's story, wrote:

The Strange Story of Bob Scobey's Last Days

There's a strange story connected with the last days of Bob Scobey, who died of cancer recently.

Long before Scobey became ill, veteran New Orleans singer Lizzie Miles once vowed to the trumpeter that she would outlive him. By early this year, it appeared that the 67-year-old singer's prophecy was about to be fulfilled. Scobey, beyond medical help, was given but a few weeks to live, while Lizzie rested at home in comfortable retirement.

On March 17, the exact day of Lizzie Miles' sudden death, Scobey rallied and, to everyone's astonishment, went back to work at his Chicago club, Bourbon Street. Announcements of his "miraculous" recovery were sent out by the club.

It was, of course, a temporary victory. Yet, Scobey, found enough new strength to work through most of May, long after ordinary men would have given up. On his final day, June 12, the 46-year-old jazzman was making plans for his next job.

But this time he didn't make it.

Gloria, Ron's wife, wrote to me of her memories.

"... I have always had ESP or whatever you choose to call it. Just after you and Bob returned from your European tour, Ron and I met you in the coffee shop of the Sahara on Mannheim Road. I believe Bob was appearing there. He had not as yet manifested any signs of his illness. Yet, sitting next to him that evening, I was overwhelmed with the knowledge that he was ill and dying. (This was July, 1962).

"I told Ron, on the way home and at first he called me a silly goose, but I was so depressed and despondent that it even touched him. Very shortly after that, Bob had the bleeding ulcer attack, and the cancer was found.

"Of Bob's illness, Jan, I can remember feeling my heart break watching him waste away to nothing, but still up on that stage blowing that horn and making 'Happy Sounds'.... his music definitely changed during those months... there was something in that horn... it seemed more melancholy, the notes seemed to touch your soul. One night, when you and Bob stopped over to the house, I opened the door and it was all I could do not to gasp. He looked so thin—so wasted, all except his face. He was smiling. During the evening, he made the comment 'everything's coming up roses'. He really believed it! I knew that night much of the strength he was displaying was you.

"Jan, you talked only positive. You thought only positive. You even fussed at him and nagged about something. You treated him so normal, it was unbelievable. He got your coat. You treated him every way but sick. Oh Jan, how much I have learned from you. My personal feeling is that Bob didn't want to give up, but most important YOU gave him reason to feel there was no need to give up. Ron and I watched you two play out your final months. We both hurt for you and felt so damn helpless...."

When friends dropped by to visit Bob at the hospital, or when they would call, Bob was always 'up' and thinking of how the other guy was feeling. Nappy Trottier another trumpet man called, to cheer Scobey up!

"... When Bob heard my voice he said, 'How ya Napo Old Buddy, how are you doing?' It made me feel as though he was trying to cheer me up! I had a lot of respect for Bob and his playing...."

LATE MARCH

Like Lazarus of old, Bob miraculously began to recover from his latest, most terrifying setback. A real struggle against death. This time he was in the hospital ten days and was anxious to come back home. He was feeling better now, as if he had a sudden remission of disease. His attitude improved so much the day before he left the hospital. Bob took a new interest in his music and wrote out a complete list of tunes for the band. They included the up, slow and medium tempo tunes; plus featured arrangements, so the band would keep things going just as if he was still there at Bourbon Street, until he could get back. He would have gone that day if anyone would have let him.

Bob's weight, now dropped to what mine was which was

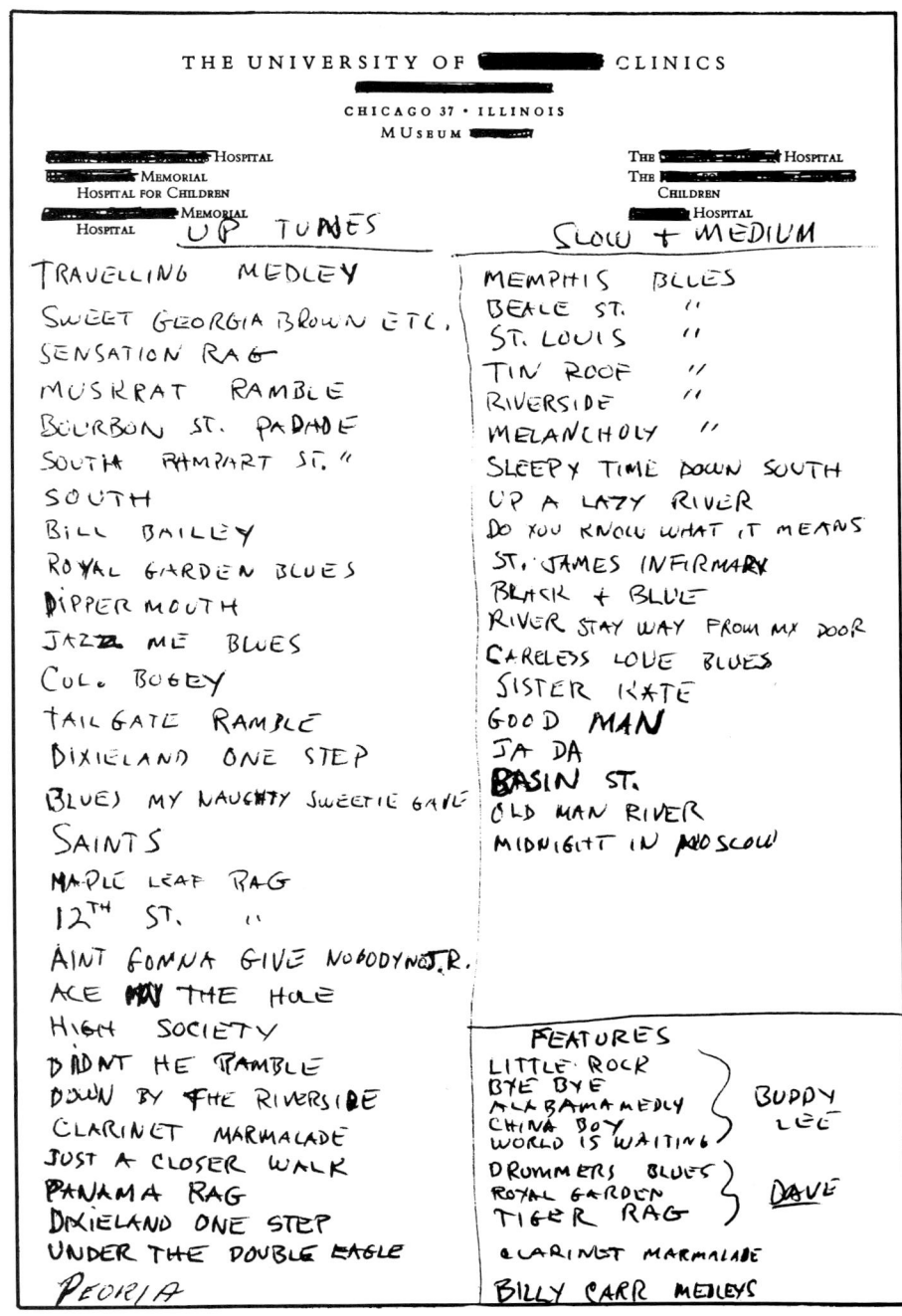

Bob's recent recovery was only a reprieve. Just as suddenly as he got well, in a few weeks he was ill again*... The ups and downs were weighing heavily on him. The malignancy within his body continued to grow. It's expansion of fluid reached a pressure point, on some vital organs or nerves, that caused a sudden painful attention to itself. I don't believe it was the tumour causing the discomfort as it was the fluid it generated during the process.

The enlargement grew to the size of a volley ball and the doctors told him to come to the hospital so the tumour could be tapped. The tapping process would drain the fluid and give him great relief. It was just as he had been warned a few months earlier; fluids would accumulate and would have to be drained, through tapping, probably several times.

We drove to the hospital in a relatively calm state. When we arrived, we went straight to the outpatient clinic.

While his tumour was being tapped, I leafed through his records (this was strictly against the rules, but somehow I wasn't noticed). I believe everyone else was too interested in the tapping procedure. I didn't go in when Bob was being treated.

I noticed this chart and started leafing through it. I came across a report based on his last stay in the hospital. A certificate, referring to his hospitalization March 12th through March 22nd, showed his cancer had metastasized and the report should not get to the family.

I pulled it out of the file and stuffed it in my purse. I was still examining the contents of the folder when out from an inner office, came an employee. She spotted me and immediately snatched the chart away from me.

It is a strange set of priorities when a clerk has a right to see records the wife may not. She was angry with me, but Bob was coming out of the room, and his presence stopped the fuss.

When Bob came out, he appeared considerably thinner. Where his waist had crowded his '36' inch trousers now you could fit two men like Bob into his pants.

He nonchalantly pulled them up and wrapped his jacket around himself.

The doctors and nurses told him to stick around for a few hours.

Bob wanted to play that night. He always left the hospital as soon as he could, and this time was no exception. No one insisted he should stay or explicitly explained what to expect. They were quite casual about it. The attendants even wheeled him to the car!

Caldwell Hospital, at 6000 South, was two miles behind

---

*The attending surgeon, Dr. George Port, wrote to me and said, *"March, 1963. Bob realized his life expectancy was very short."* But I didn't believe it was!

CERTIFICATE OF PROOF OF ILLNESS

Policy # G-1947-C-2433

Submitted in lieu of your form No. Cert # 411

COOLEY, Robert   Date APR - 8 1963

1917 N. Kenneth,   Chicago,   Ill.   Unit No. 79-21-61

46 Sex M   Legal Status M   Color W   Occupation Band Leader

Date of appearance of first symptoms:
Weakness and abdominal pain

Date admitted to: 3-12-63   Discharged 3-22-63

Diagnosis: Carcinoma of stomach with carcinomatosis

DIAGNOSIS STRICTLY CONFIDENTIAL DO NOT RETURN FORMS TO PATIENT OR RELATIVES

Date and name of operation:
none

Prognosis: (type and period of disability) Improved - Return to clinic when necessary

Remarks: X-Rays: 3-12-63 chest, abdomen
            Intravenous solution

Estimated length of disability following hospitalization: uncertain.

STATE OF ILLINOIS } ss.
COUNTY OF COOK   }

                                    Taken from records
Sworn to before me this _____ day of
_____ 19 ____   _____ HOSPITALS AND CLINICS

_____   Charles R Goulet
Notary Public   Superintendent
Address: _____

THE NUMBER AND VARIETY OF FORMS MAKES NECESSARY SUBMISSION OF THIS FORM IN LIEU OF YOUR FORM. WE SINCERELY TRUST IT WILL FULFILL YOUR NEEDS.

---

us when, without any advance warning, Bob went into grand mal convulsions! When total body convulsion occurs, the eyes roll back into the head, the tongue protrudes and is in imminent danger of being bitten and badly lacerated, or even swallowed. Arms and legs, neck and head, the entire body goes completely rigid and jerks in rapid, massive, convulsive movements.

It sounds bad enough, but when someone you know and love suddenly convulses it is absolutely terrifying and shocking. I never imagined anything like this could happen to the human body. Bob's spirit just seemed to leave him and, instead, a contorting monster seemed to possess his body. One minute he was seated upright in the car and the next, his body was flopping over the seat like a loose rag. He was making strange choking noises.

I believe now the pressure release inside triggered his state, but, in no way did I relate to it at the time. Remember, I was also a new driver and I had no warning about what was occurring beside me, on the seat. I had no idea of how to help or what to do and I was in a bad spot to stop the car.

I panicked! I started to speed along Lake Shore Drive. Where were all the traffic police? 60—70—80, I was traveling 100 miles an hour, and no one came to my rescue!

Soon I was to the Planetarium about 1200 South. Still no one had stopped me! All the time Bob continued moaning, winding, and twisting out of shape.

Suddenly, Bob's movements ceased. I pulled over to the exit near the Planetarium. The only way I could think of helping him was to give him a shot of compazine. I kept wondering, what is the right thing to do? The shot was all I had with me and I had to try it. There wasn't any place to phone for help. I wouldn't leave Bob alone and run up to the Planetarium for help, as I was afraid Bob might die while I was gone. So I gave him the shot. In an instant, he started to come out of it.

"Bob, Bob, are you okay?" I asked him with tearful relief.

When he appeared conscious, I ran to the nearby water fountain and moistened a pillow case I found in the car. The coolness seemed to help and Bob composed himself again.

I got back in the car and began to cry and carry on.

"Bob," I said, *"we will have to go back to the hospital. You passed out on me and I don't know what is going on. We need help!"*

"Jeannette, please, I want to go home. Please take me home, I'll be okay! I just felt a little faint that's all."

Sure enough, his composure was back. We talked very little the rest of the way. I was angry with him. He wouldn't go back to Caldwell Hospital.

Often, we would leave the hospital and no sooner get home, some 15 miles away, and he needed an ambulance or help to get him back to the hospital! It was becoming downright foolish having care so far away from home.

We pulled into the parking lot next to the building where we lived. I hurried to the other side of the car where Bob was sitting.

"Here, Bob hang on to me, just in case you start to feel weak again!"

We slowly started walking to the door which lead to the

foyer of the building.

Unexpectedly, Bob suddenly lost consciousness again and slipped from my arms. He fell against the glass, entrance door, pushed it shut and blocked it with his body, so that it was impossible for me to open it!

All his body wastes, pent up so long by the tumour obstruction, released and saturated his clothing and the carpet beneath him.

He regained consciousness, but he had lost all of his strength and could do nothing to help himself. I tried to lift him. His loose trousers had slipped away during my frantic exertions, leaving him partly nude. That must have added to his self-consciousness and embarrassment.

I felt a hot flash of anger toward the medical staff who should have foreseen the consequences of the drastic, internal arrangement that must have occurred when Bob's tumour was tapped. Any logical person with medical experience, especially a trained staff, should have predicted some kind of reaction to the release of the internal pressure. Sure, they suggested we stay, but they did not tell us what could happen, nor did they insist we stay. The advice was too casual and matter of fact.

Bob had a good healthy ego and sense of pride in his appearance. He loved to dress well, wearing fancy clothes; mixing with people at all sorts of social gatherings. Now this proud man was reduced to a smelly, sick, helpless, shrunkened animal, stripped of all his dignity.—He was a sorry sight now—truly pitiful! I tear now, in compassion for him as I think of it.

There we were, helpless and alone. I wished someone would get off the elevator or walk in to help us.

Soon someone was coming—a man walked toward us from the other side of the glass door. He perceived our problem. He started to push as I tugged Bob toward me, on my knees. Inch by inch, we moved him. At last the door was open.

The kind stranger helped me carry Bob to the elevator. The moments passed, I don't remember if I even spoke, other than a thank you, as the passing of time jelled into an eternity.

We reached our floor and I helped Bob to the door of our apartment. Bob leaned against the door while I held him with one hand against my side (much the way you would hold groceries), and tried to open the door with the other hand. Bob had started to recover slightly and was trying to stand on his own.

We were no sooner inside and laboring toward the bedroom, when Bob fainted again. As he fell, he struck his trumpet lip a smashing blow against a desk and now lay on the floor, bleeding profusely. I panicked again, but this time I was able to regain my composure quickly. I slowly lowered Bob's head to ease his bleeding, first aid fashion. Then I phoned for help.

I reached Dr. Port and he told me to bring him back to the hospital, immediately. I told him I couldn't handle Bob any more, so he suggested an ambulance. I thanked him and put the phone down. I turned to Bob telling him of the doctor's orders. Bob refused,

"I don't want to go back to the hospital Jeannette, and that is all there is to it."

He was very weak, but conscious and his objections were clear and insistent. I argued desperately with him.

"Bob, you're bleeding badly, you're too much for me and we must have help. You could faint again and you are just too heavy for me to handle." Bob quietly remarked,

"Let me rest a little while, I'll get my strength back, you'll see, everything will be okay again."

I became furious, then crying again, I just sat on the bed while he was still on the floor. I felt so ineffective and helpless. Then, I looked down, and there was Bob, smiling and trying to make me feel better.

"Don't worry Jeannette, it will all be fine, I'll take a warm bath, go to bed and I'll awake feeling good again, You'll see, Honey."

Moving slowly, practically crawling our way, we made it to the bathroom and I ran the bathwater for him. I helped him into the tepid water and he sank gratefully into it's relaxing and healing warmth. When Bob got out of the tub, he rested on the toilet seat, gathering his resources to make the few steps to the bed on his own. He was deliberate and economical in his movements. Bob wanted to stay home and not return to the hated hospital, so he was on his best behaviour. He reached his bed, still moving cautiously and without incident. He closed his eyes and slept all that afternoon and into the evening. His lip was split, still puffy and discolored.

About 8 o'clock that evening he awakened alert and ready to go. The club's entertainment started at 10 p.m. and he insisted on making the gig! Would you believe it? . . . . After the ordeal he had suffered through, nearly dying enroute from Caldwell Hospital and ending all the turmoil with a fat lip, 'Tiger' wanted to go to the club and blow his horn! I listened to his plans in utter amazement and unbelieving wonder. I was nearly as exhausted as I knew he must be, but obligingly, probably drained of my spirit to fight, I did exactly what he asked . . . . We went to Bourbon Street so he could play his horn!

MAY 1963

Our circumstance was getting worse! We were no longer kidding ourselves that it wasn't. We continued to feel Bob would make it, even so, the soaring medical costs, added to our other living costs and those of his family, all supported by a lesser income, made things tougher each day. Our rent alone was $400 a month and that was high in 1963. We had held on to the apartment because of the unbreakable lease, and hoped things would soon be better. Now we had to do something drastic.

One day, during a visit with Bob's parents, he proposed to me that we move into his house in Highland Park. My face froze and went lifeless. I was not expecting that suggestion because his ex-wife was living in the house, and even if she had agreed to move out, *"Me!, move into another woman's house?!"* *"Things can't be all that bad!* I realized, although his ex-wife lived there by Bob's sufference, it was still his house. He had to go to her and ask her to leave so we could have a place to stay. I was so discouraged, so forelorn. All the same, I was the bookkeeper and no one knew better, the sorry state of our finances, and how high the bills were piling We had to move!

The children and Ethel were to stay with us. Only his ex-wife would leave. It wasn't inconvenient to her, for she had her own, rather bizarre, life style and had other resources. When we came in, I found the two boys shared a room, and Ethel, the maid, and Adrienne shared the other. The carpets were all shabby, frayed and soiled. Everything appeared smokey and discolored from the dirty oil heat coming from the basement. The walls were dark and the entire house had fallen into disrepair. The house was basically classy, and I began to figure ways of cleaning it up and making it more livable for everyone.

Bob called the gas company, and for a few dollars down and a few more dollars a month, they converted the system to gas and added air conditioning for the coming summer. Then, while the basement, oil stove was out of the way, I had two new rooms added downstairs so that Bob jr., and Kyle each had their own private room, all to themselves. They enjoyed their new privacy. We rearranged things a little more so that Ethel and Adrienne each had separate rooms. We painted the walls, a cheerful, gleaming white, laid new, blue carpeting and finally the place began to acquire a fresh charm. We moved in our furniture and now it seemed like our home and not something borrowed. We were making the best of things.

'Bobby Lewis', a horn man like Scobey, worked closely with him on the 'International Hour - American Jazz' a CBS television show. Lewis saw the erosion of Bob, because of cancer, and its effects, in a way I could not.

". . . . This may have been Bob's last appearance because his body was pretty well consumed by the "Big 'C'" by this time. Yet, weak and drawn, just a shell of what he once was, (and believe me, because I am a trumpet player, playing the trumpet is very physical and only the healthiest and strongest can do it justice), Bob reached into that unknown, and played with that spirit and drive he was so well known for! . . . ."

It wasn't Bob's last appearance but it should have been. What was he using for stamina? I knew his intakes, he wasn't on uppers or anything like that, whatsoever. Everytime he was finished with a job he was exhausted but he would never let his friends or fans see it. John D. Walraven, a fan observed,

". . . . I can still recall him sitting down during a May '63 Bourbon Street session and having a 'milk on the rocks' with me and talking about going to Canada to see someone up there about his disease. His last tune that evening was 'Sidewalk Blues' and it was a knockout. One of my favorites by him, as my favorite trumpeter, among many good cats.

"What a shame he and Clancy Hayes were taken by the same illness . . . ."

Gail Brown was the hostess for a benefit Bob had agreed to perform:

". . . . I met Bob Scobey the first time in 1961. We chanced by Bourbon Street for an after dinner drink. I had little knowledge of Dixieland music—but from the moment I stepped into the dimly-lit club and felt the vibrations of the sounds and the feelings of the musicians transmitted through their instruments—I was a believer!

"I thought it would be great if Bob Scobey and his band played for a benefit Infant Welfare group, so I phoned. I was very frightened, but as soon as Bob took the call, he placed me at ease. He was so pleasant I felt I was speaking to an old friend and he eagerly agreed to perform for our benefit. The fact he was so kind and willing to help—was something else. I can't explain that. He didn't have to do it and his action must have been out of the goodness of his heart!

"The benefit was a huge success! Everyone agreed it had been great fun and so I was asked to contact Bob Scobey again. He was just as willing and we made arrangements for

BOB SCOBEY
JAN SCOBEY
©Jan Scobey 1976

the following year.

"During the following year an item appeared in The Tribune's Tower Ticker column and mentioned that Bob Scobey had been in the hospital and cancer had been diagnosed. I could hardly believe that vibrant man could have an evil fate such as cancer attack him. My family and I were sick at heart.

"My Infant Welfare group wanted me to contact him to see if the benefit would still be held (I can't blame them for their concerns, but certainly it was one of the hardest things I've ever had to do). I was to call Mr. Scobey and, in effect, ask him if he planned on being around for the benefit.

"Mr. Scobey sounded hurt, (and I don't blame him) that I had to ask.

"He said, 'We have an agreement, I'll be there!'"

"The night of the benefit arrived. What can I say? The music was great—as always. But it had to be one of the most depressing events that any of us ever attended. The shock of seeing a man; that had been so vivacious and full of energy the last year; changed into a quiet, mournful skeleton of a man; was very difficult to accept.

"He was still playing with the band. No one could believe it! Where he got the stamina, and yes, nerve, we couldn't figure out.

"At one of the intermissions I asked to see him, so I could thank him. I was sent to a dark corner where I found him sitting in a booth.

"He looked terribly depressed and small. As I stumbled over my words of thanks, a spark of life came into his face. He looked proud and defiant, too! I remember going down to

having great financial worries himself, and he answered a call way beyond friendship. Gloria, his wife, confirmed it.

> *". . . . Ron was not in particularly good financial shape at that time, he was a marvelous husband about taking his wife into consideration about finances. His feelings were always that it was our money, not just his. There could have been much easier times for Ron as far as being able to help you, however, there was never any question that he would . . . somehow.*
>
> *"Perhaps it was disloyal that we never felt the hope that you felt in the Canada trip. We did feel that it was hopeless, but you two had such bravery, such a will to live and to keep on trying, we did what we could and hurt that it was so little.*
>
> *"To speak of Ron for a minute, Jan. He had invested considerably in that club and if Bob had lived, the club, therefore Ron and Bob would have had a great success. When Bob became ill and died, Ron took a terrible financial beating, but I never heard him once becry his misfortune, only his loss of a friend.*
>
> *"Jan to summarize . . . for me there was never just a Bob Scobey. I never really knew him before you. There was Bob and Jan Scobey. The two of you have left the memories of important lessons learned, among the most important lessons of my life. Lessons of evaluating people, lessons of 'Happy Sounds', of living and loving and hoping, without reason for hoping.*
>
> *"I pray that my own personal strength is never tested the way Bob and you were. Losing John (my son) was quite enough, but should the powers that be, see fit to place me in similar circumstances, I hope that I will always remember the bravery and lessons of love I learned from you.*
>
> *"Please, when you are writing your book remember what I have said. If you are writing about those final months, you cannot separate Bob from Jan, they became one entity for a while. Who is to say who gave who what strength? . . . ."*

Upon reflection of her words, how true it is . . . Gloria's last question . . . Upon recalling, I too wonder, WHO GAVE WHO WHAT STRENGTH?

and more than three times, learned men drained my energy, by saying, *"Bob will die...."* I wouldn't believe them... Not this time...

I continued questioning the physician and asked him to pinpoint his reasoning.

"Bob has a bowel obstruction! The tumour in the intestinal tract had enlarged and is preventing normal bowel functions. Eventually, the body waste, not permitted to pass from the body, will be toxic!"...

In other words, the cause of death would be the bowel obstruction, not cancer.

"Why don't you operate?" I inquired. *"Remove the tumour and, if you had to, re-route the intestine to make a by-pass arrangement—a colostomy."*

"The cancer has spread too far and Bob is so emaciated he won't live through an operation!" Dr. Scarlatesco went on.

I ached when I heard the truth. Bob was so emaciated!

Dr. Scarlatesco mapped out his strategy of treatment and described it to me.

"First, Bob can be expected to stay here three weeks. We can concentrate on giving him healthy foods, Vitamins B-12 and B-15, and intravenous feeding supplements."

Feeling progress, I went in to tell Bob about the new program.

All Bob could hear was, *"three weeks in the hospital"*.

Bob, as usual, rebelled against being kept on his back. He refused to stay in the hospital.

We originally thought, when we went to Canada, we would have Bob diagnosed; the doctor would prescribe Laetrile; and after a few days, with drugs in hand, we could go back to the United States. This long-term stay was totally unplanned for.

I went and talked to the doctor again about Bob's continuing fetish against staying in hospitals.

"You can take an apartment close by and be Bob's nurse, since you have been able to help him until now!" the doctor indicated.

"I'll make a list of things you can purchase at a surgical supply house and health food store."

With the compromise, I went back to Bob and told him he didn't have to stay in the hospital, but we had to stay in Canada a few weeks so the doctor could observe the positive affects of the drug.

"Bob, you know the solution to this would be to take an apartment close by."

"Okay," he agreed.

I had to go back to Chicago for the supplies we needed for long-term housekeeping. Subsequently, we would save money by not renting everything.

I waited till about six in the evening before I departed.

"I'll go to sleep," Bob assured me.

"I'll fly back to Chicago, load up the car with all our necessities and drive back all night, and be here to see you before you awaken," I calmly replied.

Bob worried about my sleep, but I placated him by saying I could sleep on the plane. When I was leaving, his spirits were up and high. He knew, when I returned the next morning, we could set-up housekeeping in a nearby apartment, so he would get his wish to leave the hospital. I secured an apartment before I left.

After reaching the airport in Montreal, with added time of custom's delay, then flying to Chicago, and getting home to Krenn Avenue in Highland Park, the clock ticked away six more hours.

When I arrived, I said a quick hello to the children and Ethel, and rushed around packing while I talked with them. I tried to bring along some help. Bob Scobey, III; age 15 then, wanted to go along, but he was so close to examinations in school and needed to stay the last few weeks or he might have had trouble passing.

"If I still need you when I get back to Canada, I'll send for you." I promised.

It was 2 a.m. now, and I had just finished loading the trunk of the car. In the darkened night, I was startled by the phone ringing. It was Bob! calling from Montreal at 2 a.m.!

"What are you doing?", he asked.

"Bob, I am nearly ready to drive back right now, I can leave in minutes." I assured him.

He was ultra-depressed. I had never known him to be that way before.

"Jeannette, fly right back, I don't want to stay here and die." he exclaimed.

I nearly dropped the phone in astonishment! It was the first time I heard him speak of death.

I retorted,

"Gee, Bob, by the time I take a plane and go through customs, with the added time back and forth to airports, and securing an ambulance, I can be there with the car and then we can go ahead with our plans according to Dr. Scarlatesco. The doctor's program looks pretty good and there is no other way to get the drug. Bob, you just awoke in the night and missed me, that's all. Relax," I pleaded, *"I'll be right there."*

Bob shouted irritably, *"No!"* *"Come and get me I want to die at home!"*

All I could do at the time was to say, *"Okay, Dear,*

face—Bob had grown pale, all the blood had been drawn from it so that his nose protruded very obviously and it looked cold and white against his dark eyebrows and hair.

I jumped out of the bed and massaged his feet, trying to get the circulation going. He had been in bed too long, unable to get up and walk around. We were still concerned with things like pneumonia, but even so, his limbs were weakened from staying in a reclining position and he just didn't feel like walking.

With evening here, Bob still hadn't had any sleep. I kept on thinking and reviewing the events of the last few days. I thought, *"he must be feeling worse, his bowels are blocked again, and he is very weak."*

It was all getting to me now, heart wrenching fears, changes were for the worse again.

It seemed to always happen, just as my hopes were at their highest, he would get worse.

JUNE 9, 1963

With all the activity of the night before, I was bushed. My nerves were ragged, by this time, from constant attendance and worry, I kept thinking, *"Maybe he will make it. Oh—I don't know!"* Bob had started to get on my nerves and I felt topsy-turvy.

This morning I told Bob I would need help from Chicago, so someone could be watching him all the time, day and night. At first, I thought of Bob Jr., But it was his last week of school, he was in the midst of exams. On Ethel's advice, I thought I better not. Besides having a man in the room under such circumstances when often times I was not dressed, and with the nursing help needed, I soon thought of Adrienne as a better alternative.

I phoned Ethel in Highland Park to send Adrienne, she was 13 and rather adult for her age, but Ethel was reluctant, giving the excuse that her mother wouldn't let her go. I relayed Ethel's message to Bob, as we were in the same room. Bob angrily shouted across the room,

'Put Adrienne on the very next plane, Ethel!"

Of course, Ethel put Adrienne on the next plane, as she always had faith in what Bob wanted to do. So I made plans to leave Bob to pick up Adrienne at the Montreal airport.

It was still morning. I told Bob it would be nice if he had a shave. I pulled myself together and called a barber to come to our apartment.

Bob had his second shot of demerol with only three hours in between. I continued to be overly concerned.

When the barber arrived, he was unprepared for what he found. I was use to Bob, others were not. To have dropped from a one-time 209 pounds to the present weight of 78 pounds, a few pounds at a time, somehow was not as obvious to me, as when others would see him, or perhaps love put blinders on me.

The barber went ahead with the shave and when he was finished, he called me outside. As I was paying the bill, he squirmed,

"Lady, your man is dying, can't you smell the room. You should get some help!"

He was holding himself together with an obvious effort. He had been totally unraveled by the experience of shaving a man, who in his estimation was already a decaying corpse.

"I know, but what can I do," I asked him?

"Thanks a lot for helping us out!" Then he left.

He brought sudden realization of Bob's true condition and I was simply shattered. I had tried so darn hard to make him well.

"Why wasn't he getting well?" "God damn life and everything!" . . .

I walked into the room and told Bob how swell he looked with his fresh shave. Off in his corner he kept his frail smile . . .

I left Bob, hopefully in good spirits, and went to the airport to pick up his daughter, Adrienne.

While we were driving back to Bob, I prepared her for the change in her dad by explaining how badly he had deteriorated.

"That's why we need your help, Adrienne. The doctor thinks your Daddy will die and our job is to make him as comfortable as we can. You may be shocked when you see how thin he is, just 78 pounds, but try to overlook it, and remember the Daddy you always knew."

"Don't worry, Jeannette," Adrienne smiled, *"I'll be a good nurse!"*

When we arrived at the apartment, being gone awhile, I must say, even I was appalled at the smell and debasement that filled his bedroom. It seemed no ventilation would rid the room of the odors.

Little Adrienne wanted to nurse her Daddy and she helped tremendously. After the barber's reaction, I was utterly amazed at her ability to adjust and accept the situation. Of course, she loved her Daddy and that made the difference. She accepted the happenings with courage.

They were so cheerful seeing each other, I should have put all the children on the plane, had I known Bob's response would be so overjoyous. I regret I hadn't done that very thing.

I immediately gave Adrienne a full share of responsi-

JUNE 12, 1963

Early this morning, in the still of the long night, around 3:00 a.m., Bob was gone.

Bob Scobey's heart was weary, weary from the fight. For a long time, longer than anyone had predicted, his indomitable will to live had kept him alive.

His feet and hands were icy. Blood could no longer flow to his extremities. His lungs could labor no longer.

Bob could, at last, relax . . . . . . He was at peace!

20 ST. JAMES INFIRMARY BLUES

ADRIENNE AND I BOTH FOLLOWED THE ambulance to the hospital. It was nearly 4:00 a.m. and quiet so early in the morning. We were both weeping, I tried to stop and comfort her.

When we arrived at the hospital the attendants put Bob on a table in the emergency room and we waited to hear from some official, the confirmation of his death. When the final word came, I remember telling them it was very important for them to do their necessary work related to donating his body to the hospital, for any transplant use, and they handed me a paper to sign, saying he willed his body to science.

Then someone told us we could leave, so Adrienne and I left for the apartment. When we arrived there, it was hard to take the empty bed, dented from Bob's long stay and soaked in Bob's waste fluids.

"Let's pack, we should leave this place as soon as possible and head back to Chicago." I excitedly told Adrienne.

We were almost ready to leave when our phone rang, it was someone from the hospital.

"Mrs. Scobey, would you please come back to the hospital? We have had to ask the coroner to evaluate the death of your husband."

That sounded so ominous and frightening! "What were they talking about?"

Adrienne and I hurried back to the hospital where they had us wait, sitting on a bench, for a long time, almost an hour and a half. It was almost 8:30 a.m. now. Finally, I asked someone for a reason for having to remain so long. They explained, they were waiting for the attending physician, Dr. Scarlatesco, to come in and give his report. That sounded reasonable and so we stayed.

I found out, when Dr. Scarlatesco arrived and talked with us, the coroner thought Bob Scobey may have died by my hand!

That suspicion nearly killed me! After I had given my very all to help him live; after finally losing him to a struggle of perserverance, trying all there was to do, this news was violent and demoralizing!

The doctor assured them he had seen the sufferer and that I had done more to get Bob well than any other person in his whole association with sufferers.

He took Adrienne and me aside into a room and explained all of this to us. Dr. Scarlatesco turned to

21 TRIBUTES TO A TRUMPETER

'At the grave side, everybody was sad, but when they turned to go home again, the musicians struck up the happy music, and, Oh Lord, wasn't it HOT! Didn't it Swing?

(*New Orleans Funeral*)

The seven men who trouped with Bob, delivered their last performance at one of their favorite old haunts before a crowd of about 400 jazz devotees.

Unable to successfully continue without their leader, their last performance was a roof-raising tribute to the man that brought them all together and gave them fame.

The emcee asked the crowd to call out their favorite Scobey arrangements like 'South', 'St. James Infirmary', 'Oh Didn't He Ramble!' The music rang out, over and over again. It seemed the crowd wanted to wear out their favorite album before the finance company repossessed the record player.

There was the college crowd, the business man, the young and the old . . . . Bob's music crossed all the lines.

When the hours had finally run out and the performers had finished with their playing, the audience went home, the place closed for the night, and the boys went their separate ways.

I wrote to many of Bob's friends and fans, asking for their personal memories of Scobey and his music. They generously contributed and many of them helped 'this book' reach a completion. At the end of all their letters, they remembered their leader, their brother musician, their friend, very affectionately.

". . . . 'Bobbyloo' he used to call me and always had a handshake and a smile. His leadership, personally and with his horn, professionalism, personality and stage presence, and performance standards were always of the highest caliber and are reflected in the true artist, as Bob was!. . . ."

. . . . Bobby Lewis, musician

". . . . But, oh! . . . those Sunday afternoons in Milwaukee. Bob will ever be remembered by all of us as bringing real musical sunshine and happiness into any place he happened to be!. . . ."

. . . . Ralph Friedman, fan

". . . . It was heartbreaking to see him in such bad shape. The world lost a great trumpet player, but, I lost one of the dearest friends I ever had. Upon his death he donated his eyes to an Eye Bank, so somewhere, there is someone seeing with Bob Scobey's eyes!

"....I was more of a fan of Bob's than I was critic, and I recall the pure joy of listening with strong emotions to Bob at his creative best.

"I pay tribute to Bob's horn, by remembering him, along with Satchmo, King Joe Oliver, Bob Shefner, Bix, and many others whom I heard in person. Rather than make comparatives let me state that I have tonal memories of them all - each unique and contributing joy to many people. I place Bob in my gallery of Gods, grateful for the privilege of

"Bill Feist said it best when he wrote, 'A plaque should be put up on Victor and Roxie's as a landmark, because of Scobey's playing there.' As far as I am concerned, Bob Scobey was the most influential and unforgettable person in my life. He gave me the advantage of having a really true, solid friend...."

....Marilyn Napier McGwynn, fan

"....When I saw Clancy last at Earthquake McGoons, he talked glowingly about Bob and the more he talked, great big tears came to his eyes. He didn't like Bob, he loved him! And so did I!...."

....Dick Rippey, fan

"....Bob not only was a master musician, he was a leader. He could organize, he was always on the phone setting up engagements or tending to other business. We couldn't even agree on who should be the leader or what songs we should play without him. There just was nobody to step in and take charge!...."

....Art Hodes, musician

"....I'm glad you're publishing a book on Bob because I always considered him THE JAZZ MAN and a really dedicated Jazz lover...."

....Bob Rippey, friend and record promoter

"....I considered Bob a very good friend, an excellent musician and he was my inspiration when I was at a really low point in life. I was able to play in many good Dixieland bands because of him. If he hadn't given me that really good pep talk when I was in High School, I would never have gotten that far in life...."

....Larry Kostka, musician

"....I became very attached to Bob not only as a sufferer who had a lot of stamina and courage and insight, but as a human being, he was a very warm and superior individual. I felt very frustrated in taking care of Bob because we admired him so much, and liked you both so much that we wanted to accomplish the impossible for him. He was an uncomplaining and brave individual who had a lot of insight into his own problems, the difficulties he had had in his family life previously and wanted very much to live and enjoy life. We wanted also to help Bob and were frustrated in our inability to be of significant help other than to ease his suffering and to let him know that he had physicians who were concerned about him. He was an unforgettable individual of very strong character and had an intellect and personality that made an impression on us all...."

....Dr. George Block

"....Bob Scobey is one of the greatest Jazz artists of all time and he left us too damn soon! We lived in different cities so I did not see or *hear Bob play as often as I would have liked, but I was able to see him occasionally and take a few photos of him.*

"He was always a great and wonderful person to talk to and be with . . . ."

. . . . George Fletcher, photographer

". . . . It can get better cold in Chicago. I mean you can have it. It's driven every one of its favorite sons elsewhere. So, why do we come back? Hard to figure. The town's been rough, and today the story is the same. The modern cats can't make it and finally leave, just like their traditional older brothers did.

"Something may bring us back . . . to find the best jazz work reserved for the out-of-town attraction, the name that plays a couple of weeks and moves on. Stick around, and you're faced with few choices. You get a gig, and it soon runs out; play the club-date routine; get a day gig, and club when you can; sell insurance. It's like Bert Williams would say: "The man who stays behind, a hero shall be . . . somebody else, not me."

"So this is the setting; this is the town that Bob Scobey came to and decided to make a go of. I never questioned him. I don't know what entered his figuring. I know he dug in, bought a home in a suburb, opened with his band at [what was then] the Continental on Walton St., near north side, and played there a good two years to many a capacity crowd.

"Maybe he heard that if you can't make it in Chicago, you can't make it anywhere, and it's true—no one need fall apart in the town. Somehow you can get by . . . . We always have. But Bob was a top-of-the-heap man. So it could have been any number of things, possibly the challenge. But whatever it was, believe me, for the boys who played it trad style, it was a blessing.

"Suddenly Dixieland became a fashionable word, and clubowners were using the same format. Scobey proved to be a shot in the arm for dear ol' Chi. Gave the newspaper guys a new something to write on. Bob was a first-rate promoter, and he kept his name and his music in the foreground.

"Funny how we met. It was '59, and I was visiting my daughter Janet in Chicago. (I live 32 miles south of the big town. It's an armed truce. I need a big town to support my profession, but I'm not fixin' to live in it.)

"The phone rang. "It's for you, dad," Janet said. (Always leave a number when you're out of the house—it may be a gig.)

"Who?" I said. "Bob Scobey?" I was surprised. I knew he was in town, but I'm not much on "openings" and I hadn't dropped in. Besides, I didn't know the man.

"Art, whatcha doing—I mean tonight?"

"Friday, and I haven't got a gig.

"Nothing. What's on your mind?"

"Well, he was stuck, and would I come in and play? I made my usual objections . . . . Haven't played for days . . . Won't have time to warm up . . . Fingers are stiff . . . . Not sure I can handle your

TRIBUTE TO A HORN PLAYER

They are all yellow and brittle now, the thick packet of newspaper clippings, written about Bob Scobey.

Yes, death is sad. A final closing of one door, but not all of them. While I wrote, I relived and remembered the times of Bob's life and career. My home was jumping with music that I had saved because I didn't want the records to wear out and probably because I wasn't ready to listen again. Now as I write, my stereo is loaded with Bob's records, playing all my favorites.

As I struggled with my pen and paper, the SAINTS CAME MARCHING IN through the rooms, filled with joy.

There are some doors, for some men, that can never be closed. LOVE, JOY, BEAUTY go on and on . . .

And the Beat Goes On!!!!!!!!

Jan Scobey

TRUMPET
As played by: BOB SCOBEY
JANSCO—Volume III JLPS 5231
© Jan Scobey 1976

WHEN THE SAINTS GO MARCHING IN

22 BOB SCOBEY'S DISCOGRAPHY

Good Time Jazz - 12001 Yerba Buena Jazz Band recordings made by Lu Watters in 1946 and later remastered for GTJ. They were recorded at the Avalon Ballroom on Post Street off Van Ness in San Francisco. Personnel: Bob Scobey and Lu Watters, trumpets; Turk Murphy, trombone; Bob Helm, Clarinet; Wally Rose, piano; Harry Mordecai, banjo; Dick Lammi, bass; Bill Dart, drums.

Minstrels of Anne St.; Jazzin' Babies Blues; The Easy Winners; Ostrich Walk; Pineapple Rag; I'm Goin' Huntin'; Ain't Gonna Give Nobody None Of My Jelly Roll; New Orleans Joys; Ory's Creole Trombone; Original Rags; Pastime Rag #5; Canal St. Blues.

Good Time Jazz - 12002 Yerba Buena Jazz Band. Personnel: Bob Scobey and Lu Watters, trumpets; Turk Murphy, trombone; Bob Helm, Clarinet; Wally Rose, piano; Harry Mordecai, banjo; Dick Lammi, bass; Bill Dart, drums.

Annie St. Rock; Big Bear Stomp; Antigua Blues; Emperor Nortons Hunch; Climax Rag; Sage Hen Strut; Trombone Rag; Down Home Rag; Creole Belles; Sunburst Rag; That's A Plenty.

Good Time Jazz - 12003 Yerba Buena Jazz Band. Personnel: Bob Scobey and Lu Watters, trumpets; Turk Murphy, trombone; Bob Helm, Clarinet; Wally Rose, piano; Harry Mordecai, banjo; Dick Lammi, bass; Bill Dart, drums.

South; Chattanooga Stomp; 1919 Rag; Sunset Cafe Stomp; Copenhagen; Panama; Working Man Blues; Richard M. Jones Blues; Weary Blues; Bienville Blues; Triangle Jazz Blues; Friendless Blues.

Good Time Jazz - 12026. Part of this album was recorded in 1949 and 1950. Between the two sessions there was a slight change in personnel. Turk Murphy, trombone; Bob Scobey, Trumpet; Bob Helm, Clarinet; Burt Bales, piano; Harry Mordecai, banjo; Dick Lammi, Tuba or string bass; Bill Napier, clarinet; Bill Newman, guitar and banjo; Squires Girsback, tuba or string bass; Stan Ward, drums.

New Orleans Stomp; Chimes Blues; When My Sugar Walks Down The Street; All The Wrongs You've Done To Me; Grandpa Spells; Trouble In Mind; Turk's Blues; Papa Dip; Struttin With Some Barbecue; 1919 Rag; Curse Of An Aching Heart; Irish Black Bottom; Trombone Rag; Dark Town Strutters Ball; Ragtime Dance; Waiting For The Robert E. Lee.

Good Time Jazz - 12006. BOB SCOBEY'S FRISCO BAND . . . recorded in Los Angeles in 1955 by Les Koenig and John Palladino, engineer. Bob Scobey, trumpet; Bill Napier, Clarinet; Jack Buck, trombone; Ernie Lewis, piano; Clancy Hayes, banjo and vocals; Dick Lammi, bass; Earl Watkins, drums.

Battle Hymm Of The Republic; Someday Sweetheart; Parsons Kansas Blues; Strange Blues; Memphis Blues; Down in Jungletown; Sweet Georgia Brown; Beale St. Blues; Mobile; Friendless Blues; Careless Love; Bill Bailey.

Good Time Jazz - 12009. BOB SCOBEY'S FRISCO BAND . . . recorded in Los Angeles in 1955, Les Koenig, Producer, Roy DuNann, engineer. Bob Scobey, trumpet; Bill Napier, Clarinet, and Bass Clarinet; Jack Buck, Trombone; Ernie Lewis, piano; Clancy Hayes, banjo and vocals; Hal McCormick, bass; Earl Watkins, drums.

When The Midnight Choo-Choo Leaves For Alabam; St. James Infirmary Blues; Home; At The Devel's Ball; St. Louis Blues; Angry; I Ain't Gonna Give Nobody None Of This Jelly Roll; Love Me Or Leave Me; I Want To Go Back To Michigan; You Can Depend On Me; Lights Out Blues.

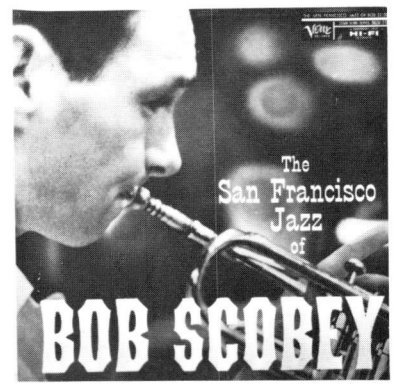

Verve Records - MGV 1011. THE SAN FRANCISCO JAZZ OF BOB SCOBEY . . . Recorded in 1957. Bob Scobey, trumpet; Clancy Hayes, banjo and vocals; Jesse "Tiny" Crump, piano; Bill Napier, Clarinet; Jack Buck, trombone; Freddie Higuera, drums; Hal McCormack, bass.

Five Foot Two Eyes Of Blue; Royal Garden Blues; Stumbling; Ain't She Sweet; Milneberg Joys; Getting My Boots; Muskrat Ramble; Trouble In Mind; Copenhagen; Somebody Stole My Gal; Lover Come Back; My Gal Sal.

RCA Victor - LPM 1344. BEAUTY AND THE BEAT . . . BOB SCOBEY'S FRISCO BAND . . . with Clancy Hayes, recorded in 1957. Matty Matlock, Arranger; Fred Reynolds, A and R; Bob Scobey, trumpet; Mannie Klein, trumpet; Clancy Hayes, banjo and vocals; Abe Lincoln, trombone; Warren Smith, trombone; Elmer Schneider, trombone; Jack Buck, trombone; Matty Matlock, clarinet; Bill Napier, clarinet; Wayne Songer, clarinet; Ralph Sutton, piano; Phil Stephens, bass; Bob Short, tuba; Freddie Higuera, drums.

The Girl Friend; Linda; Miss Annabelle Lee; Mandy Is Two; Mickey; Alice Blue Gown; Calico Sal; Sweet Lorraine; Lulu's Back In Town; Sweet Substitute; You Must Have Been A Beautiful Baby; Rose Of Washington Square.

RCA Victor - LPM 1473. BING WITH A BEAT . . . Recorded in 1957. Bob Scobey, trumpet and leader; Frank Beach, trumpet; Matty Matlock, clarinet; Dave Harris, tenor sax; Abe Lincoln, trombone; Clancy Hayes, guitar; Ralph Sutton, piano; Red Callender, bass; Nick Fatool, drums; BING CROSBY, vocals.

Let A Smile Be Your Umbrella; I'm Gonna Sit Right Down And Write Myself A Letter; Along The Way To Waikiki; Exactly Like You; Dream A Little Dream Of Me; Last Night On The Back Porch; Some Sunny Day; Whispering; Tell Me; Mack The Knife; Down Among The Sheltering Palms; Mama Loves Papa.

RCA Victor - LPM 1448. SWINGING ON THE GOLDEN GATE . . . Recorded in 1957. Bob Scobey, trumpet and leader; Dick Cathcart, trumpet; Matty Matlock, clarinet and arranger; Abe Lincoln, trombone; Warren Smith trombone; Jack Buck, trombone; Ralph Sutton, piano; Red Callender bass; Bob Short, tuba; Sammy Goldstein, drums; Clancy Hayes, guitar, banjo and vocals.

Sunny Disposish; Carolina In The Morning; Feet Draggin' Blues; It Happened In Sun Valley; I Can't Get Started With You; Come Back Sweet Papa; Wabash Cannon Ball; New Orleans; Ain't-Cha Glad?; Let's Dance The Ragtime Darlin'; Snag It; Waiting For the Robert E. Lee.

RCA Victor - LPM 1700. COLLEGE CLASSICS . . . BOB SCOBEY'S FRISCO BAND . . . Recorded in 1958. Bob Scobey, trumpet; Clancy Hayes, banjo and vocals; Jack Buck, trombone; Doug Skinner, trombone; Pete Dovidio, clarinet; Clyde Pound, piano; Tom Beeson, bass; Dave Black, drums.

Wedding Bells Are Breaking Up That Old Gang Of Mine; I've Been Working On The Railroad; Let The Rest Of The World Go By; We'll Build A Bungalow; I've Been Floating Down The Old Green River; Let Me Call You Sweetheart; Absinthe Frappe; Put On Your Old Grey Bonnet; Shine On Harvest Moon; The Whiffenpoof Song; There's A Long, Long Trail; You Tell Me Your Dreams I'll Tell You Mine.

RCA Victor - LSP 1567. BETWEEN 18TH AND 19TH ON ANY STREET . . . BOB SCOBEY'S FRISCO BAND . . . Recorded in 1958. Bob Scobey, trumpet; Jack Buck, trombone; Doug Skinner, trombone; Pete Dovidio, clarinet; Clancy Hayes, banjo and vocals; Clyde Pound, piano; Tom Beeson, bass; Dave Black, drums.

The Five Piece Band; Whistling In The Dark; My Extraordinary Girl; Little Girl; Cake Walking Babies From Home; A Sunday Kind Of Love; Black & Blue; I'm Not Rough; Woodchopper's Ball; Struttin' With Some Barbecue; West End Blues; Muggles; Save It; Pretty Mama; Undecided; Bob's Blues; Between 18th and 19th On Chestnut Street.

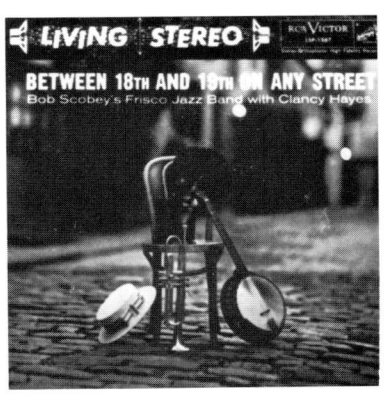

California Records - M-1501. SCOBEY & CLANCY RAID THE JUKE BOX . . . BOB SCOBEY'S FRISCO BAND . . . Recorded in 1958. Bob Scobey, trumpet; Clancy Hayes, banjo and vocals; Pud Brown, clarinet; Jack Buck, trombone; Doug Skinner, trombone; Stan Wrightsman, piano; Bob Short, string bass & tuba; Dave Black, drums.

Bye Bye Love; Yellow Dog Blues; Singing The Blues; Tammy; Round And Round; All Shook Up; Love Letters In The Sand; Marianne; C.C. Rider; So Rare; Blueberry Hill; Don't Forbid Me.

RCA Victor - LPM 1889. SOMETHING'S ALWAYS HAPPENING ON THE RIVER . . . Recorded in 1958. Recording Engineer Ray Hall, Produced by Fred Reynolds. Bob Scobey, trumpet; Rich Matteson, Tuba and bass trumpet; George Duvivier, bass; Jim Beebe, trombone; Gene Schroeder, piano; Brian Shanley, clarinet; Clancy Hayes, banjo and vocals; Toni Lee Scott, vocals; Dave Black, drums; Bob Scobey, vocals.

Something's Always Happening On The River; Floating Down To Cotton Town; Down By The Riverside; Alexander's Ragtime Band; River Stay Away From My Door; Riverside Blues; Row, Row, Row; Dixie; Swanee River; Mississippi Mud; Riverboat Shuffle; Glad To Be Me.

RCA Victor - LPM 2086. ROMPIN' AND STOMPIN' . . . Produced by Fred Reynolds, recorded in 1960. Bob Scobey, trumpet; Brian Shanley, clarinet; Jim Beebe, trombone; Art Hodes, piano; Rich Matteson, tuba; Clancy Hayes, banjo and vocals; Dave Black, drums.

Colonel Bogey March; The Pearls; Kansas City Stomp; Buddy Bolden's Blues; Skit-Dat-De-Dat; The Chant; Shake It And Break It; Canal Street Blues; Fidgety Feet; Dallas Blues; Black Bottom Stomp.

Sesac Recordings - N2251/52. Recorded in 1960 at Coliseum Tower, New York; No information regarding personnel was on the record jacket. Bob Scobey, trumpet; Clancy Hayes, vocals; Jack McConnell, clarinet; Floyd Bean, piano; Dave Black and Bobby Christian, drums; Doug Skinner and Ralph Hutchinson, trombones.

Frisco Jazz Parade; There's Nothing In Dixie; Too Much Mustard; Memories Of Bunk; Georgia Blues; My Heart's In Dixie; Sudan; Hobo Blues; Bourbon Street; Tailgate Romance; Cable Car Swing; Don't Count Your Kisses.

KRAFT FOODS—JELLY 'n' JAM and all that JAZZ. BOB SCOBEY PLAYS FOR KRAFT . . . Recorded in 1960 in Chicago. Bob Scobey, trumpet; Buddy Lee, banjo; Tommy Smoot, piano; Connie Milano, bass; Bill Hanck, trombone; Bill Napier, clarinet; Dave Black, drums.

When The Saints Go Marching In; Under The Double Eagle; Maple Leaf Rag; Georgia Camp Meeting; Peshtigo Court Stomp.

RCA Victor - LSP 2982. THE BEST OF DIXIELAND . . . Released in 1964. This album is loaded with Jazz Greats. All the side men, some 96 musicians, are too numerous to mention. Many have since found success in leading their own bands. Louis Amstrong; Turk Murphy; Mugsy Spanier; Bourbon St. Dixielands; Henry Red Allen; Bunk Johnson; The Dukes of Dixieland; Bob Scobey; Pete Kelly and His Big Seven; Jimmy McPartland; Tony Almerico; Original Jazz Band.

Rocking Chair; Tiger Rag; I Wish I Could Shimmy Like My Sister Kate; High Society; St. James Infirmary; Saints; Tin Roof Blues; Mississippi Mud; Oh Didn't He Ramble; South Rampart St. Parade; Milneberg Joys; Livery Stable Blues.

JANSCO RECORDS - RLPS 5231. SCOBEY AND HIS FRISCO BAND . . . This album was recorded by Bob Scobey in 1960 and was issued on the Ragtime Label. It was acquired by Jan Scobey, purchasing it outright from Bob Scobey's estate and the label changed to Jansco Records. Bob Scobey, trumpet; Richard Nelson, trombone; Bill Napier, clarinet; Tommy Smoot, piano; Buddy Lee, banjo; Dickie Phillips, electric bass; Dave Black, drums.

Rampart St. Parade; Basin St. Blues; Clarinet Marmalade; Misty; Bye Bye Blues; When The Saints Go Marching In; Under The Double Eagle; Sleepy Time Down South; Drummer's Blues; Bourbon St. Parade; Wabash Blues.

JANSCO RECORDS - JLPS 6252. THE GREAT BOB SCOBEY AND HIS FRISCO BAND . . . Produced by Jan Scobey, recorded in 1956 by Stan Page at the Jenny Lind Hall in Oakland: issued in 1966. Bob Scobey, trumpet; Clancy Hayes, banjo and vocals; Lizzie Miles, vocals; Bill Napier, clarinet; Jack Buck, trombone; Jesse "Tiny" Crump, piano; Bob Short, tuba; Ralph Sutton, piano; Hal McCormack, bass; Freddie Higuera, drums.

I'm Blue Turning Grey Over You; Five Foot Two; I'm Confessing That I Love You; In New Orleans; It Ain't No Fault Of Mine; Maple Leaf Rag; Sugar Blues; I'm Sorry I Made You Cry; Nobody's Sweetheart; Ela Ba.

JANSCO RECORDS - JLPS 6250. THE GREAT BOB SCOBEY AND HIS FRISCO BAND . . . Produced by Jan Scobey, recorded in 1956 by Stan Page at The Jenny Lind Hall in Oakland; issued in 1966. Bob Scobey, trumpet; Clancy Hayes, banjo and vocals; Lizzie Miles, vocals; Bill Napier, clarinet; Jack Buck, trombone; Jesse "Tiny" Crump, piano; Bob Short, tuba; Ralph Sutton, piano; Hal McCormack, bass; Freddie Higuera, drums.

Wang Wang Blues; My Honey's Lovin' Arms; I Ain't Got Nobody; Then I'll Be Happy; Mack The Knife; Georgia On My Mind; I Can't Give You Anything But Love; Please Don't Talk About Me; I'll See You In C.U.B.A.; Panama Rag.

MY OPINION

If you have never purchased Bob Scobey albums and would like to acquire some of them, I have carefully reviewed his works to aid you in your selections of his recordings.

I have listened, more carefully, to all of the albums in the discography and I tend to be a perfectionist. I was very familiar with Bob Scobey's work and the artists surrounding him, (at one time I was a band leader and trumpet player) and I have talked and listened to many musicians. I am also personally acquainted with many of Bob Scobey fans and have heard their comments.

My review lists only the finest albums and his best works are at the top of the list. This analysis is based, primarily, from the point of view of Bob Scobey's artistry and listening enjoyment.

Jansco records are still produced. Other recordings may be difficult to find.

1.) JANSCO RECORDS - RLPS 5231 - BOB SCOBEY & HIS FRISCO BAND. This album is an instrumental. The sounds cover a wide range of feeling; from Misty, a mood tune, to the rip-roaring excitement of Bourbon St. Parade! I believe it successfully captures the entire range of Bob Scobey's musical skills and types of playing.

2.) RCA VICTOR - LPM 2086 - ROMPIN' AND STOMPIN'. This album is equally as exciting as the JANSCO RLPS 5231. It features a wide library of 'Jelly Roll Morton' tunes, all fine classics of Dixieland Jazz. There are tremendous intricacies in the solo playing; as well as an outstanding ensemble performance. RCA has discontinued issuing this album. Sometimes they are available through jazz societies or record collectors. Perhaps with enough requests RCA may find it lucrative to re-issue.

3.) Good Time Jazz - 12023 - DIRECT FROM SAN FRANCISCO. This recording offers you many of the most requested tunes played during Bob Scobey's stage performances. They are the top favorites in 'Dixieland Jazz' music.

Bob had a top notch band of musicians that played together like a well oiled, fine machine. The sound is thoroughly 'warmed up' the way a second set can sound in a night club or concert performance. There are several superb vocals by Clancy Hayes that adds spice.

4.) JANSCO JLPS 6250 and JLPS 6252. THE GREAT BOB SCOBEY & HIS FRISCO BAND. Bob Scobey and band plays in about the same period as item three above, with the added delight of Lizzie Miles singing the blues. It has a good range of musical selections and the acoustics of Jenny Lind Hall, where it was recorded, give it that special *"live"* sound.

5.) RCA VICTOR - LPM 1889 - SOMETHING'S ALWAYS HAPPENING ON THE RIVER. I'm in favor of this album because of one very superior performance of "River, Stay Away from My Door". Both, the genuinely melancholy trumpet of Bob Scobey, and the expressively

A WIDOW'S EPILOGUE

I received a letter from Dr. Port, the surgeon who performed Bob's operations and headed his chemotherapy treatment. I have included parts of his letter in Volume II, *"Cancer? What you can do!"*

After writing this book and receiving his letter, I have come to some conclusions: (1) I was the first to tell Bob he had cancer, just before his second operation. I believe, we should have been told his condition, together. (2) After Bob's second operation, Bob was told he had 'terminal' cancer, evidenced by the will he made in October, 1962. (3) Bob never told me he had 'terminal' cancer. Somehow, I never faced up to this fact until about the last month. (4) I should have been told, instantly, as soon as diagnosed, he had 'terminal' cancer. It should have been suggested we read all we could about cancer and take courses that would aid us in, not only coping with the disease and situation (which turned out to be a necessity), but to acquire knowledge to make our own decisions as to the course of care and treatment. We certainly should have been told about Bob's diabetes mellitus, even before we went to Europe. All these things might have avoided his death. (5) If we had done some of our own research, I would have advised Bob not to suffer his second operation. (6) Through my research, I would have realized, the only possible way of eradicating cancer is by first repairing the immunological system—through quality nutrition—through psychological assistance—through rest and relaxation and other therapies (presented in greater detail in Volume Two. (7) Finally, after reviewing the percentages of cures and the miserable affects (which are truly horrible) from 5-Fluorouracil, I would have shown Bob the facts, advised him not to accept chemotherapy for his specific type of cancer, but to keep searching for another answer. Bob did voice a psychic feeling about hormone treatment. It would have been his best try, if he went no further to research his condition.

Of course, these conclusions are based on knowing Bob's condition was 'terminal' and may also be applied to an early, curable diagnosis of this disease.

All of my detailed research, conclusions and offers of help to the sufferer, are in Volume II. The future can hold victory for sufferers who are subjected to any illness.

WIDOWHOOD

What follows applies to all widows or widowers who, married only a brief time, lose their spouse. It is human nature, I suppose, for relatives and acquaintances to feel 'you haven't earned the right to claim full rights as a wife or husband. This can be very painful if you are on the receiving end of this kind of prejudice.

You are either married or you are not! I was an exceptionally, loving wife and partner to Bob—as his lover, in our social relationships, in his business, and at last, as his final, only, caring companion. I helped him more than anyone had in his entire lifetime. Still, the prejudice can exist, so if the situation applies to you, be ready to cope with it.

After Bob died, my saddest experience was to realize most people did not consider I had earned the right to be his wife! In their eyes, the marriage of a year and a half was too brief. In spite of my having cared for Bob, unceasingly, for the entire ten months of his terrible illness, until his passing, they considered the time of our union too short to have given our marriage a 'real legitimacy' . . . It is sad, but true, and widows and widowers, married only a brief period, should be prepared for this.

The probate court, social security officials and the veteran's administration did not consider me . . . officially . . . as Bob's wife! In their bureaucratic opinion, our marriage was not long enough . . . But when it came time to pay his bills, I was, once more, considered his wife!

In every love story that ends sadly, you seldom read about the way life must and does continue, in practical ways, afterward. This chapter deals with the time after the mourners go home and the widow goes to her empty house . . .

NO MORE SCOBEY BAND

The band broke up. Dave Black and Bill Napier went back to San Francisco. The rest of the guys spread out and went on their separate ways. After the last job at Buddy Beek's, there was no more Scobey Band!

NO MONEY

When I returned from Canada and went to the Glencoe Bank, I discovered my account was frozen! I could not make a single withdrawal, although it was a joint account. It had been 'locked up' at the direction of the Internal Revenue Service!

The account contained approximately $2500, nearly all I had and it was held for nine months! I had written checks to pay the band, a few days before Bob's death, but because of the account 'freeze' they were not allowed to clear, since they had been received by the bank after Bob's death. I had to pay the members of the band from private funds. Luckily, I had kept a small account of my own, under my maiden name, even though I was married to Bob. It was from these funds I was able to handle the payroll from time to time and, in March of 1963, make the down payment for our new Cadillac.

NO HOME

I moved out of the house on Krenn Avenue, Highland Park, within a week or two of Bob's death. I thought at the time the property was held in joint tenancy with his ex-wife, and I just wanted to get away from everything that reminded me of the bad times.

Upon reflection, I know I should have stayed in the house as long as I could. Had my mind been on it, I would have checked to see what my legal claim was on the property. I could have, at least, lived there until the court settled everything. Since Bobs' death, I was still having ex-wife

JEALOUSY

A widow's lot is awkward for another reason. Jealousy! You don't fit into a married group anymore. You are a 'fifth wheel.'

The women are often fearful that your sympathetic situation (especially if you are at all attractive) is tailor-made to steal their husbands.

I did not accept dates with men for a long time. Bob was still very much on my mind. I had close friends, mostly women. I didn't want the inevitable complications, at that time, which usually result in a prolonged association with a man. I am, and always have been, a straight, heterosexual female, but during this period of mourning I was even accused of being a lesbian because of these friendships. It was the big joke around Rush Street. Try to just fluff off gossip and persecution.

It needs to be emphasized again, at this point in my story, I relate my personal experiences only to possibly help others who would otherwise fall into similar pitfalls.

TAXES

Of course I had very little money. I had been burglarized and much of the $10,000 had gone to pay bills that Bob and I had before he died, plus Uncle Sam still had his hand outstretched. I had foolishly signed a joint tax return, just seven weeks before Bob died. At the time of signing, I had great optimism and believed he would still make it and, looking to our future, to save him a few dollars in taxes, I accepted joint responsibility. If I had not signed the return, I would not have been liable for the taxes. I could have avoided this added burden. Instead, I was saddled with a $2500 tax bill, and a lien was put on my property and insurance policies.

The best information and advice I can give you is to arm yourself with information. Take a mini-tax course. Read the will carefully. Fight for every cent someone wants to take from you. Do not be concerned with how others may feel about you because you act this way, as I foolishly did. People, you deal with, know you are in a weakened condition because of your loss. Keep all your personal business secret, especially from the attorneys.

PROBATE

The calamities continued to mount. When a widow walks into a courtroom, it is an arena where her grief and defenselessness count for very little. I had no attorney at first. I foolishly assumed the man who drew up Bob's will would support me after Bob's demise. No way! He was now an officer of the court and responsible for probating the will.

Instead of backing me up, the way Bob and I thought he would, and carrying out Bob's wishes as they were requested in his will, he put his influence toward giving away (what I considered personal possessions and part of Bob's bequest to me) the few remaining assets of his estate.

Courtrooms are cold places, colder still for this widow, who was a newlywed. Parasites came out of the woodwork. An ex-wife, old 'friends', even someone who loaned Bob money before he died, tried to get it out of my hide.

I suggest, widow or widower, fight for yourself, do not give an inch, unless it is a stiff court order, and then still question it. I had to part with some of my husband's most personal belongings including the cadillac for which I paid the $800 down payment. I should have refused the forced sale, requested by the attorney, and taken this matter to court for besides losing the car, I was never even re-imbursed for the down payment!

Whatever Bob had, we acquired together during the year and a half of our marriage; scrimping, saving, paying bills. When I met Bob, he had heavy, heavy financial troubles.

Musical tapes, Bob kept for nine years and never produced in record form, were really part of his personal possessions. These were never edited and he never thought of them as material to issue on record. Yet the courts and the attorney who witnessed the will called in other record companies to bid on acquiring them, as well as the one album he did issue. After the record companies refused, not being interested in the tapes, whatsoever, the property remained assets of the estate.

I was forced, in a highly emotional state, to go to an auction of the tapes (my own personal property). In the sad state of mind I was in, with the yearning desire to see music produced from the tapes, especially since I was still in mourning, I was pushed into bidding $6,250! The tapes were not worth two or three hundred dollars, at the time. Since the other creditor was against me, and the courts allowed her claim (feeling Bob's debt was my debt), this unfair pettiness skyrocketed the cost of the tapes.

The court required all available funds must remain in the estate to pay bills. All possessions, even personal possessions willed, had to be included in the estate for this purpose. Well, there were no bills because I had foolishly paid all of Bob's debts, except for the privately secured loan. I should have left them unpaid and forced everyone to put in their claim to the estate. I would have been much better off. Most of these bills had absolutely nothing to do with me nor were they my expenditures.

I had paid the Canadian doctors, bills from Caldwell Hospital, the funeral expenses, house repair bills, department store bills, children's dental bills, back rent, maids bills and so on. These are items I should have let the estate handle and not paid from my rapidly depleting personal funds.

The personal possessions I had, which could raise some money, were taken from me by the court. Some were later returned, but most were sold and the proceeds given to the ex-wife for child care (already provided for by social security benefits) and to pay the one large loan, Bob had made previous to our marriage.

The worse part of this experience was the effect it had on my frame of mind. I had no fight left . . . . So again, beware!

COLLECTING LIFE INSURANCE

LAST WILL AND TESTAMENT
OF
ROBERT A. SCOBEY, JUNIOR

I, ROBERT A. SCOBEY, JUNIOR, being a resident of the City of Chicago, County of Cook and State of Illinois, and being of sound and disposing mind and memory, do hereby make, publish and declare this to be my Last Will and Testament, hereby revoking expressly any prior Wills or Codicils by me heretofore made.

ITEM ONE: I do order and direct that all of my just debts and funeral expenses, and the expenses of administration of my estate be paid as soon after my death as may be practicable.

ITEM TWO: I give and bequeath my mortal remains to the UNIVERSITY OF CHICAGO HOSPITAL AND CLINICS, and direct that they be employed in their certain hospital and clinic known as Billings for use in scientific research, I request that my eyes be placed in an eye bank for subsequent use, all at the discretion solely of the duly constituted authorities of such hospital.

ITEM THREE: All household goods, jewelry, wearing apparel, and automobiles, if any, which I may own at the time of my death, I give and bequeath to JEANETTE M. SCOBEY, my wife.

ITEM FOUR: All of the rest, residue and remainder of my estate I do give, devise and bequeath as follows:

I direct my Executor to divide my entire estate aforementioned into two separate portions consisting of one-third of said estate and two-thirds of said estate respectively, and as to same, I give, devise and bequeath the said one-third portion to JEANETTE M. SCOBEY, my wife.

The remaining two-thirds portion I do give, devise and bequeath to THE FIRST NATIONAL BANK OF HIGHLAND PARK, Highland Park, Illinois, as Trustee, in trust nevertheless, upon the following uses and purposes:

ITEM FIVE: In the event that at the time of my death, any of my children shall then be minors, then I direct the nomination and appointment of JEANETTE M. SCOBEY, my wife, as Guardian of the Person of said minor child or children.

IN WITNESS WHEREOF, I have hereunto subscribed my name and sealed this Instrument this 11 day of October, A. D. 1962.

Robert A. Scobey, Jr. (SEAL)

ASSETS AFTER BOB SCOBEY'S DEMISE

John Hancock Life Insurance $10,356.00
Estate, widow's award 4,173.00*
Bank Account 2,500.00
San Francisco Musician's Union 2,000.00**

                                                       $19,040.00

* I put in $10,175.00 of my money, by relinquishing the cadillac and paying for the personal tapes. And received less than 50 percent return as a widow's award.

** This insurance policy was paid after a two year delay.

IMMEDIATE COST OF BOB'S DEMISE

Personal, Pre-marriage debt to Jeannette at time of death $6,545.00
Purchase from estate, Scobey tapes, part of personal property .. 6,250.00
Lease cost of apartment 500.00
Burial Expenses 285.00
Car taken away 3,925.00
Car depreciation, loss for quick sale 675.00
Internal Revenue taxes 2,500.00
Bob's Parents 150.00
Children's clothes 131.00
Moving costs 340.00
Band Payroll 1,600.00
Maid 105.00
Groceries and Xmas Presents 400.00
Cadillac deposit 800.00
Doctor bills and hospital, etc. 800.00

                                                              $25,006.00

No employment, but immediate cost of living for
eight months before finding work .... ?

$25,006.00 Paid out
- $19,040.00 Taken In

$ 5,966.00 Loss

PRESIDENTIAL CERTIFICATE OF HONOR

When I received this certificate of condolence from the President of the United States, at the time I thought: Wow, how thoughtful! In retrospect, since the government is so aware of their deceased taxpayers, to freeze the account of money so that the widow does not have access to it, to put a lien on her property to pay her husband's taxes and, at the same time, disallow her marriage when it came to benefits because she wasn't

". . . . MILWAUKEE SENTINEL . . . THE MAGIC OF SCOBEY IS MISSING . . .

"A good Dixieland band needs more than a name. Unfortunately, Jan Scobey and her Dixiecats made this simple truth only too clear Sunday.

"The raven haired beauty, wife of the late and great jazz musician, Bob Scobey, played a one night stand with her newly formed group at Buddy Beek's supper club, 2575 N. Downer Ave. The magic behind the Scobey name was gone.

"Jan Scobey was married to the 46 year old trumpet player about a year and a half before he died of stomach cancer last June. His own band kept the widely known name for a time, but in October played together for the last time at a memorial tribute here.

"The widow gathered her own musicians, continued her singing lessons, bought a few gowns and started playing the circuit.

"Individually the musicians deserve praise. Eddie Davis is a swinger on the banjo, as witnessed by his ultrafast offering of "After You've Gone." Likewise Bob Ballard plays a hot trumpet and Jug Berger displays nimble fingers on the clarinet and a passable Louis Armstrong voice when he gets before the microphone.

"The others, Gena Rasbury on piano, Jim George on trombone and Bob Cousins on drum, all are able performers.

"However, as an ensemble, the group is about as flat as a punctured tire. If it doesn't swing on the classic "Battle Hymn of the Republic, it just doesn't swing at all.

"Mrs. Scobey, as lovely as she is, has a lot to learn about this jazz business.

"In all fairness, it must be considered that the group has been together only about six weeks, that the bistro's sound system was far from perfect and that Mrs. Scobey has had limited vocal experience.

"The 29 year old singer admitted that jazz was foreign to her until she met her husband. She didn't even know of Scobey's national fame when they met.

"She has no illusions about any success in trying to duplicate the Scobey sound and it appeared neither did the unusually sparse crowd at Beek's.

"Jan's Dixiecats have a long way to go in getting any kind of professional sound at all.

"It's as Louis Armstrong said: "If I have to explain it to you, you'll never understand it . . . ."

By Bernice Buresh

What the reporter didn't know was, 'Louis Armstrong' spirited me on! On one occasion I was appearing with my band at the Riviera in Lake Geneva. I was opposite Louis *"Satchmo"* Armstrong! The Papa of Jazz! Oh, was that a thrill!! And to top it off, when it came time to introduce my act, Louis wanted to do it. He went on for more than five minutes about Bob Scobey, his talents and their love for one another.

He told his audience of 2000 people that I was to carry on Bob's work, in presenting Dixieland Jazz. *"We need some young, beautiful chicks in*

this biz, or we will lose dixieland jazz as an art form."

I really appreciated his warm introduction. I was a novice in the business of entertaining and needed his support, desperately.

Yes, this was a high spot in my life and somehow made it all worth while. There have been other great happenings, but I respected and admired Louis so much. This evening had great, personal significance to me.

RECORDING COMPANIES

With all the big record companies issuing so many records, perhaps 31 albums, Bob never received royalties. Only one company sent a few hundred dollars from time to time. I feel even they short changed Bob. All of them curbed down their promotion of his records and took most of them off the market after his death.

I was able to acquire the tapes of the not-previously-issued Scobey tunes (these were personal but I had to pay the $6,250 to the estate to get them). After I paid off the first loan, I borrowed money again to edit the tapes and finally issued the albums.

Bob Claypool, record reviewer of the Houston Post covered these new releases.

Sunday, March 18, 1973, THE HOUSTON POST

JAZZ

".... Every devoted Dixieland buff is familiar with the work of Bob Scobey, a superb trumpeter-band leader who, before his untimely death in 1963 (at the age of 46), managed to lay down some of the finest Dixieland music ever recorded.

"For those knowledgeable fans, and for listeners who would simply like to have some great Dixieland, no better study of Scobey's music can be found than that contained on the three records reviewed below. All three records were released by Bob's widow, Jan Scobey, on her own label, Jansco Records.

THE GREAT BOB SCOBEY AND HIS FRISCO BAND, VOLUME I, Bob Scobey, Jansco Records, JLPS 6250

"The personnel for this record and for Volume II, both recorded in 1956, includes Scobey on trumpet, Clancy Hayes (banjo and vocals), Lizzie Miles (vocals), Bill Napier (clarinet), Jack Buck (trombone), Jesse "Tiny" Crump and Ralph Sutton (piano), Bob Short (tuba), Hal McCormick (bass) and Fred Higuera (drums).

"For me, the highlights of Volume I are the rousing instrumental "Wang, Wang Blues," a bluesy "I Ain't Got Nobody," sung by Lizzie, the catchy "I'll See You In Cuba," sung by Clancy, and the carefree closing number "Panama Rag." Other cuts include "My Honey's Lovin' Arms," "Then I'll Be Happy," "Mack The Knife," "I Can't Give You Anything But Love," "Georgia On My Mind," and "Please Don't Talk About Me."

THE GREAT BOB SCOBEY AND HIS
FRISCO BAND, VOLUME II, Bob Scobey,
Jansco Records, JLPS 6252.

"Like Volume I, this album features selections ranging from hard-roaring Dixieland to quiet, bluesy stuff. Eight of the ten cuts are vocals, with clancy Hayes singing "Five Foot Two," "In New Orleans" and "I'm Sorry I Made You Cry." Lizzie Miles sings "I'm Confessing That I Love You," "It Ain't No Fault Of Mine," "Sugar Blues," "Nobody's Sweetheart" and a tremendous rendering of the Creole classic "Ela Ba.

"Two fine instrumentals, "Blue, Turning Grey," and "Maple Leaf Rag" round out this fine album.

BOB SCOBEY AND HIS FRISCO BAND,
VOLUME III, Bob Scobey, Jansco Records,
RSLP 5231.

"Volume III differs from the first two LP's in the series in that it showcases Bob's 1960 group, minus Lizzie Miles and Clancy Hayes. But, despite their absence, this album rates as my favorite of the three. The selections (all instrumentals) are wonderfully arranged and executed, and there seems to be more musical maturity and depth here than on the earlier recordings.

"With the help of Dave Black (drums), Bill Napier (clarinet), Richard Nelson (trombone), Tom Smoot (piano), Buddy Lee (banjo) and Dickie Phillips (electic bass), Bob makes a program of Dixieland standards sound better than they ever have before.

"Selections, all excellent, include "Rampart Street Parade," "Basin Street Blues," "Clarinet Marmalade," "Misty," "Bye Bye Blues," "When The Saints Go Marching In," "Under The Double Eagle," "Sleepy Time Down South," "Drummer's Blues," "Wabash Blues" and "Bourbon Street Parade."

"It makes for first-rate Dixieland, and is the best memento yet of a fine artist who died too soon . . . ."

BOB CLAYPOOL

I wrote the liner notes (the descriptive copy that appears on the reverse of a record album jacket), composed the art for the album cover and promoted the records around the country.

It was a good feeling of accomplishment when the first albums rolled off the press in 1966. I am fulfilled that I kept Bob's music before the public.

With no royalties from the record companies and all business taken care of, the estate closed February 25, 1968, five years after Bob's death. Be prepared for a long, drawn out probate!

TIME FOR OTHERS

I was fortunate to have the strength and support of the other members in my band to put on a benefit for the American Cancer Society. The receipts were good and our performance brought in $1800 for the Society. I donated a dollar from each record I sold of Bob Scobey's music—doing something for others helped relieve my own personal stress!

BE A SURVIVOR

1.) Establish two individual bank accounts. Withdraw all accounts immediately should you lose your spouse.
2.) Avoid important decisions for several weeks, perhaps even months, after the death of your partner. Move about your business affairs deliberately and slowly!
3.) Consult with a social worker or counselor and discuss all your problems fully. They are more knowledgeable and objective than a friend.
4.) Ask the local Police Department for security advice and suggestions. You and your home are especially vulnerable to burglary.
5.) Carefully review your spouses' will before and immediately after death. Don't rely on the attorney's interpretation of the will intent. Be prepared for a battle!
6.) When your spouse has reached a critical state in his or her illness, think twice before submitting a joint return to I.R.S. - Ask for an extension if possible.
7.) Take a mini-tax course which you can usually find at a nearby adult education center, often for very little or no cost.
8.) Before death, sign over (both partners) all personal property in writing. This contractual agreement may prove invaluable as a supplement to the will.
9.) Check Insurance policy beneficiaries. An ex-wife may still be designated. Get a confirmation before death from the office that will handle your claim. Know who the beneficiary is.
10.) If childrens' custody may become a problem, try to take care of this matter before death or make the wishes of the decedent and survivor clear and definite. Don't depend only on the will.
11.) During probate, request the court to summarize and make known, as part of the court records, the available survivor's benefits (Social Security, Veteran benefits and others), especially to minor children.
12.) Start your new life eagerly, with a positive attitude no matter how great the temptation is to sink into self pity and depression. Work at it vigorously and constantly until it becomes a habit! Reach out for new Happiness!

Yes, this time had its rough spots, but life always goes on. Like tributaries flowing to the mighty river; all my times with Bob, the sad as well as the happy, each played a part in giving me added richness of experience in my life.

I am stronger and better able to meet all adversity. These times have given me a love of life and a profound sense of the importance of living each moment fully, forthrightly and honestly, free of guilt or deception, joyfully, completely and with all my heart and energy.

My dearest wish is that something I have said may enrich and aid your life in some way. It doesn't matter if you are a musician or plumber; a dixieland fan or a rock and roll fan; or just one who enjoys a good story!

Happiness Always,

Jan Scobey

P.S. Today I am happily married to the wonderful guy who helped me tremendously, beyond love itself, to complete this work. Besides the superior graphic design of this book, Gene Paleno, helped with the editing of my story. The future does hold an even greater love, if you let it happen. AND THE BEAT GOES ON!!!

(TO BE CONTINUED)

SPECIAL ACKNOWLEDGEMENTS

To GEORGE FLETCHER who is known as "The Jazz Man" because of the many fine photographs of musicians he has taken, reflecting his skill and sensitivity; and because of his popular Des Moines radio program, "The Jazz Man" (Station WHO).

George Fletcher has been interested in Jazz since he first booked band dates for Grinnell College way back in the thirties.

He later became close friends with Nesuhi Ertegun, the well known dixieland record producer, and it was as a result of their friendship that George was able to meet many Jazz Greats and photograph them.

Many of these prints are in the New Orleans Jazz Museum, in their permanent collection. He is a member of many jazz clubs throughout the states. He contributed many photographs in this book, but his finest, I believe, is the one chosen for page 196. George Fletcher Photography is located at 10445 Juan Calle, Des Moines, Iowa, 50322. Many thanks, George!

It is with deep feeling, I wish to give special gratitude and thanks to the following friends for their photographic, memorabiliac and essayic contributions. Without their unceasing contributions, this work could not have been so precise.

George Fletcher

Ed Lawless

DOCTOR ED LAWLESS of San Francisco, who so kindly contributed many of the photos in this story.

MARILYN NAPIER MC GWYNN of Alameda, who kindly gave of herself in remembering the times with Bob Scobey, and contributed so many of the photographs in this book.

E. SHORTIE SHORT of Alameda for her memoirs and gem photographs.

CHRISTINE PALENO of Arcata, for her tremendous support and editing.

JIM GOGGIN of Walnut Creek who diligently researched articles and the discography.

JIM BEEBE trombonist with the Celebration Associates, for his contribution of memoirs which helped me tremendously to complete the Bob Scobey Story.

AMERICAN RECORDING SOCIETY

DAVE BLACK of Alameda, California

DR. GEORGE BLOCK of the University of Chicago

ROBERT BORDEAUX of San Francisco, California

RED CALLENDER of Encino, California

CHICAGO PHOTOGRAPHERS - Chicago

BOB CLAYPOOL of Houston, Texas

HELEN CORONADO of San Francisco, California

DOWN BEAT of Chicago, Illinois

NOEL DRADY of San Francisco, California

EBONY MAGAZINE of Chicago

ROSE and BEN FALK of Castioga, California

NORMAN GOLDBERG of Madison, Wisconsin

SENATOR S. I. HAYAKAWA of Mill Valley, California

ART HODES, of Park Forest, Illinois

LARRY KOSTKA of Harvard, Illinois

MEL BENJAMIN of Laurel Photo, North Hollywood

BOBBY LEWIS of Wilmette, Illinois

SAM LINSCHOOTEN of Leiderdorf, Holland

MOSS PHOTOGRAPHY of San Francisco, California

BILL NAPIER, of San Carlos, California

LOU PALENO of West Los Angeles, California

PLAYBOY ENTERPRISES of Chicago Illinois

CLYDE POUND of Kailua, Hawaii

RCA VICTOR and DON BERHKEIMER of Hollywood, California

DYANN RIVKIN of Hollywood, California

ERNEST ROOK of San Francisco, California

ABE SAPERSTEIN of Chicago, Illinois

DUNCAN P. SCHEIDT of Pittsboro, Indiana

ADRIENNE SCOBEY of Portland, Oregon

And OUR dearest friends in time of a crisis . . . Ron and Gloria.

If by chance I have overlooked anyone I would appreciate hearing from you and I will include your courtesy in the very next edition. Thanks once again for being so nice!!!

Jan Scobey

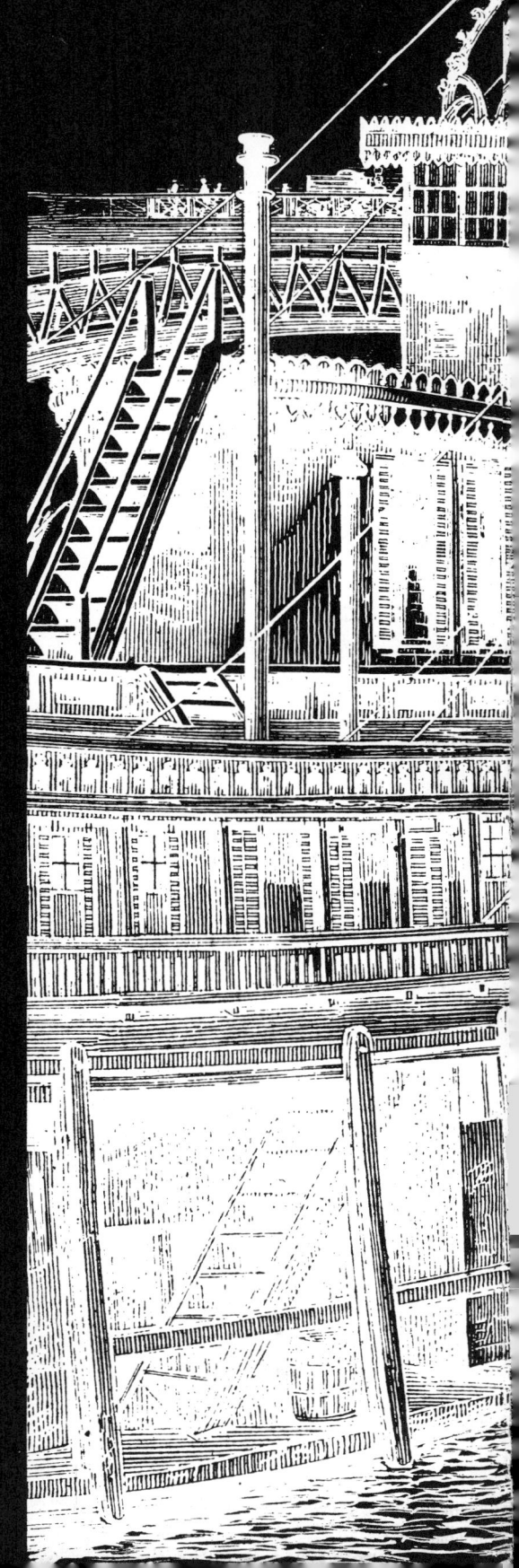

Aren't you glad you came with me?

INDEX (Continued)

San Francisco Symphony 19, 90, 91
St. Cyr, Johnny 36
Saperstein, Abe 205, **206**, 209, 210, 216, **217**, **218**, 223, 301
Scarlatesco, Dr. 277, 278, 281, 284, 291, 292
Schneider, Dlmer 310
Schroeder, Gene 312
Scobey, Adrienne 15, 16, 177, 225, 226, 236, 269, 279, 286, 287, 288, 289, 292, 293, 324, 325
Scobey, Bob III 177, 225, 226, 269, 279, 280, 286, 324, 325
Scobey, Kyle 177, 225, 226, 269, 279, 324, 325
Scott, Bud 38
Scott, Toni Lee **137**, 140, **156**, **158**, 159, 160, 165, **169**, 183, 312
Sesac 140, 173, 313, 316
Shanley, Brian 140, **151**, 156, **158**, 160, 164, 165, 183, 312
Shavers, Charlie 187
Short, Bob **80**, 89, **97**, 98, 101, 116, **122**, 135, 182, 308, 309, 310, 311, 312, 314, 332
"Shortie" 118, 297, 320, 321
Showboat 76, **120**, 121
Shuffle Inn 183
Singleton, Zutty 38, 96
Skinner, Doug **134**, **137**, 183, 311, 312, 313
Smith, Bessie 109
Smith, Charles Edward 37
Smith, Warren "Smitty" **130**, **131**, **134**, 135, 182, 310, 311
Smoot, Tommy **169**, **173**, **175**, **187**, 195, 250, 262, 313, 333
Snow, Frank **120**, **123**, 308

Songer, Wayne 310
Sousa, J.P. **27**, 64
Southern, Jeri 93
Spanier, Mugsy 313
Stacey, Jess **86**
Stardust Hotel 149, 155, 156, 157, 158, 168, 170, 171
Stegmeyer, Bill 123
Stegner, Bentley 195
Stephens, Phil 310
Stewart, Rex 187
Stillman, Roger **186**
Storyville Club 85, 97, 103, 114, 182, 260
Storyville District 33, 35, 71, 119
Sudmeier, Will 308
Sullivan, Ed 205
Sullivan, Joe 37
Sundry, Dr. Vince 243, 244
Sutton, Ralph **114**, **115**, 116, **130**, 134, 136, 309, 310, 311, 314, 332
Swetina, Heidi **74**, 75
Teachemaker, Frank 37
Teagarden, Jack 121, 186
Terry, Clark 195, 214
Thomas, Wade 20
Tin Angel 58, 77
Tough, Dave 37
Traill, Sinclair 212, 213, 214
Treniers 213
Trent, Jack 21
Trottier, Nappy 258
Typhany Club 78
Verve Records 69, 119, 123, 127, 254, 308, 310, 316
Victor & Roxie's 58, 67, 71, 72, **73**, **76**, 136, 181, 296
Walraven, John D. 270
Ward, Stan 59, 307
Watkins, Earl **76**, 77, **88**, 307
Watters, Lu 21, 40, **41**, 46, 47, 48, 51, 53, 54, **55**, 56, 57, 58, 61, 64, 89, 140, 181, 211, 220, 263, 306, 309

Watters, Pat 53, 54, 56, 57, 320, 321
Weiss, Joseph 19
Weitzel, Tony 195, 262, 263
Welsh, Alex 212
West Coast Records 55
Wiggins, Jack **169**
Williams, Clarence 35, 103
Wittwer, Johnny 61
Wright, Virginia and Marshall 119
Wrightsman, Stan 78, **79**, **80**, 93, 308, 312
Yerba Buena Jazz Band 38, 40, 41, 45, 46, 47, 48, 50, 53, 54, **55**, 56, 57, 58, 61, 62, 64, 67, 74, 98, 157, 220, 306
Young, Trummy **83**
Zack, George 162, 165
Zardi's 85

Ma Rainey	109	
Manne, Shelley	**78**, 89, 308	
Manone, Wingy	58, 64, **300**	
Mares, Paul	37	
Marsala, Marty	93	
Marx, Karl	43, 44	
Matlock, Matty	93, **95**, **130**, 134, 135, 310, 311	
Matteson, Rich	156, 159, **160**, 161, 162, 183, 213, 300, 312	
Mayle, Gene	89	
McCormick, Hal	93, 98, 101, **120**, 307, 308, 310, 314, 332	
McCoy, Ethel	151, 152, 177, 225, 226, 269, 273, 279, 286	
McConnell, Jack	313	
McDonnell, Tommy	168, **170**	
McGwynn, Marilyn Napier	**73**, 74, 208, 297, 298, 320	
McNaughton Foundation	273, 277, 281	
McPartland, Jimmy	37, 313	
McRae, Carmen	93	
Mellon, Andrew	43	
Melody Magazine	211, 212	
Mielke, Bob	57, 58, **74**, 75, **84**, 88, 309	
Milano, Connie	195, **198**, 313	
Miles, Lizzie	92, 96, 97, 98, **99**, **100**, **102**, 103, **104**, **105**, **106**, **107**, **108**, **109**, **115**, **116**, **119**, 182, 252, 254, **255**, 257, 301, 309, 314, 315, 332, 333	
Mole, Miff	213, 214	
Mordecai, Harry	**41**, 42, **55**, 123, 306, 307	
Morgan, Freddy	156, 160, **161**, 164, 165, **169**, 172	
Morton, Ferdinand "Jelly Roll"	**26**, 35, 38, 47, 62, 119, 138, 140, 183, 315	
Mulligan, Gerry	92	
Murphy, Turk	21, **22**, 40, **41**, 46, 48, 53, 54, **55**, 56, 57, 59, **60**, **65**, **70**, 88, **89**, 140, 181, 211, 268, 297, 306, 307, 313	
Napier, Bill	58, 59, **73**, **81**, **85**, **86**, **87**, **88**, **93**, 98, 116, **120**, **123**, **124**, **131**, **173**, **175**, **179**, **187**, 195, **198**, 208, 250, 263, 297, 300, 307, 308, 310, 313, 314, 319, 332, 333	
Nelson, Marvin	**90**	
Nelson, Ricky	**169**, **173**, **175**, **187**, **245**, 250, 314, 333	
Newman, Bill	**59**, 307	
Nicholas, Albert	35, **70**, **71**, 73, 309	
Nichols, Red	213	
Nichols, Marshall	309	
Nixon, President	44	
Noone, Jimmy	45	
Norman, Gene	82, **83**	
Nunez, "Yellow"	37	
Oliver, Joe "King"	26, 35, 36, 37, 38, 40, 47, 62, 64, 71, 103, 109, 119, 140, 195, 198, 254, 296, 301	
Ory, Kid	36, 38, **39**, 46, 61, 64	
Pacific Records	78	
Page, Stan	309, 314	
Paleno, Gene	5, 6, 335	
Patman, Repr. Wright	43	
Pearson, Mack	156, **161**, **169**, **172**	
Perez, Manuel	71	
Petrillo	28	
Phillips, Dickie	**173**, **175**, **187**, 314, 333	
Phillips, Wally	250	
Picou, Alphonso	35	
Pierce, Norm	296	
Pioneer Inn	58	
Pioneer Village	75, 136	
Perazzi, Horace	21	
Plantation Cafe	71	
Playboy	149, 262, 272	
Pollack, Ben	37	
Pound, Clyde	**135**, 136, 137, 138, 311	
Preservation Hall	254	
Preview Lounge	**141**	
Previn, Andre	93	
Prima, Louis	164	
Probert, George	**70**, **71**, 72, 309	
Quilligan, Larry	**61**, 62	
Radsliff, Leon	119, **120**, 121, **122**, 123	
Raft, George	148	
Ragtime Records	73, 187, 193, 201, 254, 301, 303, 304, 305, 313, 316	
Ramsey, Jr. Fred	37	
Rand, Sally	56	
Rappolo, Leon	36, 37	
Rasbury, Gena	**330**	
RCA Victor Records	26, 69, 127, **128**, 129, 134, 135, 136, 138, 162, 300, **310**, **311**, **312**, **313**, 315, 316	
Remington, Dave	**330**	
Reynolds, Fred	127, 129, 296, 310, 312	
Rhinehardt, Bill	186	
Rich, Buddy	214, 272	
Rippey, Dick	**89**, 90, 298	
Rivkin, Dyann	178, **179**	
Robertson, Zue	36	
Robinson, Edward G.	148	
Rook Ernest	93, **94**	
Rose, Wally	41, 48, **49**, **55**, 56, 61, 89, 303, 309	
Rosebrook, Dave	19	
Roundtable	85, 252, 321	
Rush Street	146, 148, 149, 262, 322	
Russell, Pee Wee	213	
San Francisco Chronicle	64, 65	
San Francisco Examiner	70, 91	
San Francisco Hot Music Society	38, 41	

INDEX (Continued)

Fatool, Nick 93, **95**, **129**, 134, 310
Firehouse Five 139
Fitzgerald, Ella 134
Flamingo 85, 113, **119**
Fletcher, George 298, 299, **336**
Fountain, Pete 254
Freeman, Bud 37
Friedman, Ralph 295
Fried, Alexander 91
Fuller, Jesse **78**
Gaslight Club 145, 146, 147
George, Jim **330**
Gillespie, John "Dizzie" 118
Girsback, Squires 48, **49**, **59**, **65**, **81**, **93**, **95**, 307, 309
Glaser, Joe 159, 160
Goggin **58**, 59, 72, 73, 296, 316
Goldberg, Norman 177, 178
Goldcoast 146, 147
Goldman 19
Goldstein, Sammy **130**, 135, 311
Goodman, Benny 37
Goodtime Jazz 50, 69, 98, 127, 255, 301, **306**, **307**, **308**, **309**, **312**, 315, 316
Grand Terrace Ballroom 71
Granz, Norm 119
Hackett, Bobby **29**, 30, 185, 186
Hall, Edmund 36
Hambone Kelly's 41, 56, 59, 61, 62, 64, 134, 136
Hanck, Bill 195, **198**, 262, 313
Handy, W.C. **28**
Hangover Club 58, 61, **64**, **70**, 76, 114
Harlem Globetrotters 205, 207, 209, 211, 263, 301
Harris, Dave 134, 310
Harris, Len 195
Hayakawa, Dr. S.I. 85, 98, **99**, **100**, 101

Hayes, Clancy 41, 42, 48, 53, **67**, **68**, 69, 70, **73**, 74, 75, 76, 78, **81**, 82, **84**, 85, **86**, **87**, **88**, 89, 92, **93**, **95**, **96**, 98, 99, **100**, 101, **106**, 113, 114, **116**, 117, **120**, **122**, 123, 129, 130, 131, 134, 135, 136, **137**, 139, 140, **150**, **151**, **156**, **158**, 159, 160, 162, 164, 165, 178, 181, 182, 183, 185, 188, 191, 211, 225, 270, 300, 307, 308, 309, 310, 311, 312, 313, 314, 315, 316, 332, 333
Heffner, Hugh 150
Helm, Bob 20, **21**, 41, 48, **55**, **89**, 306, 307
Herman, Woody 185
Higuera, Freddie **49**, 72, **81**, **93**, 98, 101, **120**, **123**, 308, 309, 310, 314, 332
Hines, Earl "Fatha" 71, 93, **96**
Hirt, Al 185, 254
Hodes, Art **138**, 139, 165, 262, 298, 299, 300, 301, 312
Hodges, Johnny 214
Holliday, Billie 134
Holzfeind, Frank 127, 139
Hoover, President 43
Horne, Ellis 41
Horne, Lena 116, 134, 214
Hotaling, Roland 86
Howard, Darnell 50, **62**, 70, 71, 181, 309
Hutchinson, Ralph 183, 313
Ivert, Jack 186
James, Harry **29**, 30, 59
Jackson, Tony 35
Jansco Records 22, 69, 117, 303, 304, 305, 313, **314**, 315, 316, 332
Jazz Man Records 21, 46, 50
Jazz Session **92**, **93**, **94**, 95

Johnson, Bunk 35, 38, 313
Johnson, Dink 38
Johnson, Jimmy 213, 250, **256**, **330**
Jones, Jonah 195, 202
Jones, Max 211, 212
Jones, Richard M. 35
Jones, Spike 172
Joplin, Scott 22, 23, 24, 25, 28, 35
Jorda, Enrique 91
Kaiser, Kay 20
Kapp, Jack 129
Keeling, Barbara **75**, 76
Kennedy, President 44
Kessel, Barney 78, 89, 308
Klatzkin, Ben 19
Klein, Manny **129**, **131**, 310
Kloss, Gerald 176
Koenig, Les 50, 307
Kostka, Larry 67, 139, 140, 250, 298
Krebs 282
Krec, Ted **82**
Krupa, Gene 37
Kupcinet, Irv "Kup" 195
Laetrile 272, 273, 277, 282
Lammi, Dick 41, 48, **49**, **55**, 72, **86**, **88**, 306, 307, 309
Laine, Jack 36, 37
Lear, Les 205
Leet, Buddy **173**, **175**, 179, 187, 195, **199**, 215, 250, 262, 313, 314, 333
Leonard, Will 195
Lewis, Bobby 183, **186**, 195, 198, 269, 270, 295, **330**
Lewis, Ernie **77**, **88**, 307
Lewis, George 36, 46, 213
Lievermann, Rolf 91
Lincoln, Abe 93, **95**, **131**, 134, **136**, 140, 296, 310, 311
Lind Hall, Jenny 71, 75, 119, 314, 315
Lingle, Paul **65**
Louden, Vern **94**
Lyon, Herb 195, 249

INDEX

Numbers in **BOLD** type indicate illustrations.

Alexander's Jazz Band   64, **73**
Allen, Henry Red   313
Almerico, Tony   103, 313
American Recording Society   33-38, 316
Armstrong, Lil Hardin   36
Armstrong, Louis "Satchmo"   28, 30, **31**, 35, 36, 38, 40, 46, 47, 50, 58, 61, 62, 64, 82, **83**, 93, 96, 103, 119, 158, 159, 160, 178, 184, 195, 198, **199**, **212**, 214, 254, 263, 296, 301, 313, 330, 331
Assunto, Frank   162, **163**, 195
Assunto, Fred   **163**
Assunto, Papa Jac   162, **163**
Austin, Claire   78, 89, 308
Bailey, Pearl   134
Baker, Chet   92
Bales, Burt   50, 59, **60**, 67, 71, 73, 136, 307, 309
Ball, Kenny   225
Ballard, Bob   **239**, 249, **251**, **261**, **262**, **263**, 272, 330
Baquet, George   35
Barber, Chris   212
Barbarin, Paul   71
Basin St.   85
Beach, Frank   **131**, 134, 310
Bean Floyd   **119**, **160**, 162, 313
Bechet, Sidney   35, 82, 103, 106
Beebe, Jim   140, **151**, 156, 159, 160, 161, 162, 181, **182**, 183, 184, 185, 186, 312, **330**
Beeson, Tom   311
Beiderbecke, Leon "Bix"   30, 37, 296
Berigan, Bunny   134, 263
Berger, Jug   **330**
Berlin, Irving   191
Bernard, Russ   **76**, 77
Bigard, Barney   35, 71
Billboard   92

Black Dave   **116**, 117, 118, 135, **151**, 156, 158, 159, 162, **169**, **173**, 174, 175, 183, **187**, 188, 195, **199**, 213, 214, 250, 262, 272, 296, 300, 311, 312, 313, 314, 319, 333
Block, Dr. George   298
Blue, Ben   155
Blue Note   78, 85, 127, 129, 139
Bolden, Buddy   33, 34, 35, 38
Bourbon Street   192, 193, 194, 195, 200, 208, 211, 239, 246, 247, 249, 250, 261, 262, 268, 270, **272**, 301, 321
Boyd   242
Brown, Gail   270, 271, 272
Brown, Pud   78 **80**, 312
Brown, Tom   37
Brunies Brothers   36
Brunies, George   37
Buck, Jack   **49**, 67, **68**, 70, 71, 72, **73**, 75, **81**, **86**, **87**, **88**, **93**, 101, 116, **123**, **124**, **131**, **134**, 136, **137**, 139, 181, 183, 296, 297, 307, 308, 309, 310, 311, 312, 314, 332
Cafe Continental   146, 147, 148, 149, 156, 159, 165, 171, 172, 178, 191, 193, 272
Calender, Red   129, 130, 134, 310, 311
Calloway, Cab   93
Campbell, Bill   182
Carey, Mutt "Papa"   38, 61
Carr, Billy   208, 301
Carson, Johnny   63
Casey, Hotso   **65**, 67
Cathcart, Dick   **134**, 135, 311
Chesrow, Mimi   152
Chicago Daily News   262, 263
China Pheasant   61
Christian, Bobby   313
Christy, June   **92**, 93
Claypool, Bob   **332**, **333**
Colyer, Ken   212
Condon, Eddie   37

Corb, Morty   78, 308
Coronado, Helen and Ben   320
Crosby, Bing   117, **128**, 129, 134, 213, 297, 310
Crosby's Bob Cats   139
Crump, Jesse "Tiny"   **81**, **93**, 98, 101, 114, **115**, **116**, **117**, 119, **120**, 123, **125**, 308, 310, 314, 332
Cousins, Bob   **330**
Darensbourg, Joe   36, **60**, 61, 82
Dart, Bill   41, **48**, 55, 306
Davidson, Wild Bill   **56**, 57
Davis, Eddie   330
Davis, Johnny   263
Dawn Club   38, **45**, 53, 55, 56, 57, 58, 61, 75
De Paris, Wilbur   213
Di Phillips, Ronnie   156, 160
Dixon, Mort   225
Dodds, Johnny   35, 36
Dovidio, Pete   **135**, 136, **137**, 311
Downbeat   139
Drady, Noel   51, 55
Draper, Dr. Benjamin   **92**
Dukes of Dixieland   158, 159, 162, **163**, 186, 212, 313
Durkin, Bill   56
Dutrey, Honore   36
Duvivier, George   312
Ebony Magazine   108, 109
Edgewater Beach Hotel   247
Edwards, Gordon "Gramps"   57, 67, **68**, 72, 309
Ellington, Duke   93, **94**, 96, 97, 116, 214
El Rancho Grande   76, 77, **84**, **86**
Ertegun, Nesuhi   46, 47, 48, 50, 71, 75, 297, 309, **336**
Evans, Doc   186, **187**, 195
Evans, Elaine   156, 172
Facks II   149, 157, 158
Falk, Ben and Rose   272, 273
Fallstrom, Bob   **187**, 188

ILLUSTRATION AND PHOTOGRAPHY CONTRIBUTORS

Armstrong, Louis "Satchmo"	31
Assunta, Frank	163
Bernard, Russ	76
Bordeaux, Robert	110
Chicago Photographers	169, 207
Cilento Studios	182, 256, **329**
Coronado, Helen	130, 131
Darensbourg, Joe	39, 60
Ebony Magazine	105, 106
Faverty, Richard	186
Fletcher, George	41, 42, 47, 48, 49, 59, 62, 64, 138, 196, 197, 198, 253, 336
Goodtime Jazz album covers	306, 307, 308, 309, 312
Goldberg, Norman	173, 179, 188
Hayakawa, Dr. S.I.	99, 100
Hulme, George	160
James, Harry	29
Jansco Records	314
Kostka, Larry	83
Kraft	313
Lawless, Dr. Ed	29, 45, 57, 60, 97, 129, 134, 136, 336
Los Angeles Public Library	26, 27, 28, 40, 52, 68, 70, 71, 129, 167, 215, 219
Merkle Press	77
McGwynn, Marilyn Napier	72, 73, 84, 86, 87, 89, 114, 157, 158, 176, 231, 234, 251, 261, 262, 263
Moss Photography	92, 93, 94, 95, 96, 115, 116
Napier, Bill	49, 85
Newbauer, Sanford	91
Paleno, Gene - cover layout, special effects	1, 3, 25, 26, 27, 32, 34, 35, 36, 37, 38, 39, 45, 110, 111, 156, 157, 165, 178, 184, 199
Pavlic, Richard	175
Playboy Enterprises	149, 150, 151
Probert, George	70, 71
Pound, Clyde	135, 137, 141
RCA Victor Records - cover photo,	128, 190, 310, 311, 312, 313
Riddle, Cliff	161, 172
Rivkin, Dyann	174, 179
Saperstein, Abe	206, 210, 218
Schiedt, Duncan P.	55, 72, 88, 128, 180
Schoenmann, Jim	245
Sesac	313
"Shortie"	60, 78, 79, 80, 81, 89, 107, 116, 119, 120, 122, 123, 124, 128, 130, 131, 132, 133, 134
Swetina, Heidi	74, 81, 82, 86, 87, 90, 121
Tamony, Pete	45
Verve Records	308, 309, 310
Watters, Pat	54

ABOUT THE AUTHOR

JAN SCOBEY is a most unusual person. She was raised in cookie-cutter conformity with 25,000 other little Polish, Catholic orphans in Chicago.

Yet, somehow, she became an absolutely unique, one-of-a-kind, individual.

Jan is one of those rare persons who has infinite faith in themselves. She is exceptionally self-reliant—a genuine "survivor" type. She has enjoyed several, successful careers; vocalist, trumpet player, bandleader, television entertainer, model, writer and artist. Jan is a renaissance woman!

As long as I've known Jan Scobey, she has been a driven person—one with all-consuming desire (even a need) to contribute something of worth and service to humankind.

Writing "He Rambled! 'til Cancer Cut Him Down." and "Cancer? What You Can Do!" helped her fulfill that wish. Bob Scobey's unusual life . . . and death . . . was also a vehicle to the greater goal of being able to help others.

When she decided to write these books, she didn't approach it, she attacked it, as she does all things, with dogged persistance, infinite attention to accuracy of detail, and total dedication and involvement.

The author is quite a woman!

Gene Palen